Robert Herbert Story

The Church of Scotland, Past and Present

Vol. 4

Robert Herbert Story

The Church of Scotland, Past and Present
Vol. 4

ISBN/EAN: 9783337425487

Printed in Europe, USA, Canada, Australia, Japan

Cover: Foto ©Lupo / pixelio.de

More available books at **www.hansebooks.com**

THE CHURCH OF SCOTLAND,

PAST AND PRESENT:

ITS HISTORY, ITS RELATION TO THE LAW AND THE STATE,

ITS DOCTRINE, RITUAL, DISCIPLINE, AND PATRIMONY.

EDITED BY

ROBERT HERBERT STORY, D.D. [Edin.] F.S.A.,
PROFESSOR OF ECCLESIASTICAL HISTORY IN THE UNIVERSITY OF GLASGOW,
AND ONE OF HER MAJESTY'S CHAPLAINS.

LONDON:
WILLIAM MACKENZIE, 69 LUDGATE HILL, E.C.;
EDINBURGH, GLASGOW, & DUBLIN.

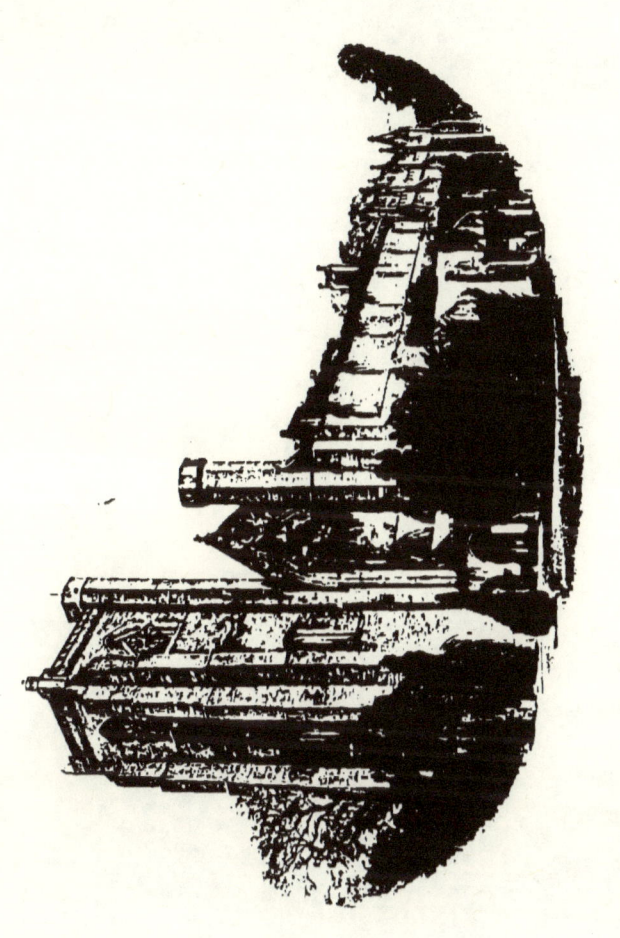

THE CHURCH OF SCOTLAND.

THE CHURCH IN ITS RELATION TO THE

LAW AND THE STATE.

BY

ANDREW MACGEORGE, Esq.,

AUTHOR OF "OLD GLASGOW;" "LIFE OF W. L. LEITCH;" "ARMORIAL INSIGNIA OF
GLASGOW;" "FLAGS; SOME ACCOUNT OF THEIR HISTORY AND USES;"
"PAPERS ON CHURCH QUESTIONS."

THE CHURCH:

ITS RELATION TO THE LAW AND THE STATE.

From the earliest dawn of our history the Church in Scotland, in all the various phases through which it has passed, has been recognized by the dominant power as an institution the spiritual independence of which was to be respected, and its endowments protected. There have been exceptions, and it is not pleasant to think that the exceptional cases, in which the Church has been assailed by acts of despotic oppression and spoliation, have occurred in post-Reformation times.

What is now called "the Church of Scotland" may, in a sense, be said to have had its origin at the Reformation, but it was not then a new Church. The Church, which always was, and which continues to be, the Church of the people, had an origin much more remote. It has passed through changes and reformations, but in historical and legal continuity the Church of to-day is the same that existed in Scotland fifteen hundred years ago. During each period of its history there was, as a rule, one religion for all, and in creed the Church and the State were at one.

What Lord Selborne says of the establishment of the Church of England is equally true of the Scottish Church. "The establishment of the Church by law," he says, "consists essentially in the incorporation of the law of the Church into that of the realm, as a branch of the general law of the realm, though limited as to the causes to which, and the persons to whom, it applies; in the public recognition of its courts and judges as having proper legal jurisdiction, and in the enforcement of the sentences of these courts, when duly pronounced according to law, by the civil power. The establishment (so understood) of the Church in England grew up gradually and silently out of the relation between moral and physical power natural in an early stage of society, not as the result of any definite act, compact, or conflict, but so that no one can now trace the exact steps of the process by which the voluntary recognition of moral and spiritual obligation passed into custom, and custom into law."[1]

One of the earliest notices we have of the recognition of the Church in Scotland by the ruling power was under the Tribal system in the early years of the Christian era. At that time, and under that system, private property in land did not exist. Personal property in movables existed, but real property, or individual property in the soil, is of later origin. The early social organization of the Gaelic, as well as of the Cymric race, was not territorial. It was based on the community or Tribe, and the oldest tenure by which land was held in Scotland was by the Tuath or Tribe, in common. The early state of the Tribe, however, soon became modified by internal changes as well as by external influences, and of the latter not the least powerful was the introduction of Christianity, and the adaptation of the Christian Church to the Tribal system. As Christianity spread, the Church came to be recognized, and practically established, in connection with the Tribes; and a grant of part of the Tribal lands, and its separation from the rest, became a necessity for the maintenance of the clergy. We have the authority of Bede for saying that it was in this way Columba acquired his world-renowned island. It was an endowment on him and his followers, as a Christian Church, by the tribe of the Picts which then inhabited the district of Britain, from which it was separated by a narrow strait.

The relations of the Church to the law and the State in Scotland in these early times is now chiefly a matter of historical curiosity. The subject is involved in obscurity, but what is known is interesting, especially from its connection with the early Church in Ireland, and it is instructive also from its bearing on our own later ecclesiastical history.

The dominion of the Romans in Britain came to an end in the beginning of the fifth century (410), and Britain ceased

---

[1] "A Defence of the Church of England against Disestablishment," by Roundell, Earl of Selborne, 1887, p. 10.

then to be a part of the Roman Empire. Her intercourse with the Continent had been almost entirely cut off, and, with the exception of a notice of the temporary prevalence of the Pelagian heresy in the British Church, all is silence for a century and a half. During this period of darkness it was chiefly in the Irish Church that the light of Christianity was preserved, and it was probably maintained there in a comparatively pure and primitive state. Certainly at that time there is no trace of any jurisdiction over the Irish Church having been exercised from Rome. The clergy were amenable to no authority but that of the prince or chief under whose protection they lived, and in spiritual matters they were independent. We know this from the account given of himself by Columbanus or Colmanus, when, with a small band of missionaries, he appeared in Gaul in 590. When asked who they were and whence they came, his answer was: "We are Irish, dwelling at the very ends of the earth. We be men who receive nought beyond the doctrine of the evangelists and apostles. The Catholic faith, as it was first delivered by the successors of the holy apostles, is still maintained among us with unchanged fidelity." They denied the supremacy of the Pope, recognizing, they said, "only one head—our Lord." They maintained that the Pope's jurisdiction as Bishop of Rome did not extend beyond the limits of the Roman Empire, and when opposed by the clergy of Gaul on account of observances which they characterized as schismatical, Columbanus, in a letter to the Pope, said in effect: "I am a missionary from a Church of God among the barbarians, and though temporarily within the limits of your territorial jurisdiction, and bound to regard you with respect, I claim the right to follow the customs of our own Church."[1]

In its first and earliest form the Church in Scotland exhibits a secular clergy founding churches; in its second we find a clergy observing rules and founding monasteries. In the earliest period there was no collective administration—each church, as it was settled, was under the charge of its own priest or minister, and he was amenable only to the lord on whose domain he had been settled, and by whom, in most cases, he had been endowed. And it was the same in Ireland. Ministering ecclesiastics came

[1] Skene's "Celtic Scotland," ii. 7, 11.

to be called bishops, but every church had its own bishop, and in many instances there were seven bishops to one church. Towards the end of the life of St. Patrick this peculiar sort of collegiate church prevailed largely. An old Culdee litany gives a list of no fewer than one hundred and fifty-three groups, in each of which there were seven bishops in the same church.[1] Then came the monastic system, but still the bishop in the Irish Church was not what the title is now understood to mean. The jurisdiction was not in him, but in the monastery, and it was exercised through the abbot as its monastic head. There was episcopacy in the Church, but it was not diocesan episcopacy. The abbot, in general, retained his presbyterian orders only.[2] The tendency of all monasteries was to encroach on the functions of the secular clergy, and not only to claim exemption from episcopal jurisdiction, but even to have within themselves a resident bishop for the exercise of episcopal functions within the monastery, to whose abbot he was subject as being under the monastic rule. Being subject to the abbot, his episcopate was only a personal dignity. At a later period, indeed, we find the subordinate functionaries of the monastery, such as the scribe, and even the anchorite, uniting the functions of a bishop with their own proper duties.[3] Ordination of a bishop *per saltum* occasionally took place. Fiacc was made a bishop by St. Patrick without having been a priest or even a deacon, "and he became chief bishop of Leinster."[4] But the Irish bishops had no territorial jurisdiction.

These monasteries had no proper central head. They consisted of an aggregate of separate communities in federal union, but where there was more than one monastery of the same order there was a superior, to whose superintendence they were subject. In monastic language, *parochia* was the jurisdiction of such a superior over the detached monasteries of the order.[5] This at least was the case in Ireland. It is interesting to notice that the early monastic church in Ireland was a Tribal institute, and its rights were interwoven with those of the Tribe. We know from the "Ancient Laws" that the rights and obligations

---

[1] "Celtic Scotland," ii. 25.   [2] Ibid. 44.   [3] "Irish Annals," quoted by Dr. Skene.
[4] "Tripartite Life of Patrick," by Whitley Stokes, part i, p. clxxxi.
[5] Reeves' "Columba," p. 336, quoted by Whitley Stokes, "Tripartite Life," part i., p. clxxxi.

of the Church and the people were mutual, as they are now. The right of the Church was protection in its property, and maintenance from its members; and what the *Tuath* or Tribe could claim from the Church was "the right of baptism and communion, and requiem of soul, with the offering (*oifrend*) from every church to every person after his proper belief, with the recital of the Word of God to all who listen to it and keep it."[1]

The relation of the Church to the civil power in Scotland was at first what it was in Ireland—that of the clan to its chief. Although a pure doctrine was preached, the earliest "conversions" were often of a very wholesale character. Clanship, as an eminent Celtic scholar (Dr. Todd) has justly said, is the true key of Irish history—political and ecclesiastical; and it was at first the same in Scotland. Upon the clan Christianity was engrafted in the monastic form. When the Christian missionaries first went to Ireland they found the clans existing there, like the Tribes in Scotland, as the primitive form of government, with numerous chieftains virtually independent, and one or more nominal kings. St. Patrick and his followers always addressed themselves in the first instance to the chieftain, and his baptism was followed by the outward adherence of the clan or sept.[2] Then followed the establishment of a monastery, and it was constituted on the model of a family. The abbot was the father, the monks his children. The society at Iona was known as "the family of Hy."

The monastic system was at an early period extended to Scotland. It was in the year 563 that Columba—saint, soldier, statesman, one of "the twelve apostles of Ireland"—landed in Iona, and preached to the Pictish people, addressing himself first to the sovereign. Within twelve years he had founded his celebrated monastery, having first converted and baptized the most powerful monarch that ever occupied the Pictish throne. At his death he left Iona the acknowledged head of the Christian Church in Scotland, having maintained the same independence of Rome as did the Church in Ireland. An interesting illustration of the separate and independent position of the Church in our Islands is to be found in the fact that in

[1] "Ancient Laws of Ireland," iii. 33. [2] Godkin on the "Old Church of Ireland."

the latter half of the fifth century, and for long afterwards, an old Latin version of the Scriptures, peculiar to the British Isles, was in use in the Scoto-Britannic churches, differing largely both from the Vulgate and from the known ante-Hieronymian versions.[1] It is questionable if the Vulgate was known to St. Patrick.

By the Pictish kings the Church was protected in the endowments which so soon began to flow into it; and there is no reason to doubt that in questions of property, and even in the enforcement of ecclesiastical decrees, the Church was to some extent then, as it certainly was afterwards, assisted, and her rights enforced, by the secular power. But the Church was not exempt from the taxations and secular exactions to which other subjects were liable, and this state of matters continued till towards the end of the ninth century. At that time the kingdom of the Picts still existed, and by a king of that dynasty the Church with its possessions was "freed from servitude, under Pictish law and custom."[2] The Church was thus liberated from the old lawless exactions of what the Duke of Argyll calls "Celtic feudalism." The introduction of charters "effected this," the duke says, "as regards all lands granted to the Church, by expressly forbidding these exactions altogether, and they effected the same object as regards lands granted to laymen by substituting definite and fixed amounts of payment and service."[3] But the exemption was not quite absolute, as reservations occasionally occur in charters granted to the Church by David and William the Lion, in such phrases as "*pro conredio regis*" and "*salvo servicio meo.*"

Meanwhile the power of the Roman party had been steadily growing, and by the beginning of the eighth century probably the greater part of the Britons of the West of Scotland had conformed to Rome. The movement was resisted by the Columban Community till the year 717, when they were expelled from the Pictish kingdom. They were the last to disappear of the Celtic Communities, and they were replaced by monks who adopted the canonical observance of Easter and the ca-

---

[1] "Councils and Ecclesiastical Documents of Great Britain and Ireland," i. 170, by A. W. Haddan and Wm. Stubbs.
[2] "Statuta Ecclesiæ Scoticanæ," edited by Mr. Joseph Robertson.
[3] "Scotland as it was and is," by the Duke of Argyll, 1887.

nonical mode of tonsure. The primacy was transferred to Dunkeld, and towards the end of the ninth century it was again transferred to Abernethy. After the expulsion of the Columban monks many of the monasteries fell into the hands of laymen.

Then came the return to the older system of a hierarchy of secular clergy, with monachism, as a separate institution, existing within the Church, but not pervading the whole. At the same time increased asceticism began to prevail, and a sect of Anchorites arose who got the name of *Cele De, Deicolæ*, or God worshippers, afterwards changed to Culdees, a body who exercised for some time a great influence in Scotland. They sprang from that ascetic order who adopted a solitary service of God in isolated cells as the highest form of religious life. They were clerics, and might be called monks, and they had a Liturgy of their own. Joceline of Furness, in his "Life of Kentigern," relates that the saint gained to himself a great many disciples whom he trained in his sacred literature of the divine law, and, educated to sanctity of life by his word and example. "They were content," he says, "with spare diet and dress, possessing nothing of their own, and living in separate huts or cells. These solitary clerics," he adds, "were called in common speech *Kalledei*." Joceline is guilty of an anachronism when he assigns the *Kalledei* to a period so early as that of Kentigern, who came to Glasgow soon after the middle of the sixth century. When Joceline wrote, however, in the twelfth century, there did exist bodies of *Kalledei* in Scotland, and in his description of the Culdean clergy before they became canons, he was probably repeating a genuine tradition.[1] The Culdees were finally brought under the canonical rule along with the secular clergy, retaining, however, to some extent, the nomenclature of the monastery, until at length the name of Culdee became almost synonymous with that of Secular Canon.[2] Like the other religious bodies they acquired lands and churches for their Communities from kings and nobles, which bishops and popes confirmed in their favour. They possessed many monasteries, and there is evidence that they had a college at Brechin. In the little island of St. Servanus in Loch Leven was one of their foundations, where, during a long period of darkness and violence,

[1] "Celtic Scotland," ii. 260.   [2] Ibid. ii. 277.

they kept alive the lamp of civilizing religion, until they were driven from their quiet dwelling to give place to another order of Churchmen. With the plantation of bishoprics, and the assimilation of the native Church to that of Rome, the communities of the Culdees became extinct and were replaced by regular Canons. By internal decay and external change the old Celtic Church was also coming to an end. The chief causes were the encroachment of the secular element on the ecclesiastical, and the policy adopted by the kings of the race of Queen Margaret. The last of the Bishops of Alban died in 1107. The old Celtic Church then practically came to an end, and was superseded by the bishoprics founded in the early part of King David's reign, and by the establishment of the ordinary cathedral staff of Canons, Deans, and other functionaries. An old Celtic community, however, still existed in Iona, but they were not protected by law, and existed only by sufferance. At length the Lord of the Isles, adopting the policy of the Scottish kings, introduced into his territories the religious order of the Roman Church. In 1203 he established the Benedictines or Black Monks in Iona, and with this the last trace of the old Celtic Church disappeared.

About 878–889, under the new dynasty of kings of Scottish race, we find the first appearance of the name "the Scottish Church," after it had been freed from servitude under Pictish law.

But although the Church was, as a rule, protected by the Civil power, the Civil power was not always able to protect her. When a priest was settled in a particular district, the lord of the manor extended to him and his church the protection he afforded to his vassals; but in the case of the monasteries, many of which, apart from their lands, possessed valuable property, not only in money and plate, but in precious manuscripts, and bells, and costly shrines, they were cast more on their own resources, and in some localities they suffered serious loss from sudden predatory attacks. These occurred more frequently after the latter part of the eighth century, when certain localities suffered so severely from the inroads of the Northmen. To provide against these the monks were obliged to follow the example of the Irish monasteries by erecting places of security for their treasures. Before the invasion of these northern hordes, the Irish ecclesiastics, as a rule, possessed their churches and monastic buildings in comparative peace, but the attacks to which they then became exposed obliged them to devise means for their own protection. There can now be little doubt that it was for this purpose the celebrated Round Towers, which have been the cause of so much controversy, were erected by the Irish monks. It is a style of building which reached Ireland from Brittany, and it is known that so early as the seventh century they were used there for purposes of protection. They were, in short, the keeps of the monasteries, although they were also used as belfries. A confirmation of the hypothesis as to their use is found in the interesting fact, pointed out by Lord Dunraven, that in Ireland these towers are found along the coast, and in the valleys of the rivers, where the churches had been most exposed to the attacks of the Norsemen.[1] In Scotland there were a considerable number of similar towers, which were no doubt used for the same purpose as those in Brittany and Ireland. Some still remain, as at Brechin and Abernethy, but there were many others, of which no remains now exist. Till a late period two were standing at Deerness in Orkney; there were three in the Shetland Islands, one in West Burra, and another at Ireland Head.[2] They were erected also, like those in Ireland, in the localities which had been found most open to attack, and into them the monks no doubt carried their more valuable possessions till the temporary storm had passed. The great height of the towers, their isolated position, and the small doorway, usually fourteen feet from the ground, made them well fitted to resist an enemy chiefly armed with bows and arrows, and whose movements were rapid and his time necessarily limited; while the approach of the foe could be signalled at once by those who kept watch at the top.

In considering the constitution of the Church in its relation to the State, it is necessary to keep in mind, not only that there has always been in Scotland a national recognition of religion in accordance with the will of the people, but that in ecclesiastical matters the lay or civil element has always been

---

[1] "Notes on Irish Architecture," by Lord Dunraven.
[2] "Early Christian Art," by Miss Stokes.

represented. In the earlier times, when the Church had no collective administration, the king or chief exercised his sovereign power in Church matters as head of all the institutions in the realm. Thus, in a Council or Assembly of the Picts, we find an ordinance of King Nectan read, which decreed that the whole Pictish nation should observe Easter according to the Latin reckoning, and that the Pictish clergy should make their tonsure after the Latin fashion. The Kings of Alban exercised the same supervision, while they were careful to recognize the rights of the Church and its spiritual independence.

The year 906 was an important one for the Church, for in that year, as we learn from the record of a Council of the Church, a great meeting was held on the Moot Hill of Scone, at which King Constantine, the second of the Kings of Alban, and Bishop Cellach swore, together with the Scots, to keep the laws and discipline of the faith, and the rights of the Churches and the Gospels.[1] This secured the rights and liberties of the Church, as amalgamated into one body. Cellach became the first Bishop of Alban, and the Primacy must now have been removed from Abernethy to St. Andrews.

For a long period the memorials of Church history in Scotland are few and imperfect. Of the Church Synods held at the end of the eleventh century, when Queen Margaret was labouring to bring the Scottish Church into conformity with that of England, the information is very scanty, but we have a glimpse of the proceedings of one of the Councils, which is interesting. We are told that in this Council, the greatest of all, the pious Queen contended for three days, almost alone, against the supporters of the Scottish usages; that King Malcolm, her husband, who spoke English, French, and Irish with equal ease, interpreted between her and the clergy; that he was ready to say or to do whatever she commanded; and that among the many abuses which the Council was thus persuaded to condemn, were the commencement of Lent, not on Ash Wednesday but on the Monday after it, so that the fast lasted thirty-six days only instead of forty; the not-partaking of the Communion on Easter day; the celebration of the Mass by certain priests in some parts of the country after an uncouth, barbarous ritual,

[1] "Stat. Eccl. Scot.," Preface, p. 19.

contrary to the custom of the rest of Christendom; the neglect of Sunday, so that the people worked on it as freely as on other days; and marriages within forbidden degrees of affinity, as between a man and his stepmother, and between a man and his brother's widow.[1]

The assimilation of the Scottish Church to the English, thus begun by Queen Margaret, continued to advance rapidly during the reigns of her sons, Edgar, Alexander, and David, although it was not for three centuries that Scotland obtained the pall of supremacy. So long as they had no metropolitan, the clergy could meet in council only by authority of the Pope, exercised by a legate in Scotland, or transmitted by rescript from Rome. In the year 1225 the clergy were empowered by the Pope, Honorius III., to meet in council without the summons or the presence of a legate, and to hold their provincial councils by the Pope's authority—the bishops choosing one of their number to be Conservator, with power to punish notorious transgressors of the Canons, and to enforce their observance by the Church. There are scarcely any other remains of the proceedings of the Scottish Councils earlier than the beginning of the thirteenth century. Within little more than fifty years after the Bull of Pope Honorius, the Provincial Councils framed or adopted fifty or sixty canons, which sufficed for the government of the Church in Scotland almost till the Reformation.[2] The Provincial and Synodical Canons may be said to date from the year 1225, and they continued till 1559, when the Provincial Council, which was called in that year to meet the advance of the Reformation, separated never to meet again.

But whatever power was claimed by the Pope or by the Church Councils, we find throughout the whole period of Scottish history—even in the time when Papal authority was at its highest—the State jealously maintaining its independent action, and any proceeding by the Church not approved by the State, was resisted or overruled by the King and the Parliament. In the beginning of the thirteenth century, on occasion of a Papal commission granted to an English and a foreign Churchman for trying an action against the Abbey of Kelso, King Alexander II. promptly interfered, and prohibited the Commissioners from

[1] "Concilia Scotiæ," Preface. p. xxii.   [2] Ibid., Preface. p. liv.

proceeding, while he intimated that anything done by them could have no effect. About the same time the State asserted its right to a seat and a voice in the Councils of the Church; and the proceedings of one of the Councils in the fourteenth century (22nd March, 1325) show that the sovereign was exercising what the Scottish Kings had long claimed—the right of presenting to all benefices in the collation of a bishop during the vacancy of the see. At this Council the claim was protested against on the part of the Papal Court, but with no practical result; and in a Provincial Council held in 1450 it was declared to be a right which belonged to the Crown by ancient and primitive use. Three years afterwards this was confirmed by Parliament.

The Church was represented in Parliament, and its heads had seats there, but only as holders of property; and although they came to be recognized as a separate Estate, they voted, like the other Estates, only as subjects. During the troubled period from 1391 to 1428, and for many years afterwards, although Provincial Councils still met, ecclesiastical questions were discussed and determined in Parliament. In one instance, when the office of prior was in dispute between two monks, an appeal was taken from the judgment of the bishop of the diocese to the Council; but the appeal was held not to be competent, and the question was decided by the King in Parliament, with the advice of the clergy present for the time.[1] Again, during the Papal schism, Parliament interfered to regulate rights of appeal in the Church courts. In 1401 it was enacted by Parliament that any one thinking himself unjustly excommunicated should be at liberty to appeal, within forty days, from the bishop to the conservator, and from him to the provincial council, where such questions should be determined so long as the schism in the Papacy should last. "To this ordinance," it is recorded, "the clergy consented during the schism, like the rest of the King's lieges." Thus, too, after the deposition of the Anti-Pope by the Council of Constance in 1417, when it had to be decided whether the Scottish Church should acknowledge Pope Martin V., the question was debated and judged, not in a provincial council of the clergy, but in a general council of the Three

[1] "Concilia Scot."

Estates of the realm. By the Act 1424, c. 3, Parliament directs the secular power to support the Church, if necessary, in punishing heretics and Lollards. So also in 1425 it was enacted by Parliament that every bishop should cause his *Inquisitores Hereticæ Pravitatis* to make search for heretics; also that he should order his clergy to make rogations and prayer for the King and Queen and their issue. So likewise in 1427 Parliament having framed or adopted a measure for expediting the procedure in secular causes in the ecclesiastical courts, ordained that it should be enacted by the Provincial Council. In two of these instances the consent of the clergy to the deliverance of the Parliament is formally set forth, and the presumption is that it was accorded in the other also. In the summer of 1427 the Parliament framed an ordinance curtailing the cost and abridging the forms of process in civil causes against churchmen in the spiritual courts; and, as if the Church had only to register the decree, ordained that it should be forthwith enacted by the Provincial Council.

Against this bold interference of the Scottish legislature in ecclesiastical affairs the Pope protested, but his interference came to nothing. At a later period, 1492, on the elevation of Glasgow to an archbishopric and metropolitan see, bitter disputes arose between the Archbishop of Glasgow and the Primate of St. Andrews, which continued till the Parliament interposed, and enjoined the archbishops to cease their contest, and submit to such judgment as the King and his Three Estates should communicate to the Pope, under penalty of suspension of payment of their rents.

The Crown exercised other rights over the Church. By a custom which long prevailed in Scotland the personal estate of a bishop lapsed to the Crown on his death, even when he died testate. In the middle of the thirteenth century the Bishop of St. Andrews procured the prohibition of this by a Papal Bull; but this was recalled by another Bull, and the right of the Crown remained unchallenged for a hundred years. It was renounced by James II. in Parliament in 1449–50, but with a reservation to the King of his right, during the vacancy, to the revenues of the real estate of the see, and to the advowson of all benefices in the bishop's collation. In the early part of the sixteenth century Parliament is found framing ordinances, declaring the steps which it was expedient that the general Provincial Council should adopt. The use of the Bible in the vernacular had been sanctioned in England in 1538, and it was by an Act of the Scottish Parliament, four years afterwards, that it was declared lawful to all men to hear and to read the Scriptures in the common speech of the country—English or Scottish. This Act was resented by the Church as an encroachment on its prerogative, but the Provincial Council was powerless to prevent it. But we are anticipating. There are matters belonging to an earlier period which fall to be noticed, especially in regard to the connection of the clergy with the administration of the law.

From the time of Queen Margaret churchmen had a large share, and exercised a powerful influence in the administration of justice, and they rendered valuable services in that important department. The Lord Chancellor was the first subject in the realm, and of fifty-four persons who held that high office down to the death of Beaton forty-three were churchmen. Of the Lords of Session, by the original constitution of the College of Justice, the President and one-half of the Senators behoved to be ecclesiastics. Most of the dignified churchmen of later times belonged to the first families in the land, and many of them were allied to royalty, and from their education, and the accomplishments of many of them, they exercised a powerful influence on the tone of society. For the same reason, to churchmen fell, in a great measure, the framing of laws. It could not be otherwise, for there were no others capable.

The jurisdiction of the courts of the Church, which came to be so extensive, was, we need scarcely say, a matter of growth. In England, by the laws of Edgar and Canute, the civil and ecclesiastical judges sat together in one Court, and this joint jurisdiction was confirmed by Edward the Confessor. William the Conqueror (*circa* 1072) separated the ecclesiastical from the civil, and required all spiritual causes to be thenceforth brought before the Bishop or his Official only. In Scotland in early times, before the reign of David I., the king exercised jurisdiction in ecclesiastical as well as civil ones. David frequently heard causes in person, but not ecclesiastical cases. He had, however, his great law officers—his justiciar, his chancellor, his constable

—each with his own jurisdiction; and then, or soon afterwards, Scotland was divided into sheriffdoms, where the law was administered in the name and by authority of the king. A separate jurisdiction was recognized in the Church, but this was always limited, as it is now. It was never allowed to encroach on civil rights, and there never was a time when the supremacy of the Pope was recognized as controlling the free action of the State, or indeed of the Church itself.

The acknowledged jurisdiction of the Church courts, however, was very large, and it was recognized and respected by the State; and when ecclesiastical sentences, pronounced in cases within the Church's own province, were resisted, churchmen looked to the State, and to the King's courts, to aid them in their enforcement. In one recorded instance the King commands his justiciar to compel payment to churchmen *de redditibus casus* and other dues.[1] The King even lent the aid of the State, on the application of the Church, to seize and deliver over to their ecclesiastical superiors apostatizing members of religious fraternities. But with demands issued from Rome in ecclesiastical matters the King did not always comply, nor indeed did the clergy, although in some instances the strenuous efforts made by the Papal See to obtain enforcement of ecclesiastical decrees by the arm of the civil power were successful. There are recorded instances of Papal Bulls addressed to the sovereign, in which he is "asked, admonished, and exhorted" to enforce the decrees of the Church, and these are followed by letters of incarceration by the King against the delinquents who had disobeyed. There are examples, also, of the great lords coming under obligations for themselves and their dependants to respect the rights and claims of the Church. In 1225 we find Earl Duncan of Carrick, in a chapter held at Ayr, solemnly undertaking to pay all his own tithes and dues, and to use his power with his men and tenants for the same purpose; also, no longer to oppress the clergy of Carrick with tallies or exactions, and to enforce Church censures by confiscation and temporal penalties.[2] At the same time we find the whole authority of Rome exerted to prevent the clergy from pleading in the lay courts.

[1] "Scottish Legal Antiquities," Professor Cosmo Innes.
[2] Chartulary of Glasgow, preface, xxvi.

At an earlier time the Church was empowered by our ancient laws to exercise jurisdiction in an interesting class of cases which concerned what was certainly a civil right, those, namely, which related to serfs who had taken holy orders. When we come to mediæval times we find what remained of the native population—*nativi* as they were appropriately called—in a state of bondage to the Saxon invaders. They were bought and sold with the land, and all their descendants became also serfs to the feudal lord, and the Church held many of these in property. Among many other examples there is a charter by King William (*circa* 1180) by which he conveys to Joceline, Bishop of Glasgow, one Gilmachoi de Conclud "with his children and all his descendants." In some cases, however, the serf was permitted to work for himself and to commute his services by an annual tribute to his lord, and thus to save money. Many of them were men of intelligence and contrived to obtain education, and in not a few instances they attained to good social positions, and filled offices of trust. Sometimes if they could amass sufficient means they purchased their freedom, and occasionally it was purchased for them by friends. There is a charter in the reign of Alexander II., when a burgess of Berwick purchases the freedom of one Renaldus, "a Neyf" or serf, "so that his wife and children and all descendants from him may go, and return, and stay wherever they please like other freemen." In this case the serf whose freedom is purchased is styled in the deed "*præpositus* (or bailie) of the town of Berwick." Not a few obtained admission to holy orders, but the mere act of ordination did not confer freedom. If he obtained ordination with consent of his lord, he was free; if ordained without his lord's consent, and without knowledge, on the part of the ordainer, that he was a serf, he was to be restored to his lord; but he was free if at the time of ordination the ordainer knew he was a serf. In that case, however, the ordainer was obliged to provide the lord with a substitute. A lord who had a right to reclaim a serf in orders was obliged to do so within a year. When the conditions which were necessary to freedom were awanting, the serf was to be deposed and degraded before being returned to his lord. In all questions as to whether a serf who had obtained holy orders could be reclaimed by his master, the Church courts had, by law, jurisdiction to decide them.[1]

But then as now, as we have said, the ecclesiastical jurisdiction was jealously defined. The Church courts were not permitted to deal with matters which touched the rights of the King. Our sovereigns, from William the Lion to Alexander III., maintained rigorously the jurisdiction of the civil magistrate, and if an ecclesiastical judge attempted to transgress the limits of his recognized jurisdiction—whether under the direct mandate of the Pope, or on any other pretext—he was liable to be restrained by the King or the Parliament. We find a brief addressed to an archdeacon, prohibiting him from entertaining in his court a plea respecting a lay fee held of the King *in capite*, "seeing that belongs to the King's court;" and there is an instance of a similar writ directed to an abbot. Our Stuart kings continued to act on the old tradition. An example is recorded in the reign of James IV., when the King interposed, and prevented the Bishop of Moray from enforcing, in an ecclesiastical court, a decreet-arbitral in a question regarding certain marches. And by the Act 1584, c. 31, the Privy Council was empowered, on cause shown, to suspend decrees of the Church inflicting ecclesiastical as well as civil penalties.

But the extent of business which fell within the allowed jurisdiction of the ecclesiastical courts was, as we have said, very great. The Bishop's Official had by law the sole cognizance, not only of suits directly concerning religion and morals and Church discipline, but also of others in their nature mixed (according to modern ideas chiefly temporal), "as to which the ecclesiastical preceded the civil jurisprudence in establishing the doctrines of moral obligation on which they depended."[2] Such were questions of *status*, of legitimacy, and of divorce; cases of slander, disputes between churchmen; questions arising upon covenant, when the covenant was sanctioned by an oath. To these was added the large class of business connected with testaments and probate, executry succession to heritage—in the time when Scottish heritage could be left by will: all these were dealt with in the bishop's court. Add to this the management and superintendence of notaries, then the largest class of

---

[1] "Q. Regiam Majestatem," c. 10.   [2] Lord Selborne, "Defence," p. 11.

"professional men." They received their appointments from the Archbishops, who had the power of suspending them,[1] and, being all churchmen or dependants of churchmen, they preferred the ecclesiastical courts to those of the sheriff. The Church courts, indeed, became the only settled and organized judicatories in Scotland presided over by educated lawyers.[2] In Glasgow, especially, there was a very large influx of suitors to the bishop's court, attracted by the exceptionally high character and reputation of the Chapter, with a great amount of civil business, which resulted from the extension of the privileges and civil jurisdiction of the bishop conferred by James IV.[3]

At an earlier period certain ecclesiastical cases of importance —such as questions concerning Church revenues, ecclesiastical buildings, and lands which formed part of the endowments of the Church—were tried by delegates appointed by the Pope. An account, or rather a judicial report, as it deserves to be called, of one of these cases is recorded in the Chartulary of Paisley, and it is interesting as an example of the regularity of the procedure observed in the old ecclesiastical courts, and the strict regard to justice, and observance of judicial forms, which characterized them. It was a lawsuit regarding a property belonging to the Abbey of Paisley, and the proceedings are recorded with great minuteness of detail. A part of the abbey lands at Kilpatrick had been unjustly seized by one Gilbert, a layman, who disputed the title of the monks, and the abbot obtained from the Pope a commission to certain delegates to try the cause. Many witnesses were examined, parties were heard, and a judgment having been pronounced in favour of the abbot, the expenses of process were taxed, and decree pronounced—the sentence concluding with an admonition to the bishop to see it put to execution. The bishop did what he could, but Gilbert proved contumacious. He was thereupon excommunicated, but as he despised that censure, the Pope's delegates applied to the King to lend the aid of the secular arm, *brachium seculare extendere*. The King, Alexander II., appears to have complied, but the sequel has not been recorded.[4] The proceedings in this

---

[1] "Liber Protocol.," No. 428.
[2] "Sketches of Early Scottish History," Cosmo Innes, p. 263.
[3] Chartulary of Glasgow, Maitland Club, No. 458.
[4] Chartulary of Paisley, Maitland Club, pp 73, 166, *et seq*.

old lawsuit, decided more than six hundred and sixty years ago (1223), would do credit to any modern court of justice.

The judicial proceedings in these Courts were conducted according to the Roman or Civil law, which, from the earliest period of which we have a record, was considered the common law of Scotland. In certain provinces, such as in Galloway, and also on the Borders, there were local or "Customary" laws; but whatever the law was for the time being, the clergy, equally with the laity, had to observe it. Even in exceptional cases, where it might be supposed ecclesiastics would be exempt, they had to submit like other subjects. For example, in the beginning of the thirteenth century, when an unseemly usage prevailed, by which, in all questions between a Scot and an Englishman, the settlement was, by the laws of the Marches, referred to the arbitrament of single combat, an ecclesiastic, be he Priest, Abbot, or Bishop, was compelled to fight in person the same as a layman. Pope Innocent III. issued a Bull forbidding the practice, under pain of excommunication, but it was too inveterate to be readily abandoned, and twenty years afterwards we find the Bishops and clergy of England petitioning the Cardinal Legate Otho for its suppression.[1] But some time elapsed before it was abolished.

Another innovation on the common law—one claimed by the Church and conceded by the State from a very early period—may be here noticed, namely, the right of Sanctuary, called in old Scottish law "the privilege of grith." It was a right which, from very early times, had belonged to the precincts of the Royal palaces, but by the Canon, and the more ancient ecclesiastical law, all churches were held to afford protection to criminals for a limited period, sufficient to admit of amends by composition—in the old laws of England called "bot" or "wergild" (blood-money)—being made for the offence. One of the ecclesiastical laws of Canute, in the early part of the eleventh century, confirmed and legalized the claim of the Church to right of sanctuary, which had existed before Canute's time. The terms of this old law are curious:—"Every church is, by right, in Christ's own grith (protection), and every Christian man has great need that he show great reverence for that grith, because God's grith

[1] "Stat. Eccl. Scot."

is of all griths the most excellent in merit and the best to preserve. . . . And if ever any man henceforth so break God's church-grith, that he be a homicide within church walls, then be that bot-less (beyond compensation); and let every one of them who is a friend to God pursue him, unless it happen that he escape thence, and seek so awful a sanctuary, that the king, through that, grant him life against full bot both to God and to men."[1] In one of the ancient canons of the Scotican Councils, among the list of misdeeds against which the Church enjoined excommunication, after the laying of violent hands on parents and priests, is denounced "the open taking of thieves out of the protection of the Church." Fugitives within the grith of church-sanctuary were supplied with food by the clergy. The Church, however, was not always able to afford this protection, and to strengthen her authority, and to support what, in the then circumstances of society, was a salutary refuge against rash vengeance, the King at times granted his special sanction to particular ecclesiastical asylums. In the Chartulary of Kelso four of these are mentioned; but it was carefully guarded in Scotland from the danger of encouraging crime by affording an easy immunity to criminals. In later times, and during a period of great misrule, the Parliament enacted that whoever took the protection of the Church for homicide should be required to come out and undergo an assize, that it might be found whether it was committed of "forethought felony," or only in "chaude mellée." In case it should be found to be of the latter, he was to be restored to the Sanctuary, and the Sheriff was directed to give him security to that effect before requiring him to leave it.[2]

The limits of the place of Sanctuary were usually defined by four crosses. In a charter by David I. to the Church of Lesmahago in 1144, the privilege of sanctuary is conferred in these terms:—"Whoso for escaping peril of life or limb flee to the said cell, or come within the four crosses that stand around it, of reverence to God and saint Machritus, I grant him my firm peace." To break the "king's peace" was something more formidable than to break the peace of the Church. By our most ancient law the penalty of even raising the hand to strike within the king's grith, was four cows to the king and one to

[1] Laws of Canute, quoted by Lord Selborne.   [2] Act Rob. II., 1373.

him whom the offender would have struck; and for slaying a man "in the peace of our Lord the King," the forfeit was nine score of cows to the king besides the asythment or composition to the kin of him slain, "after the assize of the land."[1] In granting the same privilege to the church of Inverlethan, Malcolm IV. (1153–65) ordains that none dare to violate its peace "and mine," on pain of forfeiture of life and limb. In later times the claim of the Church to rights of Sanctuary was jealously scrutinized by the civil courts, and cases are recorded, such as that of the Friars Preachers of Glasgow in 1553, when the right claimed by ecclesiastics to the privilege of grith was rejected.

The recognition by the law, in cases of homicide, of the payment of money to the relatives of the slaughtered man as a satisfaction for the wrong, survived in Scotland till after the Reformation, and the "Letters of Relaxation," with the "Letter of Slayance," which followed the discharge by the relatives, were accepted by the Church as a sufficient atonement. An example of the Church's action in the matter occurs in the records of the Presbytery of Glasgow in the end of the sixteenth century. The Minute of the Presbytery is as follows:—"Ordenis Jo^n Levingstoun in Inchevold to produce this day viii dayes before thame Lettres of Relaxation fra the horne, and respet (respite) he hes fra the slauchtir of umq^{ll} Jo^n Adame: As also ane Lettir of Slayance for the said slauchtir fra the said umq^{ll} Jo^{ns} wyfe and bairnis, kin, freindes, and alyance, for the said slauchtir. And ordanis the minister of Campsie to summond the said umq^{ll} Jo^{ns} wyfe and bairnis before thame this daye viii dayes that thai may declair gif thai be aggreed w^t the said Jo^n Levingston and satisfeit for the said umq^{ll} Jo^n Adames slauchtir."[2] In Glasgow, at a later period than this, the ministers appear to have, at their own hands, practised the ancient custom of commuting offences for a money payment. In 1630 there occurs in the records of the Presbytery a minute "censuring the ministers for dispensing with public repentance for money."

The protection afforded to criminals by places of sanctuary was subsequently extended to debtors. After the Reformation

---

[1] "Leges inter Brettos et Scotos."   [2] Presbytery Records, 7th February, 1595.

it was to the latter only that the right remained available,[1] and even to that extent it was confined to the precincts of the Royal palaces. In this way a defined district round the palace of Holyrood has, down to our own day, been used as a place of sanctuary for debtors. In the Act, 1696, c. 5, "the Abbey" is referred to as "a privileged place," to which a debtor may "flee for his personal security." The privilege has never been formally abolished, but it has fallen into disuse since the alteration of the law as to imprisonment for civil debt.

In the early history of the Church there arose, out of the question of the celibacy of the clergy, another innovation on the common law, affecting the position of ecclesiastics in questions of succession. In the early monastic Church of Ireland celibacy was enforced upon the monks, but when the rule was broken in upon, under the influence of the secular clergy, marriage came gradually to be permitted. The consequence was that a direct descent from the ecclesiastical persons themselves came in place of the older system of succession, and Church offices came to be hereditary in families. The next step was that the abbots and superiors did not take orders, but became virtually laymen, providing a substitute to perform the ecclesiastical functions, but themselves retaining the name, and all the secular privileges and emoluments of the abbacy. The performance of the Church services was either entrusted to a secular priest, or it fell to the *Cele De*, when there was such a body connected with the monastery, or to both combined. In the old chartularies we find repeated instances of the acknowledged marriages of priests, and of their sons succeeding to their livings; and in the Chartulary of Kelso there are abundant instances of the sons of clergymen appearing along with their fathers, and plainly taking their rank and style from them. In England marriage had been so general among the clergy that Pope Pascal II., writing to Archbishop Anselm in A.D. 1100, took notice of the fact, and that "the greater and better part of the English clergy were clergymen's sons;" for which reason he considered that, as to them, the observance of the Roman rule must be dispensed with.[2] It was not till 1139 that celibacy was rigidly enjoined by the great Council of

[1] Bankton's "Institutes," iv. 39. [2] Wilkins' "Concil.," quoted by Lord Selborne.

Lateran, and in Scotland it was first effectually enforced by David I. among his other Roman reforms. So late as 1185 we find Pope Urban III. empowering the Bishop of Glasgow to remove the sons of priests from churches which they claimed to hold as of hereditary right, and of which their fathers had been the last incumbents. In many instances, however, the effect of the enforcement of celibacy, when the benefice had become hereditary, was, not to restore the clerical character of the possessors, but to convert them into purely lay families, who retained the lands for their own use.[1] It was in this way that the Abbot of Brechin, who had been secularized, appropriated to himself and transmitted to his family the territories which his predecessors had administered for the Church. The best effect of the enforcement of the celibacy of the clergy at that time was to prevent them from becoming a hereditary caste.

But, apart from the licentiousness of the priesthood—confessed and condemned through all the three centuries of Scottish ecclesiastical legislation—there was an evil, less conspicuous perhaps, but not less fatal: the failure of the Church in the due exercise of its right of collation. At no time during the three hundred years that preceded the Reformation does it appear that the Scottish bishops succeeded in making orders an indispensable qualification for the benefice. It was bad enough to see in the diocese of Glasgow, at the close of the twelfth century, sons formally claiming their fathers' churches as of hereditary right, while the Pope, professing to condemn the practice, yet empowered the bishop, by ignoring it, to suffer its continuance. But the champions of the Romish Church themselves, in their conflict with the Reformers, acknowledged and bewailed that rich livings, with the cure of thousands of souls, were held by boys, by infants even, by men deformed in body, imbecile in mind, hardened in ignorance, old in wickedness and vice.

As the period of the Reformation approached, the state of religion in Scotland had become deplorable. Even to the most partial and tolerant among the supporters of the Papacy, it became evident that something besides the burning of heretics

[1] "Celtic Scotland," ii. 338.

must be done to amend matters. As the evil could not be concealed, it must be acknowledged, and remedies enforced. Evidence of this is found in the legislation both of the Church and of the State. An Act was passed by the Scottish Parliament in 1540, which declares that "the unhonestie and misreule of kirkmen, baithe in witt, knowlege, and maneris, is the mater and caus that the kirk and kirkmen ar lychtlyit and contempnit." On the part of the Church, again, many Statutes were passed for reforming abuses. At a General Convention and Provincial Court which met in the Blackfriars Church at Edinburgh on the 27th of November, 1549, at which many eminent ecclesiastics were present, the Statutes then passed or ratified were prefaced by a remarkable confession. It bears that the root and cause of the troubles and heresies which affected the Church were the corruption, the profane lewdness, and the gross ignorance of Churchmen of almost all ranks. It enjoins the clergy to put away their concubines, to dismiss from their houses the children born to them in concubinage, not to promote their sons to benefices, nor to enrich their daughters with dowries from the patrimony of the Church. Prelates are admonished not to keep in their households manifest drunkards, gamblers, brawlers, buffoons, blasphemers, nor profane swearers. The clergy in general are exhorted to amend their lives, to dress modestly, to keep their faces shaven and their heads tonsured, and to abstain from secular pursuits and especially trading—and more of the same kind. One canon sets forth that even in the most populous parishes few of the parishioners come to mass or sermon; that in the time of service those present indulge in jesting and irreverence, and that sports and secular business go on in the porch and churchyard. Parliament also came to the aid of the Church with further legislation for the reform of abuses. There is one Act against the swearing of abominable oaths; another to enforce the sentences of the Church against persons who frequented places of worship while the curse of the Church was still upon them. Parliament also passed Acts against the Reformers; against persons accused of heresy; against those who made disturbance in time of divine service; against the liberty of the press in the publication of books concerning the faith, books of ballads, songs, and blasphemous rhymes. And one Act is directed against those who, "to the great slander of the Christian people, eat flesh in Lent and other forbidden days."

Other Acts were passed by the Parliament, the object of which was to prop up the falling Papacy, for the existing state of things was to be maintained, and the faith of the Church vindicated, at all hazards. By one of these Acts it was made death to question the Pope's authority, and the heads of the Church showed they were in earnest by the martyrdom of Walter Mill so late as 1558. With that "Act of faith" the power and jurisdiction of the Pope may be said to have come to an end in Scotland. Yet in March of the following year one more Provincial Council assembled in Edinburgh, at the instance of the Queen Regent, and once more stringent canons were enacted for reforming the lives and manners of the clergy. Former injunctions were repeated, and others added chiefly affecting ecclesiastical law and order. Rectors who could not themselves preach were appointed to find substitutes at their own charges; the forms of process in the Consistorial courts were ordered to be abbreviated; the manner of appointing executors to persons dying intestate was amended; and the rule of the secular law fixing twenty-one years as the age of majority, was to receive effect in ecclesiastical courts.

But it was too late. The old system was doomed; and looking to the ignorance, the indifference to duty, and the terrible licentiousness of the clergy in its later years, which all attempts at reform failed to reach, no one can regret its fall.

Yet before entering on Reformation times, we cannot, in justice to the "old Church," leave it without a word, in passing, as to the debt we owe to it—at least to the ecclesiastics of its earlier history—and the services which it rendered to the State in return for State protection. Even to the princely prelates of the later times, with all their vices, civilization owes something, but to the older Churchmen, apart from what they did for religion, we owe a debt which is not sufficiently recognized. We have referred to the service rendered by ecclesiastics in the department of law, in the framing of statutes, and the administration of justice. In the monastery was to be found all that tended to progress and refinement. The laity, as a rule, had no education of any kind, and many even of the highest rank among them could neither read nor write. When all was darkness, and violence, and disorder without, there were cultivated within the abbey walls the arts of peace and civilization. The monasteries were the first, and for a long time the only, educational institutions in the kingdom; and it is to the old Church, at a later time, that we are indebted for our Universities. We find the monks always zealous for the welfare of their tenants; encouraging agriculture, and every improvement of the soil; leading the way in an adventurous foreign trade, and in all arts and manufactures, while they cultivated extensive hospitality and charity. To the old monks we owe the production and the preservation of many precious manuscripts, and to them we are indebted for our invaluable Chartularies. Writing formed a most important part of the monastic occupations. The art of beautiful penmanship and illumination spread from Ireland, side by side with religion, to Iona, and thence to Melrose, Lindisfarne, and other monasteries in Britain. Columba was noted for his skill in the art. "Scribe" was a title of honour, and it was frequently used to enhance the dignity of a bishop. Many of the manuscripts which remain to us, including copies of the sacred Scriptures, are wonderful monuments of the conception, skill, and patience of the old ecclesiastics. The Book of Kells, with its marvellous decorations, and other illuminated Irish manuscripts, belonging to a period not later than the end of the seventh century, are not inferior in splendour to any extant in Europe. Architecture, music, and painting, with the sculpture of stones and crosses, and inimitable metal work in croziers, bells, and shrines, were all likewise cultivated in the monastery. To the old Church, again, we are indebted for our grand old cathedrals and abbey churches—many of them of singular beauty, and adorned with stained glass. And they were not erected in haste. They were the result of careful study and matured design, and the building of some of them extended over long periods of years. The old Churchmen, too, worked from no mean or unworthy motive. Their motives, to use the words of Professor Cosmo Innes, were "the interest and honour of the Convent, the honest rivalry with neighbouring Houses and other Orders; above all, the zeal for religion which was honoured by their efforts, and their strong desire to render its rites magnificent, and to set forth in a worthy manner the worship of the Deity. All these gave to the works of the old monks a principle and a feeling above what modern art can ever hope to reach."[1]

To return. In England, as is well known, the ruling powers took the lead in the Reformation; in Scotland it was the act of the people, and it was in Acts of the Scottish Parliament that the will of the people was expressed, and the faith of the Church and its new form of government—previously adopted and settled by the Church itself—received State recognition. The "First Covenant" had been signed in 1557, and in 1560 Parliament passed the Act by which the ancient recognition of the Church by the State was renewed, and the national establishment of the Protestant faith was effected. By that Act the first Confession of Faith was adopted, and in the same year the first General Assembly was held. The Parliament of 1560 met without Royal authority, but its proceedings were "ratified and approved" and "of new" re-enacted by the first Parliament of James I. in the celebrated Act of 1567. The Confession of Faith was not imposed on the nation by Parliament. It was framed and adopted by the Church independently, and was then, to use the words of the Statute, "exhibited to the Estates of Scotland in Parliament, and by their public votes authorized as a doctrine grounded upon the infallible Word of God."

By other Acts passed in 1560—and all formally repeated or re-enacted in 1567—the jurisdiction and legal position of the Church were made more clear. By one, the jurisdiction of the Pope was abolished. By a second, all Acts of Parliament "made in time past not agreeing with God's Word, and now contrary to the Confession of Faith," were repealed. By a third, the celebration of the Mass was declared idolatrous, and was made penal. Parliament proceeded on the ground that the Mosaic law against idolatry was still binding on nations, and applying the Statute to it, as a civil crime, it was enacted that the third lapse should be punished with death.

By the Act of 1567 the Church, as established in its present faith, was formally recognized and defined. It declares "the

[1] Preface to Chartulary of Kelso. Bannatyne Club, p. xliv.

ministers of the blessed evangel of Jesus Christ whom God has now raised up among us," and their successors "agreeing with them, that now lives in doctrine and administration of the sacraments, and the people of this realme that professes Christ as he now is offered in his evangel, and do communicate with the holy sacraments, as in the reformed kirkes of this realme they are publicklie administrat according to the Confession of Faith, to be the only true and halie kirk of Jesus Christ within this realme."

The Act, 1579, c. 69, declares that "our Soveraine Lord with advice of his three estaites of the present Parliament has declared and granted jurisdiction to the Kirk quhilk consists and stands in the preaching of the trew worde of Jesus Christ, correction of maners, and administration of the halie sacraments."

By the Act, 1592, c. 116—which has been called the Charter of the Church—the present Presbyterian order was statutorily recognized and fixed, and the powers and jurisdiction of the Church were defined. Its terms are important as stating what are the Courts of the Church which have jurisdiction, and as defining what are their statutory powers.

It "ratifies and apprevis the General Assemblies appointed be the said Kirk, And declares that it sall be lauchfill to the Kirk and ministers, every zeir at the least, and oftener *pro re nata*, as occasion and necessity sall require, to hold and keepe generall Assemblies: Providing that the King's Majesty or his commissioners with them to be appoynted be his Hienesse be present at ilk general Assemblie, before the dessolving thereof, nominate and appoynt time and place quhen and quhair the nixt generall Assembly sall be halden: and in case neither his Majesty nor his said Commissioners beis present for the time in that Toun quhair the said general assembly beis halden, then and in that case it sall be lesum to the said general assemblie, be themselves, to nominate and appoynt time and place quhair the nixt general assembly of the Kirk sall be keiped and halden, as they haue been in use to do thir times by past. And als ratifies and apprevis the Synodicall and Provinciall Assemblies to be halden be the said Kirk and Ministers twise ilk zeir, as they haue bene, and ar presently in use to do, within every Province of this Realme: And ratifies and apprevis the Presby-

teries and particular Sessiones appoynted be the said Kirk, with
the haill jurisdiction and discipline of the same Kirk, agreed
upon be his Majesty in conference had be his Hienesse with
certain of the Ministers convened to that effect: Of the quhilkes
articles the tenour followes: MATERS to be intreated in Provinciall Assemblies: Thir Assemblies ar constitute for weichtie
maters necessar to be intreated be mutuel consent and assistance
of brethren within the Province, as neede requiris. This assembly hes power to handle, ordour, and redresse all things omitted
or done amisse in the particular assemblies. It hes power to
depose the office bearers of that Province, for gude and just
cause deserving deprivation. And generally thir Assemblies hes
the haill power of the particular Eldershippes quairof they are
collected. MATERS to be intreated in the Presbyteries. The
power of the Presbyteries is to give diligent laboures in the
boundes committed to their charge. That the kirkes be keeped
in gude ordour. To enquire diligently of naughty and ungodly
persons, and to travel to bring them in the way againe be admonition or threatning of God's judgements, or be correction. It
appertaines to the Eldershippe to take heede that the word of
God be purely preached within their boundes, the sacraments
richtly ministred, the discipline interteined, and Ecclesiastical
guddes uncorruptly distributed. It belangis to this kinde of
Assemblies to cause the ordinances maid be the Assemblies,
Provincialles, nationals, and generals, to bee keeped and put
in execution, to make constitutions quhilk concernis to prepon
in the Kirk, for decent ordour in the particular Kirk quhair
they governe: Providing that they altar na rules maid be the
Provincial or General Assemblies. And that they make the
Provincial Assemblies foresaids privy of the rules they sall
make: And to abolish constitutions tending to the hurt of the
same. It has power to excommunicate the obstinate, formal
process being led and dew interval of time observed. ANENT
particular Kirks gif they be lauchfully ruled be sufficient Ministry and Session. They haue power and jurisdiction in their
awin congregation in maters Ecclesiastical. And decernis and
declaris the saids Assemblies, Presbyteries, and Sessiounes, jurisdiction and discipline thereof foresaid to be in all time cumming
maist just gude and godly in the selfe, notwithstanding of quhat-

sumever Statutes, Acts, Canone, Civill or Municipall laws, made
in the contrare." By a later Act (1640, c. 20), the powers and
jurisdiction of Presbyteries were further defined.

It will be observed that there is in the Act of 1592 no speci-
fication of "the matters to be entreated" in General Assemblies,
but as these Assemblies are, in a subsequent clause, described
as "the general meeting and representatives of the foresaid
Presbyterian Ministers and Elders, in whose hands the exercise
of the Church government is established," it may be inferred
that, except that its jurisdiction extends over all the inferior
Church Courts, it does not extend beyond the class of matters
which the Act declares to be vested in Provincial Synods,
namely, "the haill power of the particular eldershippe quhairof
they are collected."[1] The minute of the very first meeting of
the Assembly, in December, 1560, bears that it consisted of
"the Ministers and Commissioners of *the particular Kirkes of
Scotland* convened to consult upon the things which are to
set forth God's glory and the well of His Kirk in this realm."
And it is the same now. It follows that the jurisdiction of
the General Assembly is confined to matters which concern
the Church within Scotland, and that no act or proceeding
having reference to matters outwith the kingdom, or which
would fall to be executed or enforced out of Scotland, can have
any force or be protected by any privilege. There is one exception to this in the case of the Chaplains at each of the
Presidencies in India, two of whom must, in terms of an Act
of Parliament of 1833, be ministers of the Church of Scotland
ordained by the Presbytery of Edinburgh, and who are declared
to be subject in all things to the spiritual and ecclesiastical
jurisdiction of that Court subject to the review of the superior
Church Courts. The General Assembly had of its own authority gone a step beyond this in 1814 by authorizing these chaplains to form Kirk Sessions, and had given seats in the Assembly
to the chaplain and one of his elders, who take their places and
vote as constituent members of the Court. For this there is
no statutory authority, and recent decisions go to show that no

---

[1] The term Eldership was applied at that time to all the Church Courts, but it was the special and familiar designation of the Presbytery ("Digest of laws and decisions of the Church," by Rev W. Mair, D.D.)

Court of the Church can, by its own authority, alter its constitution by admitting to a share of its judicial functions any but members recognized by law. In the Strathbogie case Lord Fullarton said:—"The General Assembly is recognized by the law and constitution of the country as a representative body composed of delegates chosen by the different Presbyteries."

The representation of the Royal burghs and the Universities stands on a different footing. How this originated in either case does not appear, but it has existed from a very early period. As regards the Universities it may have had its origin in their *quasi* ecclesiastical character, and the professors being among the doctors in the Church, a class distinguished from the pastors. In the case of the Royal burghs, as we shall find, their representatives were elected by the Kirk Sessions for some time before that right was exercised by the magistrates and town councils.

There was another constituency which in former times sent a representative to the General Assembly in circumstances somewhat analogous to the case of the Indian chaplains. This was the church of Campvere, in the island of Walcheren. Indeed it still stands on the roll of the Assembly as a Church entitled to send a representative, although the right has not been exercised for many years. Campvere had been a settlement of Scottish merchants from the middle of the fifteenth century, and there was a church there, the ministers of which were appointed by the Commissioners of the Royal burghs in Scotland. The last appointment was made in 1790. By an Act in 1641 the General Assembly, certainly without any legal authority, invited the congregation at Campvere to send its minister and an elder to represent them in the Assembly, and this they did, the practice being continued till the end of the last century, when the settlement was broken up. In connection with this obsolete representation an interesting reminiscence of Home, the author of the tragedy of "Douglas," was communicated to the writer by the late Dr. Struthers, minister of Prestonpans:—"The Revd. John Home, the poet," said Dr. Struthers, "after resigning the pastoral charge of Athelstaneford, having, through the influence of the Marquis of Bute, obtained from the Government the position of Conservator of

Scots privileges in the Netherlands, with a Civil List pension of considerable amount, was for years a conspicuous figure at the meetings of the General Assembly, which he regularly attended as representative elder for Campvere; and on State occasions he invariably presented himself robed as Conservator, and with cocked hat and sword. The late Earl of Wemyss once told me that one of the earliest things he remembered was that in 1803 or 1804, Home, attired in this way, accompanied by 'Jupiter' Carlyle, attended an evening party at his (Lord Wemyss') grandfather's, every one of the guests at which were said to have been at the battle of Prestonpans."

Besides the courts of the Church specified by the Statute there is another body called the Commission of the General Assembly, which sits and exercises judicial functions in Church matters. It is certainly not a continuing court of the Church, for it would have no existence but for an annual nomination by the Assembly—a nomination which may or may not be made. The Commissioners appointed consist of the whole members of the Assembly for the year, with the addition of one person named by the Moderator for the year, and persons who were not members of Assembly because of their commissions having been found informal, are also added.[1] Power is committed to them to deal with "private processes" at certain specified diets, and also "to cognosce and finally determine as they shall see cause in every matter referred to them by any Act or order of Assembly," besides various other business, including the taking up and finally disposing of matters which had been *sub judice* of the Assembly, but which it had not time to overtake before its rising. In practice the Commission has been in the habit of exercising very large powers, including the cognoscing of processes against ministers, pronouncing final sentences in these, and following them up by sentences of deposition. In addition to appointing this Commission the Assembly takes the extreme step of prohibiting "the Presbytery of Edinburgh, or any other Presbytery within twelve miles thereof," from meeting during those weeks in which the Commission sits.

[1] "The Constitution and Law of the Church of Scotland," by a Member of the College of Justice.

It has been questioned whether there is any legal authority for the continued appointment of this Court. There can be no doubt that the General Assembly had, from a very early period, at its own hand, appointed Commissioners to act during the intervals between the meetings of the Assembly. In 1642 we find an Act in these terms:—" The General Assembly, considering the laudable custom of this Kirk for to appoint some commissioners in the interim betwixt Assemblies for prosecuting of overtures, and presenting the other desires of the Kirk to his Majestie, the Lords of the Counsell, and Estates of Parliament, &c. Therefore the Assembly thinks it necessary, before their dissolving, to appoint, &c., with full power to meet and convene at Edinburgh, to consider and perform what they find necessary for the ministerie by preaching, supplementing, preparing of drafts of one Confession, one Catechism, one Directory of public worship (which are always to be revised by the next Assembly), and by all other and lawful ecclesiastical ways for furtherance of this great work, in the union of this land, in religion and Kirk government, &c." By a subsequent Act, 1647, a commission is appointed with full powers of censuring "complyers and persons disaffected to the Covenant"—a declaration being added that "ministers shall not be deposed but in one of the quarterly meetings of the Commission."

This practice continued, but the first statutory power given to the General Assembly to appoint commissioners, or "visitors," was by the Act 1690, c. 5, which was passed at a time when there were great and exceptional disorders in the Church. It contains the following clause:—" And to the effect the disorders that have happened in this Church may be redressed, their Majesties, with advice and consent foresaid, do hereby allow the general meeting and representatives of the foresaid Presbyterian ministers and elders, in whose hands the exercise of the Church government is established, either by themselves, or by such ministers and elders as shall be appointed and authorized visitors by them, according to the custom and practice of Presbyterian government throughout the whole kingdom, and several parts thereof, to try and purge out all insufficient, negligent, scandalous, and erroneous ministers, by due course of ecclesiastical process and censures; and likeways for redressing all other

Church disorders. And further, it is hereby provided, that whatsoever minister, being convened before the general meeting and representatives of the Presbyterian ministers and elders, or the visitors to be appointed by them, shall either prove contumacious in not appearing, or be found guilty, and shall be therefore censured, whether by suspension or deposition, they shall *ipso facto* be suspended from, or deprived of, their stipends and benefices."

That this enactment gave power to the General Assembly to send "visitors" to inquire into and redress the disorders then prevailing in the Church, is very plain; the question is, whether it authorized the continued appointment of Commissions, and the delegation to them of the statutory powers of the Assembly after the exceptional state of matters had passed away. The professed object of the statute is to deal with the disorders "that have happened" in the Church, and which then called for immediate and exceptional remedies. A great many parishes were without ministers, and others were filled by men who, in the words of the Act, were "insufficient, negligent, and scandalous" in their conduct, and "erroneous" in their doctrine; and what was required was, not a Court sitting in Edinburgh, but "visitors" who should go into every parish to fill up the vacancies, and to "purge out" delinquent incumbents. The General Assembly itself appears to have understood the Act in this sense. They met shortly after it passed (16th October, 1690), and immediately proceeded to act on the special power which it conferred. They appointed not one Commission but two—one "to be a Commission for visiting the whole Presbyteries on the north side of the Water of Tay," with power to cite parties, and to cognosce and finally decide "in planting of vacant churches, constituting elderships, and trying and purging out all insufficient, negligent, scandalous, and erroneous ministers, conform to the particular instructions given them thereanent." The visitors appointed by the other Commission were to act on the south side of the Tay, and their duties were, *inter alia,* "the purging and planting of the City and Presbytery of Edinburgh," and other special matters. It is important to note, too, as showing the understanding of the Assembly as to the scope and intention of this Act of Parliament, that their minute bears that "the said Commission is only appointed *ad hunc effectum, et pro præsenti ecclesiæ statu.*"

The appointments in subsequent years varied in their terms. In 1695 the members "to be sent north by way of mission" were separated into divisions. One of these was directed "to repair to its post in the province of Angus and Mearns." Another was to go to Aberdeen; another to the province of Moray; and a fourth to the province of Caithness. It was some time before the exceptional disorders in the Church could be met, and in order to deal with them we find the Assembly in 1700 appointing a Commission to visit the Presbytery of Zetland, and to "assist the brethren of the said Presbytery in their Presbyterial work." With this view "the brethren of the said Commission that lives besouth Tay" are directed "to meet at Edinburgh upon the first day of April next, and be in readiness to take their voyage, and with the first fair wind to go to Zetland."

In subsequent years the Assembly appointed not two Commissions, but one only, and this it continues to do.

On one occasion recently the Commission was required to perform an act under statutory authority—also in exceptional circumstances. It occurred under the Patronage Abolition Act, when certain regulations required to be framed at a time when the General Assembly was not sitting; and to meet that one occasion the framers of the Act introduced a provision authorizing the Commission of the General Assembly, at a meeting to be specially called for the purpose, to frame the regulations. The time within which it was empowered to deal with this matter was limited to the period between the passing of the Act and the next meeting of the General Assembly; and with that solitary occasion the power thus conferred began and ended.

The question whether the Commission is a tribunal of the Church was for the first time raised judicially in the Culsalmond case—and the importance of the doubt then suggested was enhanced by the fact that it was raised, not at the bar, but by the Court itself. It was not decided, as the judgment for the presentee went on other grounds; but the question was regarded by the Court as a grave and important one. The Lord President, expressing the mind of the Court, and having no doubt the terms of the Act of 1690, which we have quoted, fully in view, said:—"I must begin by adverting to one question to which the attention of counsel was directed by the Court itself, and which, though it had not been made the subject of discussion in the Bill Chamber, appeared to be of essential importance —namely, whether the Commission of the General Assembly of the Church of Scotland, from which that proceeding emanated which has been brought before us, is a tribunal or judicature of the Church established and recognized by the laws and constitution of the realm. Called upon, as the counsel on both sides suddenly were, to argue this question, they have discharged their duty in a most able and satisfactory manner. But although we have bestowed upon their arguments the greatest possible attention, yet, considering the shape of the present proceedings, and that we are only now in a discussion in the Bill Chamber, it appears to me, and I believe also to all your Lordships, that it would not be proper or decorous finally to dispose of such a question, involving interests so extensive and important both to the Church and to the whole people of Scotland, without farther and more deliberate consideration, and probably by availing ourselves of the assistance of our brother judges." There the matter rests at present.

Before leaving the inquiry as to the constitution of the Church, it is necessary to refer to the Confession of Faith— that known as the Westminster Confession, which superseded the earlier Confession of 1560, and which forms part of our statute law. It was approved and adopted by the General Assembly in 1647, and by the Act 1690, c. 5, it was "ratified and established" by Parliament. The Confession, which is embodied *verbatim* in that Act, provides that "Synods and Councils are to handle or conclude nothing but that which is ecclesiastical, and are not to intermeddle with civil affairs which concern the commonwealth." The Act of 1690, which ratifies the Confession, also "establishes, ratifies, and confirms the Presbyterian Church government and discipline, that is to say, the government of the Church by Kirk Sessions, Presbyteries, Provincial Synods, and General Assemblies, ratified and established by the Act 1592, and thereafter received by the general consent of this realm to be the only government of Christ's Church within the kingdom." The action of the State in reference to the meetings of the General Assembly will be noticed afterwards. We shall also advert further on to the early history and constitution of Kirk Sessions, when we shall have occasion to notice the jurisdiction exercised by these Courts, and by Presbyteries, in the earlier period of the Church's history.

Of the other Acts of Parliament relating to the Church, the most important is the Statute 1707, c. 6, "for securing the Protestant religion and Presbyterian Church government," commonly known as the Act of Security. The terms of the proposed Union between England and Scotland were at that time under discussion, and by a previous Act of the Scottish Parliament, 1705, c. 4, it had been provided that the Commissioners were "not to treat of or concerning any alteration of the worship, discipline, and government of the Church of the kingdom, as now by law established." This provision is narrated in the Act of Security, and on the preamble that it is "reasonable and necessary that the true Protestant religion, as presently professed within this kingdom, with the worship, discipline, and government of the Church, should be effectually and unalterably secured," the Queen, with the advice and consent of Parliament, "doth hereby establish and confirm the said true Protestant religion, and the worship, discipline, and government of this Church, to continue without any alteration to the people of this land in all succeeding generations." The Act of 1690, which embodies the Confession of Faith, and ratifies and confirms it, with all other Acts of Parliament "relating thereto," is then expressly confirmed. A provision follows that the Confession shall be subscribed by the Professors, Regents, and Masters in the Universities of St. Andrews, Glasgow, Aberdeen, and Edinburgh, and by "all bearing office in any University, College, or School, as the confession of their faith;" and this is followed by an enactment that "none of the subjects of this kingdom shall be liable to, but all and every one of them for ever free of, any oath, test, or subscription within this kingdom contrary to or inconsistent with the foresaid true Protestant religion and Presbyterian Church government, etc., as above established." It is then enacted that the Sovereigns of Great Britain "shall, in all time coming, at his or her accession to the Crown, swear and subscribe that they shall inviolably maintain and preserve the present settlement of the true Protestant religion, with the government, worship, and discipline, rights and privileges, of this Church, as above established by the laws of this kingdom." And then follows this important stipulation:—" It is hereby statute and ordained that this Act of Parliament, *with the establishment therein contained*, shall be held and observed in all time coming *as a fundamental and essential condition of any treaty or union to be concluded between the two kingdoms*, without any alteration thereof, or derogation thereto, in any sort, for ever. And also that this Act of Parliament, and settlement therein contained, shall be insert and repeated in any Act of Parliament that shall pass for agreeing and concluding the foresaid treaty or union betwixt the two kingdoms, and that the same shall be therein expressly declared to be a fundamental and essential condition of the said treaty or union in all time coming."

In fulfilment of these stipulations, the Act of Security which contained them was inserted, and *verbatim* repeated, in the Act of Union which followed. It is declared to be an essential and fundamental part of the Articles of Union, "and everything in the said Articles and Act are hereby for ever ratified, approved, and confirmed." In terms so stringent was the maintenance of the Established Church in Scotland secured by the solemn sanctions of an international treaty. Mr. Gladstone said truly that now "it is not option or discretion, but plighted faith, which entails upon us the support of the Scottish Church."[1]

In regard to the subscription of the Confession a relaxation was, by an Act passed in 1853, permitted in the case of Professors other than Theological Professors and Principals. Instead of the form previously required, a declaration was substituted that they should "never endeavour directly or indirectly to teach or inculcate any opinions opposed to the Divine authority of the Holy Scriptures, or to the Westminster Confession of Faith," and that they should "not exercise the function of their office to the prejudice or subversion of the Church of Scotland as by law established, or the doctrines or privileges thereof."[2]

The Reformation made little material change in the law courts,

---

[1] "The State in its Relation with the Church," 2nd Edit., 1839.
[2] This declaration was abolished by the Universities Act of 1889.

but in one important department Queen Mary did a good deed. The Consistorial jurisdiction fell, and its officials closed their courts, when the Statute passed which confirmed the Reformed religion. There was then no judicatory left to confirm Testaments, and Consistorial cases either remained untried, or were carried to the Court of Session—still more frequently to the local courts of the Reformed Church. But about three years after the Reformation, the Queen, by a writ under her Quarter Seal, appointed four Commissioners, sitting in Edinburgh, to exercise, by themselves or their deputies, the jurisdiction formerly exercised by the Officials and Commissioners of the Archbishops and Bishops. "A priest of the old faith, who abjured Calvin, but had learned to follow Luther, an official of Lothian who had become a Judge of the Court of Session—Sir James Balfour, perhaps the ablest lawyer of the age—was placed at the head of the tribunal; and the rules which he framed for its procedure—the first declaring that its language should no longer be Latin—seem to show that he exerted himself not unsuccessfully to reform the abuses so long complained of in the old Consistorial Courts."[1]

It may be noticed here that although the Church asserted —and was entitled, in virtue of her statutory rights, to assert—a large measure of independence of the State, this was not then claimed to the extent to which it was strained in recent times. The Church recognized in the Privy Council a considerable power of direction and control in ecclesiastical matters. The question, what these powers were, was incidentally discussed in one of the leading cases decided in 1843, immediately before the secession of the Free Church party.[2] It was admitted on both sides that previous to the Union the power of keeping all other tribunals in their proper places—the Church not excepted—was vested in the Privy Council. As we have already stated, the Privy Council was expressly empowered by Parliament (1584, c. 31) to stay and suspend the decreets of any judgments inflicting pains and penalties, ecclesiastical as well as temporal, on cause shown. But the Non-intrusionists maintained that shortly after the Union all the judicial functions of that Court ceased,

---

[1] Mr. Robertson, Preface to "Stat. Eccl. Scot." clxxviii.
[2] The Stewarton Case, 20th January, 1843.

without being transferred to any other Court. This, as was pointed out by Lord Medwyn, in the learned opinion which he gave in the case referred to, was a mistake, as a large portion of the jurisdiction of the Privy Council had certainly come to be exercised by the Court of Session. That Court, his Lordship said, had not succeeded to the powers of the Privy Council in matters regarding the public administration of the State—they could not, for instance, exercise the prerogative of calling and adjourning the meetings of the General Assembly, nor of appointing Fasts and Thanksgivings; but many powers, he said, were now exercised by the Court of Session which were formerly within the jurisdiction of the Privy Council. The abolition of the Privy Council was, indeed, considered a hardship by the Church. In a representation made to Parliament by the General Assembly at the time of the Union, allusion is made to the injury which would arise, in consequence of the cessation of the jurisdiction of the Privy Council, "with which the Church might correspond anent Fasts and Thanksgivings." These ecclesiastical acts were admitted, at the time, to be in the province of the State to direct, "and it is very apparent," Lord Medwyn added, "that as to these and other matters the abolition of the Scottish Privy Council has tended greatly to the silent and gradual enlargement of the Assembly's powers."

In treating of the relations of the Church to the State after the Reformation, an important matter for consideration is the property which belonged to the Church before that period. That it continued to belong to the Church after that event, equally as before it, has never been seriously questioned. What now remains to the Church is but an insignificant remnant of its once ample possessions, but small as it is, as it is maintained by some that the State is entitled to confiscate it "because the State originally gave it," it will be interesting to refer shortly to the manner in which the Church did acquire its endowments. Even if they had been the gift of the State, they would not the less have, in law, become the indefeasible property of the Church; but how little ground there is for the assertion as to the origin of these possessions, a glance at this part of the Church's history will make very plain.

We have it on the authority of Selden—a safe guide—that

in England all the endowments of the Church proceeded from the voluntary action of individuals; and it was the same in Scotland. They began at a very early period. The old monasteries were most of them amply endowed, but even before the time of the monasteries, and before the time of written charters, the proprietors of land had settled ministers on their estates, and endowed them either by gifts of land or by burdening their estates with the payment of tithes. In our earliest charters we find land sold or granted under the burden of these payments, as charges then affecting them, and recognized as the patrimony of the Church; and this occurs in charters by the Sovereign, as well as in the more numerous class of grants by the barons and other great landowners. In the Chartulary of Glasgow there is a curious charter by King Malcolm (*circa* 1160) in favour of the See, of the lands of Conclud, granted to compensate the bishop for the king's transgression against the Church, in having, in a charter of certain lands to two of his nobles, omitted to reserve the Teinds belonging to the Church. We find also, about the same time and afterwards, various Royal and Papal Writs, enjoining and enforcing the payment of tithes, as dues acknowledged to be the property of the Church.

The endowments were made, no doubt, from various motives. From the earliest times of which we have any record the support of religion was recognized by the dominant power as a public obligation, and the endowments of the clergy were recognized and protected. Before the time when there was personal property in land, the Tribes, as we have seen, out of the land which they held in common, endowed the Church, as the Picts endowed Columba with the gift of Iona. Afterwards, when the land came to be held by individual proprietors, these invited ecclesiastics to settle on their estates, and endowed them, because, apart from higher motives, they found it the most efficient way to civilize the often lawless hordes who dwelt on their properties. The great Anglian families, and Normans of high blood and name, who afterwards became the chief landowners in Scotland at and before the marriage of King Malcolm with the Saxon Princess Margaret, acted in the same way. They were of the progressive party, and friends to civilization and the Church. In many cases they found churches already on their manors which had been endowed long before their time. These they respected, and if churches were not already there they erected and endowed them from their own private resources, and their estates became parishes. Not at once, however. The parochial system, in Scotland as in England, grew up gradually. Bede, writing at the end of the seventh century, mentions cases of noblemen building churches on their manors, and between Bede's time and the ninth century many such churches were built, and endowed with tithes, by the lords of the soil. "Out of these foundations chiefly," Selden says, "came those kind of parishes which at this day are in every diocese." The term "parochia" in earlier times did not mean what we understand as parishes. It signified a diocesan organization.[1] In monastic language, as we have already explained, it meant the jurisdiction of a superior over the detached monasteries of the order. What we understand as the parochial system was not generally established either in England or Scotland till the twelfth century.

The priests thus settled by the great landowners were, there is every reason to believe, not only presented to the cure by the Lord of the Manor, but they received investiture from him, or rather they received no investiture but the presentation. We know that this practice prevailed in England until the latter part of the twelfth century, and in a letter to Archbishop à Becket it was condemned by Pope Alexander III. as wrong in principle, and "against the constitutions of the Holy Fathers."

The settlement of these Manorial churches, however, in whatever way effected, was attended with the most beneficial results. The system was in after times shamefully encroached upon by so many of those churches, with their lands and tithes, being conferred on the monasteries and bishoprics—sometimes by the arbitrary act of the Lord of the Manor himself, and sometimes by the despotic action of the Sovereign; and there followed from it the greatest evil under which the Church ever suffered—the want of a stated parochial clergy. The transfers were made, no doubt, under an obligation on the abbot or bishop to supply

---

[1] "Ancient Facts and Fictions concerning Churches and Tithes," 126, by Lord Selborne.

the cure, but as a rule this was not done, or done so inadequately as to be practically useless—the revenues transferred being in most cases appropriated by the monks or bishops. In the Chartulary of Glasgow, during the reigns of King Malcolm and his successor William the Lion, there are recorded no less than twenty-seven grants of such churches to the Cathedral of Glasgow alone. Of these twenty-one are the gifts of subjects, while only six are granted by the King. A list of Collegiate churches existing in Scotland at the time of the Reformation, with the names of the founders, is given by Mr. Laing. They are thirty-eight in number, and of these only four were founded by the Sovereign. Of the remaining thirty-four almost all had existed, as privately endowed chapels or parish churches, long before they were enlarged and further endowed by the great landowners who erected them into Collegiate charges.

The grant of "a church" was often very valuable. It carried with it all the parochial rights, all the tithes of the parish, all the dues paid at the altar and at the cemetery, the manse and the glebe, and all lands belonging to the particular church. If the grant was made to a Churchman he might enjoy all these in person; if to a Cathedral and Chapter, or to a Convent, the recipients might, as patrons, present any qualified person, leaving the emoluments either to be apportioned by the common law, which was quite precise in the matter, or to be modified by special compact with the presentee. Too often, however, they presented no one, leaving the parish vacant while they appropriated the emoluments to themselves.

Apart from the endowments of Manorial churches, we know, from our valuable collection of Chartularies, as well as from other sources, how ample were the endowments made to the monasteries and to the Episcopal sees. There are charters to the Priory of North Berwick by Duncan, Earl of Fife, and by his son Earl Malcolm, which show that it was well endowed by private benevolence before the end of the twelfth century.

The diocese of Moray, which long ranked as the greatest of the northern bishoprics, was very largely endowed—the great family of De Moravia being among its most munificent benefactors. The Abbey of St. Mary of Neubotle possessed great estates in six counties—Edinburgh, Haddington, Linlithgow,

Lanark, Peebles, and Stirling. Among these were grants by Robert de Quinci, and by his son Seyer de Quinci, Earl of Winchester; by Philip de Evermel, Lord of Lynton; by the Lindesayes; by "the good Sir James Douglas;" and by many others, all private benefactors.

The possessions of the See of St. Andrews, derived from private benevolence at different epochs, were situated in various localities throughout that vast diocese, which extended from the English border to Aberdeen. Its possessions went even beyond this, and included property, in land as well as tithes, far beyond the Grampians. Among the "Memoranda" in the Chartulary of the diocese—which were engrossed in the twelfth century, but bear to be extracted from an ancient Gaelic volume recording the foundation by Brude, King of the Picts, of the Celtic Monastery of St. Serf—there are described many gifts of lands and freedoms bestowed on that house before written deeds were in use. It contains a long list of nobles and other benefactors, and it is interesting to note one by Macbeth and his celebrated Queen, who, we learn from the record, bore the unpoetical name of *Gruach filia Bodhe*. From a record of the Priory of Monymuse, another ancient house of the Culdees which merged in the Priory of St. Andrews, we learn that it brought into the possession of the Church the fruits of the munificence of the old Lords of Mar. In many of these grants the *nativi* or serfs are conveyed along with the lands. Before the end of the thirteenth century a great part of these ample lands and baronies were held by the monks *in dominico*, in their own hands, and cultivated by their serfs from their several Granges.

The Monastery of Paisley was richly endowed, and from its Chartulary we know that almost all the grants were made by Alan, the Steward of Scotland, and other noblemen and gentlemen, from their own resources.

In the case of Melrose there are some grants by the King, but far the greater number are endowments from nobles and other landowners. From these latter sources the Monastery acquired large possessions in Ayrshire from the successive Stewards, and wide territories in Eskdale from the Lords of Avenal, as well as rich endowments in other parts of the kingdom—all the gifts of subjects.

The restoration of the old bishoprics, and the erection of new sees, were made the occasion of ascertaining and defining many of the possessions of the Church, acquired before the time of written Charters, and afterwards lost sight of. Alexander filled up the See of St. Andrews; he also erected the bishopric of Moray, and revived that of Dunkeld, while David, who ruled as Earl, was reconstructing the dormant bishoprics in the southern districts. For this purpose he caused inquiry to be made as to the possessions of the Church, which had been greatly encroached upon, or lost sight of altogether, with a view to their restoration. In a celebrated *Notitia* of this Prince (A.D. 1120),[1] we have an enumeration of the large endowments which belonged to the See of Glasgow in the early part of the twelfth century—many of them acquired long before that time. Professor Innes truly observes that there is no more instructive record for ecclesiastical antiquities than is afforded by this Inquisition—a document by which, he says, "the full light of history first falls on Glasgow." It records an Inquest by the Good Men of the Country, directed to be made by David, who is designed in it Prince of the Cumbrian region, in order to ascertain the possessions which then belonged to the see. It relates the foundation of the Church, and the ordination of Kentigern as Bishop of Cumbria. It mentions the death of the saint, and that he was succeeded by many bishops in the see, but that the confusions and revolutions in the country had at length destroyed all traces of the Church, and almost of Christianity. The restoration of the bishopric by David is then stated, and the election and consecration of John, who had been tutor and afterwards Chancellor to the Prince, and who has been commonly called the first Bishop of Glasgow. This is followed by a record of the possessions of the Church "in all the provinces of Cumbria which are under his (David's) dominion and power." The district thus designated extended from the Clyde on the north, to the Solway Firth and the march with England on the south, and from the western boundary of Lothian on the east to the river Urr on the west, and it included Teviotdale, which had remained a part of the diocese

---

[1] Chartulary of Glasgow, Maitland Club, where a facsimile of one of the leaves of it is given.

of Durham, when the Lothian churches north of the Tweed were transferred to St. Andrews, but which were now reclaimed as properly belonging to Glasgow.[1] The possessions thus ascertained and confirmed to the see of Glasgow were large and valuable, and they must have consisted of endowments made in very early times, for it is extremely improbable that during the dark periods of confusion and anarchy which immediately preceded the reign of David, the Church received any accession of property.[2]

Notitiæ such as this of David were the admitted and approved mode at that time of ascertaining and establishing Church property and Church privileges which had been acquired before charters came into general use. They contained a record of the tradition and belief of the country as to these—*titres narratifs*, as the learned fathers of St. Maur aptly call them. And such titles were the more unquestionable because the right of the Church was proved, as the Duke of Argyll observes, by the verdict of an Assize of powerful men, who had the strongest personal interest to call the Church's right in question.[3] Some ceremony, doubtless, accompanied these gifts of land before the time of charters. Traces exist of a usage of having solemn processions or perambulations around the lands conveyed, and there are indications of the occasional use of symbols of a kind that we are apt to associate with feudalism.[4]

Previous to the Reformation, the Church in Glasgow, among other endowments, possessed the baronies of Glasgow, Carstairs, Ancrum, Lilliesleaf, Ashkirk, and Stobo, besides Eddleston, called in the *Notitia* Penteiacob. The portion of these lands which came to be called the Regality of Glasgow embraced the city and a large district adjoining, comprehending the Barony parish, the parishes of Cadder and Govan, and a large portion of the parish of Old Monkland. Besides the general property of the see there were separate endowments for each of the numerous altars in the choir and nave, as well as for those in the crypt. These consisted of tenements in the city and other properties;

---

[1] "Celtic Scotland," ii. 375.
[2] Professor Innes, Preface to "Origines Parochiales," 24.
[3] "Scotland as it was and is."
[4] "Scotland in Times Past," by Mr. Burnett, Lyon King of Arms, in *Scottish Review*, January, 1888.

and in addition there were special endowments for the general services of the cathedral—all the gifts of private donors.

We need not go into the details of other endowments. They occurred all over Scotland, and not a few of them had been made before the old Church had conformed to Rome.

Among these endowments we have mentioned gifts by the Crown, but when we read of grants of lands, or teinds, or "churches" made by the King during the process of assimilating the native Church to that of Rome, begun by Queen Margaret and resumed by her sons, and at other times, it must not be supposed that these were in any sense State grants, or gifts from national sources. If we except some grants in our own times, so small that they may practically be left unnoticed, there is not to be found in the whole history of the Church any trace of an endowment granted by an Act of State. The endowments made by the King fall under the same category as those made by subjects. They were acts of personal benevolence like the others. This cannot be explained better than in the words of the distinguished lawyer already quoted. "There is no principle," writes Lord Selborne, "on which gifts by Kings, made not by public Acts of State, but as territorial landowners, can be distinguished for this purpose from gifts by private persons. They were made in times when Kings could hold and grant lands or other property as freely as their subjects. What these kings granted, whether to ecclesiastical or to lay corporations, or to private individuals, ceased absolutely to be theirs when so granted away. The titles so created were the same in point of law, to all intents and purposes, as if made by private persons, and a possession of centuries has followed upon them." And what is true of the lands is equally true of the teinds. "Whatever else may be doubtful," says Lord Selborne, "this is quite certain, that they never were the property of or payable to the State. They never entered into and never were granted out of the general public revenue, and never became part of it under any law, ecclesiastical or temporal."[1]

As little did the "churches" we have mentioned—those conveyed to the See of Glasgow, and the many others granted to Cathedrals and Monasteries in all the dioceses of Scotland—

[1] "Defence," 184.

ever belong in any sense to the State. They were churches, or rather the revenues of churches, founded and endowed by subjects, which were thus, by a despotic act of the King, diverted from their legitimate purpose and conferred on the great religious houses.

At the Reformation all the endowments we have mentioned, in whatever way acquired, were the indefeasible property of the Church, and up to that time they had been recognized and protected as such by the State.

The spoliation to which the Church was subjected after that period has been partially made up from private sources by various valuable endowments in recent times. Within the last fifty years there have been added to the Church more than 366 new parishes, with churches, and many of them with manses, all erected, and each parish permanently endowed with a minimum stipend of £120. These are exclusive of forty Parliamentary churches erected into parishes. In addition to all this the late Mr. James Baird of Cambusdoon made an endowment of half a million sterling, which is held in trust for "objects and purposes in connection with the Established Church of Scotland, all of a religious character." These recent endowments might become an interesting question with reference to the position taken by those who seek the disendowment of the Church. These parties do not—in the meantime at least—pretend that such endowments could, with justice, be confiscated by Parliament, but they contend that the older endowments might. In this, however, they are inconsistent. The title of the Church to the one is no better—or worse—than its title to the other. It can make no difference, to use the words of Lord Selborne, " whether the land was given, or the Church built, yesterday or a thousand years ago; in both cases the origin and lawfulness of the gift, and the nature and certainty of the subsequent title and enjoyment, have been the same. What is true of land with a Church built on it, is of course equally true of any other private endowment. If the longer period of enjoyment did make any difference, it could only be in favour of, not against the title. It is true that if what was given yesterday were taken away, the donor might be living to feel personally the wrong, while the donor of a thousand years ago would not be.

But, in each case alike, the donor's personal and individual right of property ceased when he gave his land to the Church; in each case alike the primary beneficial interest passed to those for whom the ministrations of the Church in that particular place were provided—to a permanent undying class, which still continues, and will hereafter continue, and who are as much interested in the gift at this day as their ancestors or predecessors may have been a thousand years ago. In all other cases titles are fortified, not impaired, by length of possession. To dissenting chapels, and other trusts for the religious purposes of dissenters, that principle was not long since applied by Parliament. Why should the Church only be deprived of her ancient endowments for no other reason than that she has been so long in possession of them?"[1]

In Scotland, as in England, the old endowments were given to provide for the religious instruction of the people, by the support of their religious teachers, in a Church which, throughout all its history, has been the Church of the people—a Church reflecting the national characteristics and embodying the genius of the national life, and which in all its vicissitudes has preserved the orderly succession of its ministry. A change was made at the Reformation—as changes had been made before—but in historical continuity, and in a strictly legal sense, it remained the same Church; and because abuses were corrected, and the faith reformed, it did not follow that the people were to be deprived of their patrimony. There was a much greater difference between the old Celtic Church and the Church after it became assimilated to the Roman model by Queen Margaret and her sons, than there was between the latter and the Church of the Reformation; yet the Church of David's time was protected, by the State and by the law, in the possession of the ample endowments which had been bestowed on the old Columban and Culdee communities. And it was properly so protected, because although radical changes had been introduced, it was still the Church of the people, and its continuity had not been broken.

But, indeed, neither the right of the Reformed Church to the endowments nor the continuity of the Church was questioned

[1] Lord Selborne, "Defence," 183.

by the State after the Reformation. On the contrary, they were expressly recognized. It is important to note this. The title of one of the earliest Acts of the Scottish Parliament after that event—1572, c. 46—is "That the adversaries of Christ's Evangel sall not enjoy *the patrimonie of the Kirk.*" But the only patrimony which the Church then had consisted of the endowments which she had acquired before the Reformation, and of which she was at that time in possession, and that patrimony, the Act declares, shall continue to be enjoyed as before by the holders of all benefices. The only condition made is the reasonable one that they shall "in the presence of the Archbishop, Bishop, Superintendent, or Commission of the diocese where they have the ecclesiastical living," give their assent to the reformed faith. Only on their failing to do this were they to be deprived "of their ecclesiastical promotions and livings." Ecclesiastics who were "forth of the realm," were to be left in possession of their livings and endowments if they conformed to the new faith; and even this was relaxed in the case of Beaton, who never conformed. He was the Ambassador of Queen Mary at Paris, and by an Act of the Scottish Parliament in 1600 he was, in consideration of his services, restored to his Archbishopric without being required to accept the reformed faith. He did not get back "the Castell of Glasgow and the right of cheising the Provest and bailleis," or the lands which had been sold or feued, but he was allowed to retain what remained of the property and revenues of the see for life.

No one at the Reformation spoke of the Reformed Church as a new Church. It was not even made a condition that Episcopacy should be abolished. When in 1572 bishops were introduced at the instigation of Morton, the measure was approved of by Knox and the other Reformers, on the proviso only that the bishops should exercise no higher jurisdiction than the Superintendents. And in 1574 we find the General Assembly complaining to the Regent of undue delay in carrying the measure into effect, "because there are sundry bishoprics vacant, such as Dunblaine, Rosse, and others, and that his Grace should take order that some qualified person be appointed thereto with all diligence." In the same way in the matter of presentations to benefices, the patrons who had exercised the right before the

Reformation—"the just and ancient patrons," as they are called in the Act of 1567—were declared entitled to exercise it after that event. In short, the faith was to be reformed, but no new Church was created, and neither Church order, nor the possessions of the Church, nor Patronage were to be disturbed. Prelacy was not abolished for nearly twenty years after this. The only essential change in Church government was the abolition of the Pope's supremacy. Neither Parliament nor the State questioned the continuity of the Church. They regarded it as having been at all times the Church of God in Scotland, and only held that in the pre-Reformation times it had fallen into error. The Act 1567, c. 3—the one which introduces the Confession—repeals the Acts passed in the reigns of the first five Jameses, and it does so on the ground that these Acts did not "agree with God's Holy Word, and that be them divers persons had taken occasion to maintaine idolatrie and superstition *within the Kirk of God*"—that is, within the Church before the Reformation—and that these Acts had been the means of repressing persons "as were professors of the said Word, quairthrow divers innocents did suffer."

But this did not last. The respect for property, and the protection of the Church's possessions accorded by Roman Catholic rulers, did not long continue to be shown by their Protestant successors. We need not go into the particulars of the process of lawless spoliation by which the Church was robbed. The sovereign and many of the great nobles combined to make a pretext of the abolition of Popery to enter on a course of unjustifiable confiscation, and without warrant of law seized on the Church's possessions—leaving to it, out of its ample means, the barest pittance for the support of the parochial clergy. Queen Mary, and afterwards James VI., made it a pretext that the maintenance of the regular clergy had been superstitious, and that *therefore* their benefices fell to the Crown. Many of them were gifted away to favourites, and others were taken possession of by nobles and influential proprietors. The King, on the resignation or death of any Abbot or Prior, appointed lay "Commendators" for life to the vacant benefice, and these in many instances, through Court influence or otherwise, prevailed on the King to change, by Royal Charter, their liferents into perpetual heritable rights. This was done by secularizing, or, in law phrase, "erecting" the monasteries and priories into temporal lordships. The recipients of these gifts were sometimes called "Lords of Erection," and sometimes "Titulars of the Teinds," because they had by these grants acquired the same title to the erected benefices—both lands and teinds—that the monasteries formerly had. The only redeeming point was that in every case the right of the clergy serving the cure to a stipend out of the Teinds was, nominally at least, recognized and reserved. The Teinds were so far spared because they were acknowledged then, as they have ever since by the law of Scotland been held to be, "the patrimony of the Kirk"—the State in this again recognizing the continuity of the Church.

Before these confiscations had been accomplished, however, some compromises had been made by the dignified clergy, with the view of saving from the general wreck a portion of the valuable possessions of the Church. By one of these a proposal was made on the part of a number of prelates to give up a portion of their revenues on condition of being allowed to retain the rest. This resulted in certain Acts of Council, in the reign of Queen Mary, under which rentals were returned of all the benefices in the kingdom, and Factors were appointed to uplift one-third of the revenues, that being the proportion fixed upon to be appropriated towards the support of the clergy serving the cures. This scheme, known as "the Assumption of Thirds," was subsequently ratified by Parliament, but it was in many ways evaded, and the ministers did not reap the full benefit of it. The Lords of Erection, as coming in place of the former beneficiaries, assumed the right of presenting ministers to the parochial churches, but in many instances they neglected or refused to fill the vacancies, in order to avoid payment of the stipends. Against these appropriations the reformed clergy strenuously protested, as being against all law. They claimed to be protected in the property which belonged to the Church as other subjects were protected in theirs, and they specially claimed that the Teinds should be left untouched. But their claim was recognized only to a limited extent. By an Act of the Privy Council in 1566, those of the temporalities which consisted of the smaller benefices—none of them exceeding £16 1s. 4d. of yearly rent—were left at the disposal of the General Assembly; and by a second Act, in the same year, there were left, for the general support of the ministers, such rents of other benefices as should amount in all to 10,000 pounds Scots (£833) and 400 chalders of victual. The General Assembly declined to accept of these, however, except as an instalment of the property which of right belonged to the Church. Their claim was renewed, accordingly, on the appointment of Albany to the Regency, and by the Act 1567, c. 10, which proceeds on the narrative "that ministers had long been defrauded of their stipends," it was enacted that "the haill Thirds of the haill benefices of this realme sall be instantlie, and in all time to come, paid to the ministers, ay and untill the Kirk come to the full possession of their proper patrimonie, quhilk is the Teinds." This Act is important, not only as a recognition by the legislature that the Teinds, at all events, which had belonged to the Church before the Reformation, continued to belong to it, but also in respect of a provision, which its terms implied, that the clergy were entitled to levy the teinds by their own collectors.

Meanwhile the revenues of the rest of the Church property—the temporalities—were, by the lawless confiscation already mentioned, being alienated to the lay Commendators or Lords of Erection. The grants no doubt were made under burden of the "thirds" of which the reformed clergy had been left in possession, but it came to be felt that these temporal lords were getting too large a share of the spoil, and that the "rights of the Crown"—as they were called—were being overlooked. Accordingly, by an Act of the Scottish Parliament (1587, c. 29), all the temporalities, consisting of the Church lands which had formed part of the benefices of bishops, abbots, and other beneficiaries, were inalienably annexed to the Crown. From the operation of this Act, however, were excepted the manses and glebes which had belonged to the clergy before the Reformation, as what now rightfully belonged to their successors in the Reformed Church. These were secured to the ministers as part of the "spirituality." There were also excepted all the teinds in the kingdom, as equally forming part of the patrimony of the Church, and this is now recognized by our jurists. Our great institutional writer, Lord Stair, says: "Teinds are acknowledged with us to be the patrimony of the Kirk, and they are not annexed to the Crown as the temporality of benefices are." As regards the temporalities, there were also excepted from the annexation to the Crown all the lands of temporal lordships which had been previously alienated, and thus a vast amount of property which rightfully belonged to the Church was left in the possession of nobles and others who had acquired it against every principle of law and justice. In this way the greater portion of what formed part of the abbey lands of Kelso is now owned by the Duke of Roxburgh, inherited from his ancestor Kerr of Cessford, who had, in the manner indicated, obtained a grant of the lands. A great part of the ample endowments of Melrose passed to the family of Douglas. The ancestor of the Earl of Elgin was enriched by the endowments of Kynloss, and those of Arbroath were gifted to Lord Claude Hamilton. In the case of Glasgow the greater part of the Church lands seized by the Crown was conferred on Walter Stuart, Commendator of Blantyre. Another, and that a very large, portion of valuable property in and around Glasgow was seized by the Magistrates, and feued out to the inhabitants at very inadequate prices, and became permanently lost to the Church. It included, as we know by a letter to the absent Archbishop from his faithful steward, Walker, "al the borrow muir of Glasgow on the south syde of the toune, and also Garngad hill on the north part." The Earl of Argyll procured his kinsman, Alexander Campbell, while yet a child, to be appointed to the Bishopric of Brechin, with an express power of "giving and disposing of all the benefices which previously had been in the bishop's gift," and the boy-bishop made use of that power by large alienations made in 1566.[1] But we need not multiply examples of what occurred all over Scotland.

While those who called themselves "Reformers" were thus enriching themselves with the spoils of the Church, "the ministers of the blessed Evangel of Jesus Christ whom God of his mercie has now raised up amongst us"—as they are called in the Act of 1567—were left to starve. Even the scanty stipends left to them out of the wreck, and their right to which had been acknowledged by law, were, on one pretext or another, unjustly

---

[1] Professor Innes, Preface to "Chartulary of Brechin."

withheld, and many of the clergy were reduced to a state of distressing poverty. The law might perhaps have compelled payment, but the unfortunate ministers could not afford to go to law, and they were reduced to privations which would appear incredible if we had not very clear evidence of it. We find an example in a Minute of the Presbytery of Glasgow in 1595, little more than thirty years after the Reformation. It bears that the Presbytery consisted of six churches—Glasgow, Govan, Rutherglen, Cadder, Lenzie, and Campsie—"and of the said sex kirkis there is the minister of Campsie, ane auld man having onlie in stipend fourscoir and sex lib (about £9), and the minister of Leinzae onlie in stipend fourtie aucht lib with the vicarage, worth twentie merkis in the zeir (altogether under £7); and the said ministers of Campsie and Leinzae throch povertie keipis nocht the dayes of presbiterie."[1] The object which the Presbytery had at this time in view, however, was not the increase of the emoluments of these poor gentlemen—which was probably at that time hopeless—but to get the General Assembly to cause the parish of Monkland and some others to be joined to the Presbytery of Glasgow, so as to increase the number of members, and thereby secure the quorum necessary for the despatch of business. At a period long after this, the stipend of the first charge in Glasgow was 500 merks, equal at that time to only £27 15s. 6d.; that of the second charge was 300 merks, equal to £16 13s. 4d.; while that of Cadder, from all sources, did not amount to £15. In many cases residence was impossible, the manses, where there were any, having been left in ruins by the heritors—the minister of Cadder had to reside and study in the steeple. So late as the beginning of the eighteenth century we find a representation by the Commission of the General Assembly to Parliament, complaining that ministers "have not only wanted manses, but been obliged to preach on the open fields, both summer and winter, for many years, by reason of the ruinous condition of the church."[2] It was true what Knox wrote, that "thair was none within the realme more unmercyfull to the poor ministers than war thei whiche had the greatest rentis of the churches."[3]

[1] Minute of Presbytery of Glasgow, 16th March, 1595.
[2] 8th November, 1700—Scottish Acts, X. Ap., p. 49. [3] Knox's "History," ii. 128.

It is not necessary to our purpose to follow the vicissitudes through which the Church passed, and the conflicts which occurred between her and the State, from this time down to the Revolution settlement. By the Act of 1560 and those which followed, the Church, as reformed, was recognized as the Established Church of the nation, and its Presbyterian form of government—settled by the General Assembly in 1589—received the sanction of the State; but it was not long before James VI. showed his determination to introduce Episcopacy, and with that view he sought to destroy every vestige of freedom in the Church. Law was disregarded, and to effect his purpose he persevered, to the end of his reign, in a course of illegal and despotic violence. When the ministers resisted and claimed their legal rights, the king replied with imprisonment and banishment. Eventually by skilful manipulation, and an admixture of craft with simulated kindness, the General Assembly was led to consent to fifty-one of its members having places in Parliament as the spiritual estate; and in thus relinquishing one of the most cherished principles of the Church, it practically consented to the introduction of Prelacy.

We need not follow the subsequent changes, but it is important to note that in all the troubles which followed—in the setting up and putting down of orders of Church government, and in the repealing and re-enacting of Acts of Parliament—no question of doctrine proper was touched upon. The Confession continued to be respected, and the State professed, at least, to recognize what remained of the endowments. To the Parliament of Charles I., 1633, which destroyed for the time all traces of Presbytery, the Church owes the settlement of the vexed question of Teinds, and the establishment of the Parochial School system.

Neither as regards the General Assembly is it necessary to our purpose to notice its proceedings in detail. The custom at first was to meet twice in the year, in June and on 25th December, Christmas Day. At its first meeting there were only forty-two members, and of these only six are named as ministers. The first seven Assemblies were held without a Moderator, and for twenty years after the Reformation, during which there were some forty Assemblies, no one was appointed to represent the sovereign as Commissioner. We have already mentioned that at its first meeting, in 1560, the Assembly designs itself "the ministers and commissioners of *the particular Kirkes of Scotland.*" The Minute of the second Assembly, 1561, commences:—"*The whole Kirk* convened in the Tolbooth of Edinburgh has decerned," &c. And in the third, that of June, 1562, the Church is first called the Church of Scotland. The designation is, "the convention of the Kirk of Scotland convened at Edinburgh." For some time disputes occurred out of the claim made by the Crown of a right to call and dissolve Assemblies of the Church. The question was raised in the second Assembly which met after the Reformation. Lethington said: "The question is whether the queen alloweth such conventions," to which Knox replied, that to take from the Church the freedom of her Assemblies was equivalent to taking from her the Evangel; but they invited the queen to appoint some one to hear their deliberations if she pleased. While the Assembly, however, claimed the right to meet, in virtue of what it maintained to be the intrinsic power in spiritual matters granted by Christ to His Church, the right claimed by the Crown and confirmed by Statute was never abandoned. The Confession of Faith provides that the Sovereign has "power to call Synods and to be present at them." The Act 1592, as we have seen, has a very express provision as to the right of the King or his Commissioners to be present at each Assembly, and to appoint the time and place of its next meeting; and the Act of 1690, which ratifies the Confession of Faith and the Presbyterian Church government and discipline, bears that "their Majesties, *in pursuance of the premises*, do hereby appoint the first meeting of the General Assembly of this Church, as above established, to be at Edinburgh, the third Thursday of October next to come." The Privy Council accordingly continued to exercise the prerogative of calling and adjourning meetings of the General Assembly by proclamation. The Act of 1693, however (1 William and Mary, c. 22), "for settling the quiet and peace of the Church," contained a provision that all ministers should be obliged to subscribe, not only the Confession, but an oath of Assurance—recognizing William as King *de jure* as well as *de facto;* and it went on to provide for summoning a special meeting of the General Assembly by royal authority. In this last there was nothing objectionable, but it was added that the members should be obliged to make the subscription of the Assurance, under a threat of being individually excluded from that Court, and afterwards of its being dissolved. This raised a storm. The Assembly had itself appointed a day for its meeting, and the ministers determined to resist and to continue its sittings though the king should dissolve. The Government was equally firm, and the Church was on the eve of an open breach with the new monarch and the State, when, on the intervention of Carstares, the king yielded. On the morning of the meeting of the Assembly (29th March, 1694) permission came to the Royal Commissioner to withdraw the threat of dissolution and relieve the members from taking the Assurance. This was all that was wanted, and the Assembly, so far from objecting to the meeting having been called by the king, expressed two days afterwards, in their letter to his Majesty, their sense of God's goodness "in disposing and enabling your Majesty to do so great things for this Church both formerly and now in calling and countenancing by your royal authority this Assembly." Four years later (13th January, 1698) they thanked the King for "having agreed to our meeting at this time when so many other weighty affairs call forth and employ your royal care." From that time there has been no collision between the sovereign and the Church as to the calling of Assemblies. Each exercises the power simultaneously. The question is thus kept open, but the perfect understanding and good faith observed on both sides has prevented it hitherto from assuming any troublesome shape.

In practice, the Assembly is constituted, and the Moderator appointed, before the Queen's Commission is handed in, and the Moderator closes the Assembly before the Commissioner gives his address. The day of the next meeting is mutually arranged beforehand. The Assembly appoints its next meeting by a special Act, which is printed in its records. The Commissioner names the same day. He does not use any special form of words at the opening of the Assembly, but at the close he says (we quote the words used at the close of the Assembly of 1889):—"In virtue of the powers vested in me by Her Majesty the Queen, I now dissolve this Assembly in the Queen's name, and appoint that the next General Assembly shall meet on Thursday, the 22nd day of May, 1890." But this is not recorded in the Minutes of the Assembly.

All the repealing Acts passed during the ascendency of Episcopacy were in their turn repealed, and by the Acts now recognized to be in force the rights and powers of the Church are defined and regulated. We have already noticed their terms. Their meaning, and their present bearing on the relations of the Church to the State, will be seen when we come to notice the great constitutional questions which were raised and decided before 1842. Suffice to say here, that under these Acts it has been found that the Church enjoys an absolute independence in spiritual matters, and that within her own domain the jurisdiction of her courts is exclusive. It was the attempt to extend that jurisdiction, by Church legislation which encroached on civil rights, that gave rise to the troubles which resulted in the Free Church secession of 1843. It was not the first time that a similar spirit had been shown by the Church. When attempted in Papal times it was more than once checked by Parliament, but even in the early years of the Reformation the ministers, under the name of spiritual independence, made very extraordinary claims to immunity from the restraints of civil law. They maintained that no civil or criminal tribunal could touch them for anything they might say in the pulpit, however defamatory or treasonable, and that they were amenable only to the courts of the Church. The claim was disallowed then, as it has been always refused by the State, and properly refused, throughout the whole period of the Church's history.

We have mentioned the efforts made by the Church in the middle ages to obtain the aid of the civil power to the enforcement of its decrees, and its only partial success in that direction, but in the first years of the Reformed Church the action of the civil power was entirely on the Church's side. The Act of 1567 "anent the King's oath," not only bound the Sovereigns "to serve the Eternal God and to maintain the true religion of Christ Jesus," but that, "out of their lands and empire they shall be careful to root out all heretics and enemies of the true worship of God that shall be convict by the true Kirk of God of the foresaid crimes." And by subsequent statutes (1572, c. 53, and 1593, c. 164) the State assigned civil penalties to the ecclesiastical judgments, giving power, however, to those whom the Church sought to punish by the secular arm, "to propone their lawful defences." We find repeated instances of special statutory power given to the Church courts to exercise jurisdiction in certain classes of crimes. The Act 1592, c. 8, gives power to the "ministers, elders, and deacons," within the bounds of every parish, to nominate one or more persons to act as Justices, with power to execute the Act of Parliament against idle beggars and vagabonds. By another Act (1597, c. 39), Kirk Sessions are empowered to try and punish drunkards. And in the following century the Statute 1640, c. 54, authorizes Kirk Sessions to deal with abuses committed by hiring shearers on Sundays, with a discretionary power to punish the transgressors "as they shall find the said abuses then to be committed to deserve." In like manner Presbyteries are empowered by the Act 1593, c. 6, to enforce an Act against holding fairs and markets on Sundays; and by the Act 1693, c. 64, Presbyteries are authorized to appoint persons to enforce the laws against Sabbath breaking, profaneness, and idle swearing, "or other immorality whatsoever." A later Act (1701, c. 11), after ratifying and approving these and other Acts to the same effect, provides that "in case any person shall be excommunicate for not answering, or for not obeying and satisfying the Church, when proceeded before them for profaneness and immorality, or who, when cited on the occasion foresaid, shall be declared by the Church to be contumacious," the Lords of the Privy Council shall represent the matter to His Majesty, that he may be duly informed of the said person as one "not fit to be employed or continued in any place of public trust, civil or military."

The powers conferred on Kirk Sessions by the Acts we have quoted were large, but these Courts—or rather what was their equivalent, the "Minister and Elders" in each parish—exercised exceptional powers before the first of these Statutes had been enacted, and before the Reformed Church had received statutory recognition. The Court of the Minister and Elders was, indeed, for some time the only ecclesiastical court of the Church, and we find it acting judicially nearly two years before the first meeting of the General Assembly. In March, 1559, as we have seen, a Provincial Council of the old Church was held in Edinburgh to devise measures to stem the advance of the reformed doctrines, but a month before that we find the "Minister and Elders" of St. Andrews already sitting, and exercising judicial functions as a Court of the Church of the Reformation. When the first General Assembly met, on 20th December, 1560, there was no other ecclesiastical court but that of the Minister and Elders. Synods and Presbyteries did not yet exist, and it was thus that the Minute of that first Assembly bore that it consisted of "the Ministers and Commissioners of the particular Kirkes of Scotland." In their proceedings these local courts usually called themselves "the Minister and Elders;" but they sometimes designed themselves "the Minister, Elders, and Deacons," sometimes "the Minister and Seniors," and sometimes "the Ministerie" of the particular church of the place; and they tried and decided causes of very varied character.

In an old ecclesiastical Register at St. Andrews we have an interesting record of the actings of one of these early Church Courts. In its first sittings we find it largely occupied in receiving the adherence to the new order of things of "Priests quhai recantet," and of these there are a large number. In some of these cases the designation of the convert is curious. We are familiar with the prefix of "Sir" in pre-Reformation times as indicating that the party was a priest, but we have not been accustomed to regard it as implying ecclesiastical knighthood. One of the priests in question is designed "Jhone Kipper, sometym in papistrie called Sir John Kipper;" and in his supplication he designs himself "Jhone Kipper, sometym knycht of ye Paips kyrke."

Cases of discipline are the most numerous of those in which these Courts exercised jurisdiction, and many of them were of a grave character. So early as February, 1559, we find "the Minister and Elders of the Christiane congregation of Sanctandrois" pronouncing judgment in a case of divorce. The proceedings, which are recorded at length, appear to have been conducted with great regularity, and with the same attention to judicial forms which characterized the proceedings of the Courts of the Church in earlier times. The petition of the husband, the answer of the wife, an interlocutor appointing a proof, a warrant for the citation of witnesses, the deposition of each witness, and a formal sentence absolving the wife, are all recorded at length. The sentence bears that the Minister and Elders in forming their judgment had consulted with "Mr. John Douglas, Rector of the Universitie, and John Wynram, sub-prior," and two others, "with whom we communicated the secretis of the meritis of the said actioun and caus."[1] There occurs soon afterwards, in the same Court, another suit between the same parties, the wife being now the complainer. The proceedings are conducted with the same regard to judicial forms, and decree of divorce is pronounced against the husband. The sentence proceeds in the name of "the minister and eldaris of the reformed Kirk of Sanctandrois," and, without calling in any assessors, finds the husband guilty, and the wife innocent and free to marry again—the husband "to be halden and repute ane dead man, and worthy to want his lyf be the law of God, quhen evir it sall please God to stirre up the heart of ane gude and godlie magistrate to execute the same with the civil sword; to quhome," it is added, "we will that this our sentence prejudge nothing but committis the same to him."

The other cases of discipline dealt with are numerous, many of them concluding for divorce. In one of these, the summons in which is dated 5th March, 1660, the Court is addressed as "My Lordis minister and elders of the Christian Congregation of Sanctandrois," and the Minute recording the finding of the Court bears that "the minister and elders decernis sentence of divorce to be put in force, and the same to be published this next Sunday." But by this time—May, 1661—Wynram had been appointed Superintendent, and the formal sentence bears to have been pronounced after "communicating the secretis of

---

[1] "Liber Registri enormium delictorum per Ministrum Seniores et Diacones congregationis Christianæ Civitates Sancti Andreæ Feliciter incipit, 1559."—*Miscellany of Maitland Club*, iii. 221.

the said actioun and caus with maister John Wynram, Superintendent of Sanctandrois, and with his avysment and consent heirto."[1] Subsequent to this, however, sentences of divorce are pronounced without the concurrence of the Superintendent, or calling in any assessor.

Wynram was one of the five superintendents appointed by "the charge and commandment of the Lords of the Secret Counsel," the others being nominated respectively to Edinburgh, Brechin, Glasgow, and Argyll. One of them, Erskine of Dun, was a layman. Their position was somewhat akin to that of a bishop, and they had charge of a certain number of churches and Churchmen in given districts. Their special work was the planting of churches and providing ministers, and by the Act 1567, c. 7, presentations by patrons were appointed to be made to them. By another Act—1567, c. 11—they were empowered to make trial of those who were appointed to teach in schools or universities, or privately. In cases of discipline they issued summonses and pronounced sentences, sometimes in their own names and sometimes jointly with the Minister and Elders. In a decree pronounced by Wynram, "with the consult and consent of the ministerie of Sanctandrois," he thus describes his office:—"We, Mr. John Wynram, Superintendant of Fyff, being called to that office as ane watcheman over his flock, to behald, examin, and try, be ye laws of God, ye conversation, lyff, and manneris of those committed to our charge."[2]

The Court of the Minister and Elders acted at first under no statutory authority, but their jurisdiction was recognized by the State. A case occurred where a person in Kirkcaldy having complained to the Lords of Secret Council against his wife and sought decree of divorce, "the Lordis," by a minute dated 2nd December, 1560, "requests the ministeris and eldaris of Sanctandrois to proceede and do justice in this actioun." The Minister and Elders tried the case accordingly and pronounced sentence of divorce.[3]

The practice as regards these early courts varied in other localities. As already mentioned it was some time after the Reformation before regular "Kirk Sessions" were appointed to each parish church, and for some time after 1592 many parishes

[1] *Miscellany of Maitland Club*, iii. 265. [2] Ibid. 322. [3] Ibid. 248.

had none. The Act of that year by which the Presbyterian order was established, confers power on the "particular kirks" to exercise "jurisdiction in their awin congregation," only "gif they be lauchfully ruled be sufficient ministry and Session." In one of the earliest records of the Kirk Session of Glasgow, we find a notice of "a license from the King and Council, and the Bishop, for holding a Session within the toun of Glasgow."[1] For some time after this, although there were several churches in that city, there continued to be only one general Session. This continued till 1648, when an arrangement was made between the Magistrates and "the Common Session," for having a Kirk Session appointed to each of the city churches, and it was "agreed by common consent that the Common Session has only a consultative vote, and not the authoritative in any matter."[2] A subsequent minute bears that "new Sessions are chosen for every quarter, consisting of Elders and Deacons."[3]

For a long time the General Session in Glasgow continued to exercise extraordinary powers. They sat in secret conclave, the whole elders and deacons being "sworn with uplifted hands to reveal nothing that shall be voted in the Session nor the voters."[4]

Like St. Andrews and too many other places throughout Scotland, there was in Glasgow a general prevalence of immorality in the end of the sixteenth century. To check this the General Session set up a "pillar" in the churches where delinquents, convicted by the Session, were obliged to stand before the Congregation, sometimes for six Sabbaths in succession, "bare foot and bare legged, and in sackcloth;" and in some instances the offenders were sentenced "to be carted through the town."[5] On a repetition, and if the offender had been excommunicated, reconciliation to the Church was to be obtained after this fashion:—He was "to pass from his dwelling-house to the Kirk every Sunday at six in the morning at the first bell, convoyed by two of the elders or deacons, or any other two honest men, and stand at the Kirk door bare footed and bare legged, with a white wand in his hand, and bare headed, till after the reading of the text, and then in the same manner to repair to the pillar till the sermon be ended, and then go out

---

[1] 22nd April, 1585. [2] Session Minutes, 17th May, 1648. [3] 15th January, 1651.
[4] Session Records, 24th October, 1588. [5] Minute of Session, 1586.

to the door again till all pass from the Kirk, and after this be received."

Absence from church was a grave offence, and the Session imposed on the Magistrates the duty of "going through the streets on Sabbath nights to search for persons who absent themselves from Church—the town officers to go through with the Searchers," and with this order the Magistrates complied. By another Minute the Session directs the Searchers on the Sabbath to pass into the houses and "to apprehend absents from the Kirk." The offences to which penalties were attached were numerous. They included "swearers, blasphemers, and mockers of piety," and many others. And the sentence of the Kirk Session was no mere *brutum fulmen*. They enforced as well as pronounced it. They caused a ward-house to be constructed in the steeple of the Blackfriars Church, and to this prison they committed offenders—the Magistrates apparently always interponing the secular arm when that was necessary, which it, perhaps, not always was, when the Session was served by stalwart beadles, as well as stout elders, who were ready to execute its mandates. An individual who had been absent from "the examination" and from the communion for several years is committed "to the steeple," and ordered to make public repentance besides. Another person is sentenced to confinement for eight days; and instructions are given "to the beddal to let *steeplers* get nothing but bread and water, or small drink, so long as they continue in the steeple."[1] The "beddal" was apparently the jailor. In 1609 there is a Minute of the Session enacting that all offenders shall pay their penalties personally before leaving the Session house, "or be put in the steeple till it be paid."

After the Reformation, the manse which had belonged to the Prebendary of Cambuslang, on the south side of the Drygate, was acquired by the Magistrates, who converted it into a House of Correction. Of this new prison the Session took advantage—the Blackfriars Church having become ruinous—and immediately afterwards there occur entries in their records ordaining persons to be taken to the House of Correction, both men and women, and, in some instances, appointing them "*to*

[1] Minute of Session, 7th September. 1604.

be *whipped every day during the Session's will.*"[1] But the Session had still more alarming penalties in store for female delinquents—notable among these being ducking in the Clyde. The Magistrates had themselves previously resorted to that mode of enforcing morality, as we find an entry in the Burgh Accounts, on 6th November, 1575, of a payment "to the officers for dowking of Janet Fawside, xld." (about fivepence). But the Kirk Session improved upon this. By a Minute in 1587 certain women are adjudged to be imprisoned and fed fifteen days on bread and water, and "to be put on a cart one day and ducked in Clyde, and to be put in the jugs at the Cross on a Monday," that being the market day. To facilitate the operation of ducking, a subsequent Minute of the Session appoints a pulley to be made on the bridge, whereby the offenders "may be ducked in the Clyde." Whatever may be said as to the right of the Session to take the law in its own hand, this sentence was quite within what the Legislature had provided for such offences. The Act 1567, c. 14, provides that persons convicted of immorality should for the third fault be ducked in the deepest and foulest pool of the town or parish and then banished. In the case of fines these were, by the Act 1649, c. 45, appointed to be paid to the Kirk Session.

The jurisdiction thus exercised by the Kirk Session is in a great measure to be explained by the fact that in the Royal burghs the Magistrates were, as a rule, members of the Session. By a Minute of the General Session of Glasgow in the end of the sixteenth century it is "enacted that whosoever shall be chosen Provost or Bailays after this shall be enrolled to be Elders of the Kirk for the year to come:"[2] and there can be little doubt that the Magistrates interponed their civic authority to enforce the decrees which, as elders, they had joined in pronouncing in the ecclesiastical court. Indeed there is direct evidence of this as regards Glasgow in the Minutes of the Session there. In repeated instances, after recording decrees for fines, the Minute adds: "Whereunto the Magistrates present interpone their authority." In June, 1603, the Session appoints the town officers to bring the stoups with the wine

---

[1] Session Minutes. 17th December. 1635.   [2] 4th October, 1599.

at the Communion; and some years later (1644) the Session desires the Magistrates "to attend the Tables in the High Kirk, and Dean of Gild, Deacon Convener, and old Magistrates in the New Kirk." It is interesting to note that it was from this combination of the secular with the ecclesiastical function that the election of the Commissioners from the Royal burghs to the General Assembly came to be exercised by the Magistrates. It is certain that for some time after the Reformation these Commissioners were not elected by the Town Councils. They were elected by the General Session—by what right does not appear, for there is no statutory authority for it. The Magistrates, individually, may have taken part in the election, but only as members of the Session—not in their civic capacity. Gradually this state of matters came to be reversed, and the Magistrates, although they had apparently no original right other than what they derived from their character as elders, engrossed to themselves the whole power of nomination, the Session only concurring. This was the practice followed in 1718, but it appears from an Act of Assembly of that year that the matter then remained in doubt, as the Assembly resolved that "until the matter be further thought upon," no Commissions from Royal burghs be received, but such as should be "consented to and approved of," not only by the minister and Kirk Session, but by the Presbytery of the bounds.[1] In practice the "consent" came to be dispensed with, but the commissions must still be attested both by the Kirk Session and the Presbytery.

Among the cases with which the Presbytery dealt in the seventeenth century was one which, in common with the other Presbyteries in Scotland, they treated with severity—namely, witchcraft; and some of their Minutes on this subject are curious. "Charming of kine" to obtain milk; "turning the riddle" to discover parties suspected of theft; rubbing "the houlat hart" (owl's heart) on a man's shoulder "to cause a man to luif (love) ane woman," and using incantations to cause mills to grind freely, are among the cases on which the Presbytery of Glasgow adjudicated, and which they visited with sentences chiefly of pecuniary fines and severe penance. On one occasion

[1] Report to General Assembly, 1846. Sess. 13.

we find the Presbytery dealing with an unfortunate medical practitioner whose success in his profession was attributed to witchcraft. The Presbytery continues his case for fifteen days, "and in the meantime inhibitis him to go out of his parochin in ony tyme cuming to cure ony diseasis, or to take the cure of any that cumis to him, in respect it is knowen that he hes na skill except he use unlauchfull meanes, as is suspectit."[1] These were lenient sentences compared with what Parliament had prescribed, for the Act 1563, c. 9, provides that to seek help from witches was an offence to be punished with death. When the civil power was slack in prosecuting these cases we find the Church repeatedly petitioning that the Acts against charmers, sorcerers, and witches should be put in force.

Among other offences dealt with and prohibited by the Presbytery of Glasgow, was "the playing of bagpipes on Sondaye from sun rising to its going down." In this limitation of the time for indulging in amusements, the Presbytery was carrying out an order which it had issued a few years before, prescribing the limits of the Sabbath. That Minute bears that they "interpret the Sabbath to be from sun to sun—no work to be done between light and light in winter, and between sun and sun in summer."[2] It was not till fifty years afterward that the Presbytery altered this, and declared that the Sabbath "shall be from twelve on Saturday night to twelve on Sunday night."[3]

The Kirk Session in Glasgow, however, and also the Presbytery, exercised jurisdiction in important matters of a different kind. The Act 1573, c. 55, had declared divorce for desertion competent, "since the true and Christian religion was publicly preached, avowed, and established within this realm, namely, since the month of August, 1560;" and after that we find both the Session and the Presbytery exercising jurisdiction in these and other matrimonial causes. An example is recorded where the Session did this in a peculiar case of separation. There came before them two married persons "who declare they are content to separate one from another till God send more love into their hearts;" and the man having undertaken to give the wife a small yearly allowance, "the Session consent to this."[4]

---

[1] 16th November, 1609.   [2] Minute of Presbytery, 17th January, 1590.
[3] 18th August, 1640.   [4] 2nd October, 1635.

In a case before the Presbytery a man and a woman—John Philpe and Helen Willsoun—appeared craving the authority of the Presbytery for their marriage, notwithstanding the allegation that a former husband of the woman was still alive. The Presbytery having, "efter tryell, founde that now it is mair than twentie yeiris since hir husband left hir, quho since that time hes not been hard of, grantis libertie to the saidis John and Helen to marie."[1]

Repeated cases also occur of the Presbytery trying cases of breach of promise of marriage. In one case it was the man who was the complainer, and the offender, Helen Bull, having confessed to "refusing to marie Johne Miller w^t quhome scho hes bein proclaimit twyse, now being of mind to marie Patrik Bryce," she is adjudged "to mak hir repentance in hir paroche kirk of Leinzae for hir inconstancie, and forder to pay penaltie to the thesaurer of hir kirk the neist Sondaye afore she enter to hir repentance."[2] So frequent were such cases of breach of promise that we find the Kirk Session of Cambusnethan enacting "that each pairtie to be proclaimt sould lay doun aucht merk, and the pairtie rewer sould lose theirs, and the other sould get their aucht merks up againe."[3] The General Session in Glasgow also took upon itself to make rules for the form of divine worship. In 1587 it enacted that "all persons in time of prayer bow their knee to the ground."[4]

We shall mention only one other example of the jurisdiction claimed by the General Session, and it is curious, not only because of the small "disruption" which followed from it, and the establishment of the first "Free Church" in Glasgow, but because, like a larger secession in later times, it arose out of a question of patronage. The Session usurped, and for a long time exercised, the right of nominating the ministers of the city churches. It was by them also that the city was in 1648 divided into four parishes—the magistrates merely concurring. Even after the magistrates had obtained from the Crown a gift of the patronage, the Session insisted on appointing the ministers, and this continued down to 1717, when the magistrates asserted their right, and it was settled judicially that the exclusive patronage belonged to them. This was the cause of a dis-

[1] 1610.   [2] 7th September, 1596.   [3] 15th January, 1560.   [4] 21st September, 1587.

ruption, for a large number of the members of the Session, and their friends, were so displeased with this encroachment by the civil power on what they considered their spiritual independence, that they left the Church, and having erected a chapel in Canon Street, they called it the meeting house of the Free Presbyterian body.[1] So history repeats itself.

The powers exercised by the Church courts, of which we have given examples, and the civil penalties annexed to ecclesiastical judgments, and enforced under the alleged authority of the Acts of 1572 and 1593, and other Statutes, continued till the early part of the eighteenth century. It was not till the reign of Queen Anne that by the Toleration Act of 1711 it was declared that no civil pain, or forfeiture, or disability, should be incurred by the "excommunications" of the Church judicatories, and that civil magistrates were prohibited and discharged to force or compel any person to appear when summoned, or to give obedience to such sentence when pronounced.

But this does not apply to those cases in which the Civil courts are bound to give assistance to the Church in carrying out the orders of its courts, made with a view to explicate its own jurisdiction. A sentence of deposition pronounced against a minister is necessarily followed by the most serious civil consequences, and the sentence will be enforced by the civil magistrate. In the same way, if in proceedings falling within the proper jurisdiction of the Church the evidence is required of a witness who refuses to attend, the Civil courts will lend their aid to enforce his attendance, as they would in any civil case. The point was raised in a case which occurred in 1874.[2] The observations of the Lord President (Inglis) in giving judgment are important, explaining as they clearly do one phase of the relation of the Church to the State. "I confess I am surprised," his Lordship said, "to see this question raised, for I never, during the whole course of my practice, entertained a doubt that the Judge-Ordinary had the power of issuing such a warrant as is here craved, and was bound to exercise that power on good cause shown. We are dealing with a Presbytery—an established judicature of the country, as much recognized by the law as the Court of Session

---

[1] Clelland's "Annals," ii. 411.
[2] Presbytery of Lews v. Fraser (Uig), 16th May, 1874, 1 R. 888.

itself. Its jurisdiction, indeed, differs widely from that of the Civil courts, but it is just as much the creation of law as that of any other Court in the kingdom. The time at which the judicatures of the Church, as they now exist, were finally settled was the period of the Revolution, and some of the statutes then passed, particularly the statute of William and Mary, 1693, c. 22, 'An Act for settling the quiet and peace of the Church,' throw much light on the question. The last section of that Act enacts 'that the Lords of their Majesties' Privy Council, and all other magistrates, judges, and officers of justice, give all due assistance for making the sentences and censures of the Church and judicatures thereof to be obeyed, or otherwise effectual as accords.' I want nothing stronger or more comprehensive than that. Whenever the Church courts are unable of themselves to carry out their own orders, made to explicate their own jurisdiction, the Civil courts are bound to step in and give 'all due assistance.' Now there is no duty more clear than that which obliges the individual citizen to obey the citation of a properly constituted court to appear and give evidence. It was quite conceivable that the Church courts might find some difficulty in compelling the attendance of a recusant witness. But the removal of that difficulty is just one of the things contemplated by the clause of the statute I have read." How fully the Civil courts recognize the independent jurisdiction of the courts of the Church, as established judicatures of the country, will be seen from decisions to be cited further on.

The Secession of 1843, which we have now to notice, was not caused by the existence of patronage in the Church, but as one of the two great classes of cases which were decided at that time arose out of the exercise of that right, it will conduce to the better understanding of these decisions if we shortly notice the history of Patronage in Scotland, and the action of the Church in reference to it previous to 1843.

Patronage, in its proper sense, existed in the Church from the earliest times. The landowners, by whom churches were first endowed, naturally became the patrons. In many instances the right remained with their successors, in others it passed to the abbots and bishops, and in others it became vested in the Crown. The king, as we have seen, exercised the right of presentation to all benefices in the collation of a bishop during a vacancy in his See. The right of presentation by lay patrons was, as we have already mentioned, fully recognized in the post-Reformation statutes. The Act 1567, c. 7, while it secured to the Church all power in regard to "the examination and admission of ministers within the realm," reserved "the presentation of lawit patronages to the just and ancient patrons;" and by the Act 1592, c. 116, Presbyteries were taken "bound and astricted to receive and admit whatsoever qualified minister presented by his majesty or laic patrons." This Act was subsequently repealed, but it was restored by the Act of William and Mary, 1690, c. 5, subject to the exception of "that part of it relating to patronages," which "is hereafter to be taken into consideration." It was taken into consideration by the same Parliament, and the matter was then settled by the Act 1690, c. 23. This statute is commonly described as an Act abolishing Patronage, but it was not so. It no doubt took the right of presentation from "the ancient patrons," but it did so only to transfer it to another body —namely, the heritors and elders of the respective parishes, by whom the minister was to be "named and proposed" to the whole congregation. The people, under that statute, had no say more than they had before. They might approve or object, but if they objected they were required to give in reasons, and the final decision was left, as before, in the hands of the Presbytery, to be "cognosced upon" by them, and by their judgment alone was "the calling and entry of the particular minister to be ordered and concluded."

Matters continued thus till the reign of Queen Anne, when, in 1711, an Act was passed (10 Anne, c. 12) by which the right of presentation to vacant parishes was taken from the heritors and elders and restored to the laic patrons. But the rights of the people remained as before. Under the one Act as under the other—by whomsoever the minister was presented, or named and proposed—the Presbytery was bound to take the presentee on trials. The people, if they objected, under the Act of 1690 were bound to give in reasons; and under the Act of Queen Anne they had to do the same. In both the decision rested with the Presbytery.

The Church protested against the Act of Queen Anne at

the time, and continued for long afterwards to do so; but it never did this on the ground that Patronage was incompatible with its spiritual independence. By no party in the Church was it ever regarded otherwise than, as Dr. Chalmers regarded it, a matter of mere ecclesiastical polity. In the proceedings in the General Assembly previous to 1842, none of the party which ultimately left the Church dealt with Patronage otherwise than as an institution in which, although they objected to it, they might acquiesce; and in whatever way they sought to secure a veto to the people, they always recognized in the patron, as a legitimate right, the initiative power of making the presentation. In 1836, when it was proposed to petition Parliament against Patronage, the Assembly refused to do so —Lord Moncrieff, a supporter of the Veto Act, and one of the greatest ornaments of what came to be called the Non-intrusion party, giving the proposal his decided opposition. Again, in 1841 the General Assembly negatived a motion directed against Patronage, and some of the most eminent men of that party again joined in the opposition. In the same year the whole party, headed by Dr. Candlish, to whom they looked as a leader, voted their approval of a Bill introduced in Parliament by the Duke of Argyll—a Bill which was expressly based on the maintenance of Patronage as a matter of principle, and which recognized and dealt with it as a system which was not disputed, and which was not to be disturbed. The Bill, indeed, quoted the much-abused Act of Queen Anne, restoring the right of presentation to the "ancient patrons," as what constituted the law, and as what was to be recognized as such and acted on by the Church. The party voted that this Bill was "fitted to provide for the maintenance and practical application of the principle of non-intrusion as asserted by the Church," and that they "could conscientiously submit to its operation if passed into a law;" and one of their historians,[1] writing after the Secession, and with the benefit of matured reflection, expresses his sincere regret that the Bill had not been accepted by the legislature. To this may be added, that in the Claim of Right, a document which the party laid on the table of the General Assembly in 1842, and which the

[1] "The Ten Years' Conflict." by Robert Buchanan. D.D.

Free Church still points to as containing an exposition of its principles and the grounds of the secession, there is not a word implying that the party left the Church of Scotland on account of Patronage.

In the face of these facts it is curious to note that when, in 1874, the General Assembly became satisfied that it had become the desire of the Church to get rid of Patronage altogether, and to confer on the people the right of electing their ministers, the leaders of the Free Church gave the proposal their strenuous opposition, maintaining that, to concede what was thus asked, would be fraught with danger to the Free Church. They left it to be inferred that Patronage was the cause, or one of the causes, of their leaving the Church in 1843, and that their "claims"—whatever the term might mean—ought to be taken into account before such a measure was conceded by the legislature to the Church of Scotland. That the removal of Patronage would strengthen the national Church, and increase her influence, and extend her popularity, by bringing her more into harmony with the feelings and the genius of the people of Scotland, they did not question. On the contrary, the fact that such would be the effect of the measure, and that it would consequently politically weaken their own Church as a dissenting body, appeared to be, and was generally regarded at the time, as the only intelligible ground of their opposition.

Between the passing of the Act of Queen Anne and the Auchterarder case, our judicial records contain no decision settling any important principle. Cases repeatedly occurred, however, in which Presbyteries refused to induct the presentees of patrons, and inducted other ministers instead. One of these, the case of Auchtermuchty,[1] is cited in the Claim of Right as one in which the Court had "refused to interfere with the peculiar functions and exclusive jurisdiction of the Church Courts, and confined its decision to the mere question of stipend." But that was not what the Court decided. By the then existing law, patrons and heritors liable in payment of stipend were entitled to retain it in any case where a presentee was illegally rejected. In the case under notice the

[1] Moncrieff v. Maxton, 15th February, 1735.

Presbytery had settled a minister in a parish in the face of a presentation by a lawful patron, and the patron claimed the stipend. No other question was raised, and the Court, having inquired into the circumstances, found that the action of the Presbytery had been illegal, and decided in the patron's favour —finding him entitled to the stipend, "as in the case of a vacancy." The presentee was not a party to the suit. Had he been so, the Court, on the very same principles in which they decided for the patron, would have decided for the presentee. They would have ordained the Presbytery to proceed with his settlement, as they did in the case of Auchterarder; and on their refusal to do so, would have found them liable in damages. As it was, there was no occasion to take further action, as the inducted minister, finding he was to get no stipend, demitted the charge within a year after the decision.

Another of these old cases was that of Culross.[1] It is also referred to in the Claim of Right as one in which the Court recognized the power and right of the Church to do as it thought proper in regard to the filling of a vacancy, and that, proceeding on the principle that the stipend could be separated from the cure, the Court had confined its decision to the disposal of the temporalities. But such was not the decision. As in the case of Auchtermuchty, the only question before the Court was one between the inducted minister and the patron as to the stipend—the latter claiming it on the ground that the Presbytery had acted illegally in the settlement. Stoddart, the inducted minister, demanded the stipend as inseparable from the cure, and contended that the Civil Court had no jurisdiction to inquire into the legality of his admission. But the Court decided, as it had done before, that it was a civil question, and that they had jurisdiction, and having found the proceedings of the Presbytery to have been illegal, they gave the stipend to the patron. They treated the proceedings of the Presbytery, in short, as absolutely null, and their decree was, not that the stipend could be separated from the cure, but that the patron was entitled to retain it "aye and until the vacancy should be legally supplied." No other question was raised, but it is clear from the principles on which the Court

[1] Cochran v. Stoddart, 26th June, 1751.

proceeded, that had the presentee appeared to prosecute *his* claim, the Court would have given him the relief asked. Equally it is clear that if the heritors had thought fit to interfere, the Court would, at their instance, have excluded the intruder from the use of the Church and from the manse and glebe. The Court actually did this in a subsequent case, that of Unst.[1] The conclusions of the Summons in that case were, "that the Presbytery of Zetland should be ordained to give due obedience to the presentation, and to proceed to the settlement of the presentee according to the rules of the Church, and that until the conclusion of the process and the settlement of the presentee in the said Church and parish, it ought and should be found and declared that the pursuer and the other heritors liable in stipend are entitled to retain and hold the same, and to prevent the said Archibald Gray from taking possession of the manse, glebe, or other rights and privileges belonging to the minister of said parish." In these terms the Court gave decree. The presentee did not appear, and the heritors seem to have taken no further action in the matter; but the minister who had been settled by the Presbytery, finding that he was to get neither house nor stipend, followed the example of the minister in Culross and demitted his charge within a few months after the decision—verifying in this the plea that for all practical purposes "the stipend is inseparable from the cure."

But the time was near when the true position of the Church towards the State and the law—her obligations as well as her rights—was to be exhaustively discussed and judicially determined. To look back, it seems extraordinary how so great a controversy could arise out of a matter apparently so small. As regards the first case, that of Auchterarder, in nothing did it concern either doctrine or discipline, and as regarded the question immediately at issue in it, nothing had occurred from without to change, in the smallest particular, either the law of the land or the constitution of the Church itself from what the Non-intrusion party admitted these to have been for more than 170 years. The attempt to make the change was made in 1834.

---

[1] Lord Dundas *v.* Presbytery of Zetland, 15th May, 1795; Bell's Fol. Cases, 170; Robertson's "Report of Auchterarder Case," i. 323.

It was made within the Church itself, and it was the Non-intrusion party who made it. It was not a question of conscience. It concerned only a matter of ecclesiastical polity—one, moreover, which was altogether a novelty—an innovation on what, on their own admission, had been the "fixed and settled" practice of the Church for more than a century and a half. It had nothing to do with patronage, or the right of patrons to present—that right having been acknowledged in principle throughout all the proceedings. It concerned only the procedure to be observed on the admission of ministers—by whomsoever nominated or presented. The novelty consisted in the Church conferring on the parishioners an absolute power of veto, which at no period of the Church's history had parishioners ever possessed—a power which, while professing to recognize the patrons' statutory right, paralysed it, and virtually made it inoperative. The other case—that of Stewarton—arose out of an attempt by the Church to introduce a still more startling innovation—one which altered not only the practice of the Church itself, but which, equally with the Veto Act, came into direct collision with statute law and civil rights.

To begin with the Auchterarder case. There had been, in the preceding years, repeated instances of what came to be called "forced settlements"—in many of which the wishes of the people were certainly overruled, and ministers settled in parishes who were unacceptable to the parishioners. This, indeed, had occurred in all periods of the Church's history, for at no previous time had the people possessed the power of selecting their ministers; but latterly more attention had been called to it, and the leaders of the party in the General Assembly which assumed to itself the name of Evangelical, and which included many, but certainly not all, of the best men in the Church, began to consider in what way effect could be given to the voice of the people. There was more than one way of doing this, and unhappily they chose a wrong way. This was by passing the well-known Veto Act.

That unfortunate measure was moved in the General Assembly of 1834 by Dr. Chalmers. The same great divine had been induced to make in the preceding Assembly of 1833 a less objectionable proposal. It might have been called a veto, but it differed in an important particular from the Act adopted by the Assembly in the following year, for the intention and principle of it, as explained by Lord Moncrieff, was "that *the Presbytery itself*, looking solely to the spiritual interests of the parish and the good of the Church, was to take the dissent of the people into consideration," and decide accordingly. In other words, if the presentee was rejected it was to be by a judicial act of the Presbytery. This was what Dr. Chalmers and Lord Moncrieff, and the other influential leaders of the Non-intrusion party, considered, in 1833, to be sufficient to meet the requirements of the case, and to give the people all they could justly ask. But the proposal was not adopted.

In the Assembly of the following year the dominant party went far beyond this and passed a very different measure. By this Act Presbyteries were directed not to take a presentee on trial at all, and not in any way to exercise their own judgment as to his qualifications, in any case where "a majority of the male heads of families, being communicants"—a new standing hitherto unknown in the Church—should intimate that they objected to have him as their minister. The whole matter of the settlement of a parish minister was thus, for the first time in the Church's history, taken out of the hands of the Church and committed to an irresponsible body of laymen.[1]

It is to be said for the party who introduced this novelty into the constitution and practice of the Church, that they first took the precaution of asking legal advice on the subject. They never for a moment pretended that they had a right to adopt such a measure unless they had the power by Statute to do so, and they were advised—wrongly as it turned out—that the Acts of Parliament by which the Church was established did give them the power. It was solely because of that opinion that Dr. Chalmers was induced to move the adoption of the measure, and he frankly confessed afterwards that it had been "a blunder." It was certainly what a Free Church lawyer, Mr. Taylor Innes, has recently called it, "new legislation." It had no sanction in any corresponding regulation in the previous history of the Church, and it was what the same writer has the

---

[1] In an Assembly of 323 members the Veto Act was carried by the votes of only 184. A minority of 139 protested against it as *ultra vires* and unconstitutional.

candour and the courage to call it, only "appropriate for a body which held itself to be independent of Parliament."[1]

The Veto Act, it may be noticed in passing, contained one very curious feature which showed the inconsistency of its promoters. It provided that in all cases in which the right of presentation fell to Presbyteries under the *jus devolutum*, the people were not to have the same power of rejection that they were to have when the presentation was made by a lay patron. However objectionable the person presented by the Presbytery might be, the people were not to be allowed to exercise the veto. Such cases, the Act declared, were not to fall under its operation, "but shall be proceeded in according to the general laws of the Church in such cases"—a tolerably distinct admission, the Dean of Faculty remarked in his Letter to the Lord Chancellor, "that this sort of veto or rejection by the people had not only never previously been heard of, but that it could be dispensed with when it interfered with the assumption of power on the part of the Church itself."

In the summer of 1834 several cases occurred of the rejection of presentees under the new Act which were not disputed, but a case at length occurred in which its competency was to be tested. Mr. Young, a gentleman possessing the highest testimonials from the Presbytery which had licensed him, was presented by the Earl of Kinnoull to the parish of Auchterarder, and vetoed. Thereupon, in conjunction with the patron, he raised an action in the Court of Session to have the Presbytery ordained to take him "on trials" as required by the Act of Parliament, and in accordance with what had hitherto been the invariable practice of the Church. The question on which the parties joined issue was this: Did the patron and the presentee, through the exercise of the veto, and the consequent refusal of the Presbytery to take Mr. Young on trials, sustain a civil wrong? If so, was the Presbytery, in fulfilment of its official duty, bound to take Mr. Young on trials, with a view to his admission if found duly qualified?

The contention of the Solicitor-General, the senior counsel for the Presbytery, was: "We maintain that as there is here no question about a civil right the action is not competent in

[1] "Mr. Finlay's Bill and the Law of 1843," by A. Taylor Innes, 1886, p. 12.

this Court." The Dean of Faculty, for the Patron, met this by the explicit admission: "If there is no illegality, if there is no wrong in violation of a civil right, we have no case." Then who was to determine what was civil and what was spiritual? That question was answered by the Procurator, Mr. Bell, the other counsel for the Church. His words were:—"I am not here to dispute, or rather I expressly admit, the clear right of your Lordships to consider and determine whether any question which may come before you is of an ecclesiastical or a civil nature." A plainer issue could not have been raised: a more explicit recognition of the right of the Court of Session to determine it, could not have been made. On another important point the ground was cleared for the decision—namely, that both parties rested their case on the Statutes.

The Non-intrusionists in their after pleadings, however, took an extraordinary position. They maintained that however the Civil courts might interpret the Statutes, they could not enforce them against the legislation of the Church. The Dean of Faculty, alluding to this startling plea, said:—"It involves a claim of divine right—of a power to legislate and regulate as bestowed on the Church by its great Spiritual Head. This is the most pernicious error by which the blessed truths of Christianity can be perverted, and its influences on the social system blighted and destroyed—an error which arms fallible man with the belief that he possesses the power and authority of the Divine Teacher whom he worships, and leads him to disregard all rights, or usages, or laws which interfere with the end which he is thus taught to believe he has a divine mission to accomplish, or with the *authority* which he believes he is commissioned to enforce. You have been told that Presbyteries cannot be directed to do the duty which law might impose—that you cannot find that they are bound to take a presentee on trials however clearly statute may impose the duty. Such is the proposition without disguise. And why? Because they are independent spiritual tribunals, and therefore you cannot compel them to do what statute prescribes. This is plainly the claim of the Church of Rome."

The accomplished counsel for the Non-intrusionists, the Solicitor-General, afterwards Lord Rutherford, did not, in opening his case, take the high ground of which the Dean of Faculty complained, although it continued to be maintained by the party both within the Church and after they had left it. The Solicitor-General, speaking of the position and rights of the Church, said:—" I do not speak of the Church of Scotland in a spiritual sense, as forming part of that universal Church which consists of all the elect in every age and Church, and under all denominations—that Church to which the promises were made, and which is assured of the guidance of the Spirit. I speak of the Church of Scotland as a national establishment, possessed of privileges and immunities, endowed with property, having an orderly gradation of judicatories, and invested with high judicial, and not judicial only, but legislative powers. In this latter sense, as regards its *privileges* as an establishment, I agree with my learned friend (the Dean of Faculty), it is dependent on the State: it derives its being and existence from the State "—"the legislation of the State," as he elsewhere said, "from whom the power of the Church is unquestionably derived."

Nothing was asked by Lord Kinnoull which could interfere with the free action of the Church in dealing with the presentee after he was taken on trials, and in requiring him to be taken on trials the Presbytery was asked to do nothing that had not been done by Presbyteries from the time of the Reformation downwards. In every instance, without exception, where a vacant parish had been filled—whoever made the presentation or selected the candidate, whether a lay patron or the heritors and elders, the Presbytery had taken the presentee on trials, and exercised their own judgment as to his qualifications, and they were asked to do nothing else now. They were asked, in short, to do only what they would, on their own showing, have been obliged to do under their model Act of 1690, c. 23, had that Statute been in force. "I ask the Court to find," the Dean of Faculty said, "that the Presbytery *must exercise their functions* in one way or another—that they must enter legally and faithfully upon the duty prescribed by Statute—*that they are bound to take the presentee on trials*, and to receive him if qualified. The mode of discharging the duty is left to them. If they enter upon it, and if they do try, they are accountable only to God for the discharge of their duty. If they execute their functions

—if they take on trials—the State trusts to their honest discharge of duty, both to pronounce a finding on the trials, and to admit and ordain if the presentee is a proper person." But the Dean, as already stated, expressly admitted that unless Lord Kinnoull's right to present, and to ask the Presbytery to take his presentee on trials, was a civil right, and unless the obligation of the Presbytery to enter on that function was a civil obligation, he had no case. Whether it was so was the question to be decided.

The case was tried with exceptional deliberation. It was heard before the whole Court, and all the judges delivered elaborate opinions. The decision was—that the right of the Patron to present, and to require the Presbytery to take him on trials, and the right of the presentee to ask the Presbytery to take him on trials, *were* civil rights; and that the Presbytery in refusing to do this, and in rejecting Mr. Young on the mere veto of the people, had "acted illegally and in violation of their duties, and contrary to the provisions of the Statutes—particularly contrary to the provisions of the Statute 10 Anne, c. 12."

This decision was pronounced on 8th March, 1838, and it was intimated by Mr. Young to the Presbytery. A marked change now took place in the attitude of the Non-intrusion party, and it became clear that they had no intention of obeying the decree. This first became manifest in an extraordinary proceeding when the General Assembly met a few weeks afterwards. It took the form of a resolution claiming for the Church an absolute "power ecclesiastical," and declaring that "this spiritual jurisdiction it will assert and at all hazards defend," and "*enforce submission to the same* upon the office-bearers and members of this Church." It was carried avowedly with the intention of maintaining the independent authority of the Church, as a practical matter, against the decision just pronounced by the Civil Court. It was not allowed to remain a dead letter. A few days after it was passed, Mr. Young was summoned to the bar of the Assembly, evidently for the purpose of being proceeded against in terms of the Resolution. But they had reckoned without their host. Mr. Young appeared at the bar accompanied by one of the most eminent counsel of the day, Mr. Hope, then Dean of Faculty, and afterwards Lord Justice-Clerk. The scene is graphically described in the "Letter to the Lord

Chancellor," written by the Dean in 1839, and his account is interesting, taking us back as it does into the middle of one of the scenes of that stormy time. After quoting a statement by Dr. Chalmers, in which he speaks of "*the difficulty we have had in prevailing on the best and ablest of our ecclesiastics to refrain from the immediate forthputting of all the powers of the Church*, in order that the Civil Courts may have time *to retrace their steps*" [all the italics in this quotation are the Dean's], and the further statement of Dr. Chalmers that "we could depose these refractory licentiates," the Dean proceeds: "*I do not doubt it.* I do not doubt the existence and fierce ardour of the intolerant spirit which Dr. Chalmers had such difficulty to restrain. I do not doubt the difficulty he had to restrain them from proceeding to deposition or expulsion of all who disputed in a court of law the pretensions of the Veto, or the authority claimed for the Resolution of 1838. For to my last hour I shall never forget the scene in the Assembly when they summoned Mr. Young to the bar, though *without notice of any charge whatever having been given to him*, to be proceeded against for contempt, forsooth, of the ecclesiastical courts of the Church, inasmuch that he intimated the judgment of the Court to the Presbytery, and called on them to give effect to the judgment. I went to the bar of the Assembly as his counsel, knowing that nothing but a resolute *refusal to plead*, and a determination to *compel* them, if they ventured to go on, *to frame a charge*, could save him from the fierce spirit of intolerance which dictated the proceedings. The disregard of all rules of justice, the heat with which they were ready to proceed to any extremity against Mr. Young, without any charge, or notice of a charge, against him, makes me but too well persuaded of the spirit of 'the best and ablest of our ecclesiastics' (!) to doubt that they have indeed been with difficulty restrained from deposing these 'refractory licentiates.'" An extraordinary scene followed, with motions, counter-motions, and divisions. Eventually the dominant party was obliged to give it up, having at last, after several divisions, a majority of only two. Mr. Young was discharged without any sentence being pronounced against him—very much, the Dean adds, quoting the words of Dr. Cook, "from the disgust and indignation which was thus excited."

The judgment of the Court of Session was appealed, and the House of Lords on 3rd May, 1839, after exhaustive arguments, affirmed the finding of the Court below.

Lord Brougham said: "Upon the statute law of Scotland the whole controversy must ultimately depend. . . . It is the province of the General Assembly, and the inferior Church courts, to take cognizance of Church matters, and to make regulations touching ecclesiastical concerns, and ecclesiastical concerns alone; and they are excluded, they are barred and shut out, from any cognizance of civil patrimonial rights; and not only of civil patrimonial rights directly, but of those things which indirectly affect civil patrimonial rights. They cannot do *per nefas* what they cannot do *per fas*. They cannot do indirectly what they cannot do directly. They have a right to make rules as to qualification, and they have a right to make rules as to who shall judge upon qualification, because qualification is admitted upon all hands to be a matter of ecclesiastical cognizance. But they have no right to make a rule as to who shall be chosen, and how he shall be chosen, when the patron presents him; and they have no right to transfer from the patron either the whole or the half—and in this case they have transferred by far the larger half—of the choice and election of the presentee."

The Lord Chancellor, Lord Cottenham, after referring to the right of the patron conferred by Parliament, said: "If such be the construction of the Statutes, of what purpose can it be to consider the supposed legislative power of the General Assembly? For it cannot be contended that there can exist in the General Assembly any legislative power to repeal, control, or interfere with enactments of the legislature; so that even if the subject matter were found to be within the legislative power of the General Assembly, it would be powerless, as to such subject matter, so far as it is regulated by Statute. It would therefore be beyond the powers of the General Assembly to interfere with the right of a patron, as secured by Statute, by adding to the powers of the Presbytery. But this legislative power claimed by the General Assembly is confined to ecclesiastical matters, and it is insisted that the matter to which the Act of 1834 applies is ecclesiastical. Now, although it is clear that if it were so the legislative power of the General Assembly would be controlled by the Statute, it is worth considering whether the matter in question can be considered as ecclesiastical. It is clear that there is nothing ecclesiastical in the right of presentation. That is a purely civil right. The adjudication upon the qualification of the presentee may be a matter ecclesiastical, but it is the right of presentation, and not the power of adjudication, which is affected by the Act of 1834."

"But," the Lord Chancellor continued, "it is argued that although the right of presentation belongs to the patron, yet that everything connected with the admission of the minister, after the presentation, is, by law, subject to the jurisdiction and direction of the Church; that the General Assembly has legislative power to make what regulation it thinks fit upon that subject, and that no complaint can be made of anything done by the Presbytery, relative to the admission of ministers, but to the superior Ecclesiastical Courts—that is, ultimately to the Assembly. The result would necessarily be that the Assembly, in its legislative capacity, might make laws destructive of the right of patronage; and having sole jurisdiction over the execution of its own laws by the inferior jurisdictions, no means would exist of questioning the legality of its enactments. This is but a mode of describing pure despotism."

In the same month in which the decision of the House of Lords was pronounced, it was brought under the notice of the General Assembly. Professing to bow to the law, as thus declared, as regarded civil matters, and on the alleged ground "that all questions of civil right, *so far as the Presbytery of Auchterarder is concerned*, are substantially decided," the Assembly instructed the Presbytery "to offer no further resistance to the claims of Mr. Young or the patron to the emoluments of the benefice, and to refrain from claiming the *jus devolutum* or any other right or privilege connected with the benefice."

But as they refused to take the presentee on trials, the deliverance of the Assembly was unmeaning. It was the merest mockery. So far as the Presbytery was concerned it had no civil right of any kind in the matter. The *jus devolutum* was a civil right, but the Presbytery could not exercise it, for it could accrue to them only in cases where the patron had failed to present, and in this case the patron had presented. The Assembly again instructed the Presbytery to offer "no further resistance" to the claims of the patron or presentee to the emoluments; but Mr. Young had never asked for the emoluments, nor could he, in any conceivable circumstance, claim them, unless and until he was inducted. The only civil right he had was to require the Presbytery to take him on trials, and that truly civil right the Assembly, in defiance of the decision of the Supreme Court, refused to recognize.

But the refusal to take Mr. Young on trials was not the only civil wrong committed by the Presbytery. What about the civil right of the patron, whose right of presentation was rendered valueless? And if these interests could be thrown aside, what about the still higher and more important civil interests involved in providing a minister for a vacancy in one of the parishes of Scotland, and the filling of a vacant place in the Presbytery—a court empowered, and bound by statute, to exercise important judicial functions in civil causes? By the refusal of the Presbytery to exercise the civil obligation of entering on the process of filling the vacancy by taking the presentee on trials, the parish would remain vacant, and one of the courts of the realm would be deprived of one of its members. So far from bowing, therefore, to the decision in those civil matters with which alone the judgment of the Court of Session and the House of Lords had dealt, the Assembly positively refused to bow to the judgment, and set it at defiance.

Mr. Young intimated the decision of the House of Lords to the Presbytery, and again asked to be taken on trials. The Presbytery referred the matter to the Commission of Assembly, and the deliverance of the Commission was prompt. "No sentence of the Civil Court," they told the Presbytery, "can justify their compliance," and they "hereby prohibit the Presbytery in any event to take Mr. Young on his trials, as they shall be accountable." Thus did the dominant party practically declare the supremacy of Church law over Statute law, even in matters concerning civil rights, and their persistence in this was the cause of the series of litigations which brought discredit on the very name of Presbyterianism.

Acting on the highest legal advice, the patron and Mr. Young now proceeded to take the only course open to them for vindicating their right. They could not force the Presbytery to take the presentee on trials, and they therefore asked the Court of Session to find the Presbytery liable in compensation for the civil loss to which their illegal refusal had subjected them. They raised an action against the individual members composing the majority of the Presbytery by which the decision complained of had been carried, concluding for £5000 in the case of the patron, and £10,000 in the case of the presentee, as damages and solatium. The Court found the action to be competent, and this decision was on 11th July, 1842, confirmed by the House of Lords.[1]

The grounds of the decision and the pleas of parties are fully stated in the opinions delivered by the Law Lords. After referring to the proceedings in the previous case, and the continued refusal of the Presbytery to take Mr. Young on trials, the Lord Chancellor, Lord Lyndhurst, proceeded to say: "I consider, therefore, the facts established that it was their duty to take him upon trial, and that they refused to do so. These are two points which do not admit of dispute. Now, my Lords, what is the rule of law as applicable to questions of this kind? When a person has an important public duty to perform, he is bound to perform that duty; and if he neglects or refuses to do so, and an individual in consequence sustains injury, that lays the foundation for an action to recover damages, by way of compensation for the injury he has sustained."

At this point we may remind the reader that a plea on which the Non-intrusionists very much relied was, that as they acted "judicially" in rejecting the presentee, their action was within the jurisdiction of the Church. But the complaint of the patron and presentee was just that the Presbytery had not acted judicially—rather that they had not acted at all. The Dean of Faculty had urged this at the bar. "I do not ask the Presbytery," he said, "to induct Mr. Young, I only ask that they shall *enter on the process of filling this vacancy* by taking the presentee on trials. When they do that, what remains is matter entirely for themselves, and within their own power; but in rejecting him solely on the fiat of the

[1] Earl of Kinnoull *v.* Ferguson, 10th March, 1843, 5 D. 1010.

people, without inquiry by themselves, *they refuse to exercise their own judicial functions*, and delegate them to an irresponsible body having no power to do any judicial act."

Dealing with this plea, the Lord Chancellor went on to say:—" Now, my Lords, what is the argument of the appellants in this case? It is said that this was the decision of a Court, the Court of Presbytery; that they were acting judicially, and that acting judicially, therefore, if they committed an error no action can be maintained against them. My Lords, I do not deny that as a general principle, and if they had admitted that gentleman upon trial, and after taking him upon trial had come to the conclusion that he was not properly qualified, *in that case it would have been a judicial decision*, and might not have afforded a ground for supporting an action, although the party should have sustained damage in consequence of it. But, my Lords, that does not apply to the present case. Here they had no discretion to exercise; they had to form no judgment. They were bound by the law to do the act; they could appeal to no tribunal. It was imperative on them to accept the party on his trial; *it was their public duty*. It bears no analogy, no resemblance to a judicial decision."

In reference to the plea of the Presbytery that the Church sufficiently obtempered the judgment of the Court if it surrendered any claim to the temporalities, Lord Campbell said:—" To the doctrine that the spiritual office of minister of a parish in Scotland may be entirely separated from the temporalities, and that the Church, renouncing the temporalities, may dispose of the spiritual office as they please, I for one beg leave to express my dissent. By the law of the land, *in passing which the Church was a party*, the temporalities are united to the spiritual office, and this office, with the temporalities, is to be enjoyed by the person, duly qualified, presented by the patron, the Church being the sole judge of his qualifications. There is a civil right to this office which the Civil courts will recognize and vindicate. A renunciation of the temporalities of the Church, with a view to retain spiritual jurisdiction, cannot be made by those who continue members of the Establishment."

In reference to another complaint by the Presbytery, which is still continued to be made in the Claim of Right—namely, that in this case damages were sought against them "for refusing to break their ordination oaths and vows," Lord Campbell said:—"The defence is explicitly and broadly put forth that the defenders are bound by the Veto law, and not by the decrees of the Court of Session or of this House, because 'they have come under the most solemn obligations to conform themselves to the discipline of the Church, and the authority of its several judicatures.' My Lords, it is impossible not to respect those who are actuated by the construction they conscientiously put upon an oath, however erroneous it may be. But, my Lords, it is my duty to say that all oaths of obedience to superiors are attended with the implied condition that their commands are lawful. From the time of St. Thomas-à-Becket till now there has been no such pretension, in any part of this island, as that ecclesiastics, in the exercise of a *liberum arbitrium* in them, are, of their own authority, conclusively to define and declare their own power and jurisdiction, and that no civil tribunal can call in question the validity of the acts or proceedings of any ecclesiastical court. In the most palmy days of Popery in England, if 'the Courts Christian' exceeded their jurisdiction—as if they were seeking to enforce an unlawful canon—instead of appealing to the Archbishop or to the Vatican at Rome, an application was made to the Courts of Westminster Hall for a prohibition; the prohibition was granted, and the law would easily have vindicated its dignity if the Bishop had insisted on proceeding in the face of the prohibition. I am not aware that the Roman Catholic Church in Scotland claimed a higher exemption from civil authority than the Roman Catholic Church in England, or that the founders of the Reformed Presbyterian Church in Scotland claimed a higher exemption from civil authority than the Roman Catholic Church to which it succeeded."

Lord Brougham had a shorter answer to the plea of conscience. "If," said his Lordship, "the Presbytery found obedience to the law of the land repugnant to their conscientious scruples, they had, if not a remedy for the grievance, at least an escape from its pressure placed within their own reach and open to them of their own free will—namely, by leaving the Church."

It was thus authoritatively settled—(1) That patronage was

a civil right which it was within the province of the Civil Courts to deal with and to vindicate; (2) that Presbyteries were under an obligation by statute law to take on trials a presentee presented by a patron with a view to his induction if found qualified, and that this was a ministerial civil duty enforceable by civil law; (3) that it was a ministerial civil duty, incumbent on Presbyteries, to fill up vacancies in parishes according to law, and that this duty could not be evaded by any attempt to separate the spiritual office from the temporalities; (4) that the Veto Act, as interfering with these civil rights and obligations, was outwith the power and jurisdiction of the Church, and illegal. And lastly, that the refusal by the Church courts to fulfil a statutory duty subjected them in damages.

The matter was now final, and it might be supposed that the only course open to the General Assembly was to rescind the Veto Act. Whatever might have been the scruples of inferior Courts, it was no question of conscience with the General Assembly. It was a mere matter of ecclesiastical polity. After the affirmation by the House of Lords of the decision in the first Auchterarder case in 1839, Dr. Chalmers, speaking in his place in the Assembly, said he had from the first entertained serious doubts as to their power to pass the Veto Act, but he had been overborne, he said—misled by what proved to be unsound legal advice. His opinion had been that the right course to have followed was for the Church to assert, as a general principle, *the right of Presbyteries* to take the fitness of a presentee into consideration, and then go to Parliament that the concurrence of the legislature might be obtained as to the effect to be given to the will of the people. He added: " I now regret with all my heart that my fears were overruled. What I then advised, if consented to, would have prevented the blunder." This opinion was shared by many of the best men of his party. Following up these views Dr. Chalmers was the first to advocate the repeal of the Veto Act, for no one knew better than he that there were other ways by which the admitted evils of forced settlements might have been avoided. In an interesting paper which he published in 1840,[1] Dr. Chalmers puts the

---

[1] " What ought the Church and the People of Scotland to do now ? " Glasgow: William Collins, 1840.

question: "What is the proper outgoing from the position in which the Church now finds itself?" and his answer is: "We have no hesitation in saying that the first step of such an outgoing is to repeal the Veto law." It was with him no question of conscience. "Had we known beforehand," he said, "that we should thereby incur the loss of the temporalities in every parish where it was carried into effect, we should not have enacted it." But his advice was not taken. The Non-intrusion party continued to the last to set at defiance the judgment of the House of Lords, and to enjoin on Presbyteries the enforcement of the Veto.

We need hardly say that these extreme proceedings, and this persistent defiance of law, were very far from being sympathized with by the Church at large, or approved by more than a minority of the inferior Church courts. The truth is, people were bewildered by the strong self-confident tone of the language used by the Non-intrusionists, while Presbyteries were overawed into enforced submission by threats of the highest Church censure, and even of deposition, if they did not obey; and this was not an empty threat, as we shall see presently. The Courts of law were assailed with the most indecent and opprobrious language. The judges were accused of having perverted justice in the decisions which they pronounced. Every one who opposed the party of the Non-intrusionists was charged with "denying the headship of Christ." One of the most influential of the leaders, Dr. Cunningham, said that he, and those acting with him, "were contending for nothing more than Christ's crown and the liberties of His Church;" and another still more influential leader of the party, Dr. Candlish, accused the members who refused to follow them as "guilty of the very sin which would hand over the Lord of the Church bound and fettered into the hands of His enemies."

Lord Aberdeen, speaking in his place in the House of Lords, lamented the spirit in which the secession, if it did take place, was to be accomplished. "Very recently," he said, "a numerous meeting was held in Edinburgh, which was presided over by the right honourable gentleman (Mr. Fox Maule) who had presented the petition and advocated the cause of the Church in the other House, and the sentiments there expressed were not such as might have been expected from persons who felt a conscientious necessity for leaving the Church because of the interpretation which had been put upon the law. It was there announced that, if they did leave the Church, a course of agitation, unprecedented in any former times, was to be adopted. The ministers were not to continue in their own parishes to minister to such of their flocks as shared their opinion on the present state of the Church. It was announced at that meeting that the Seceders were to go through the country from end to end; that they were to preach the Gospel throughout Scotland as if it were a pagan country in which the Gospel was unknown; they were to intrude themselves into parishes occupied by men as pious, as learned, and as exemplary as themselves; in short, every means was to be taken to injure and destroy the Establishment. Indeed, one of their leaders made no secret of what was the course they would adopt and the hopes which they entertained. He said: 'When we shall leave the Establishment we shall take every step within our power, and use all the influence that remains to us, to bring down the Establishment. When we leave the Establishment do we not say that it is made up of men who are guilty of the heinous sin of Erastianism, and will it not be our duty to use all the energies we can command to bring down the heinous thing?' He further said: 'It is not the excitement of a public meeting which incites me to make use of such language. No, I have long pondered on this in my own mind, and the result has been a conviction that the reasons for leaving the Church shall also be reasons for subverting and pulling her down. If it is impossible *for us* to remain in the Church, it follows, as a natural consequence, that we cannot leave her unassailed when we come out of her.' Throughout," added Lord Aberdeen, "*it has been a clerical agitation*," and he believed that "the glorious campaign of preachers" promised by the speakers at the Edinburgh meeting was absolutely necessary in order to keep the people in that frame of mind so desirable for their ends.

Under this "reign of terror" it required no little courage in Presbyteries to do their duty, but there were not wanting instances in which they did it. A notable example occurred in the Presbytery of Strathbogie, after the decision of the House of Lords in the first Auchterarder case. A Mr. Edwards had been presented by Lord Fife's trustees to the vacant parish of Marnoch, and rejected under the Veto Act, against the private judgment of the majority of the Presbytery, who acted, as they did not hesitate afterwards to confess, under fear of the censures threatened by the dominant party in the General Assembly. The presentee thereupon raised an action against them, similar to that in the Auchterarder case, and obtained a judgment finding that the Presbytery was "bound and astricted" to take him on trials, and, if found qualified, to receive and admit him according to law. This judgment having been intimated to the Presbytery, the majority—now ashamed of their weakness—resolved to obey the decree, and having taken the presentee on trials and found him duly qualified, they resolved to proceed with his ordination. At this point they were arrested by the Commission of Assembly, and suspended from their office for a time—the minority being instructed to supply ministerial services in their parishes. Against the intimation of this order the Court of Session granted interdict. The majority, in consequence of the peculiar position in which they had been thus placed, having delayed proceedings, the presentee raised another action against the Presbytery and the individual members, concluding for decree requiring them to proceed and complete the induction, with an alternative conclusion for damages. After certain procedure in this action the Presbytery was summoned to the bar of the Court of Session. They appeared, and the majority stated frankly that they could not resist the decree asked. They stated, in effect, that they were as satisfied as the Court was that they were bound to proceed, but they were coerced, they said, by the orders of the General Assembly. As important civil rights were involved, the Court was left no option in the matter. With the decision of the House of Lords before them there was only one course open to them, and, after hearing the minority of the Presbytery, they ordained the Presbytery to proceed. Do your duty, the Court said in effect, and the law will protect you. But in adopting this course, the Court specially disclaimed either the right or the power to do a spiritual act. "We cannot ourselves ordain," the Lord President said, "*but we can ordain the Presbytery to do its duty.*"

This was in accordance with what has always been recognized as trite law both in England and Scotland—namely, that where any individual or body of men refuses to do an act which, from their position, they are bound, officially and ministerially, to do, no matter what it is, the Courts of law will, at the instance of any party having an interest, compel them to do it under pain of damages to the party aggrieved by their refusal. In the second Auchterarder case Lord Brougham said:—"To compel men and bodies of men to exercise faculties which they have received from heaven is one of the most ordinary acts of legislative, of executive, and of judicial power," and the same doctrine was laid down by the Lord Chancellor. But it is also Church law—the doctrine taught by the fathers of the Church. One of the most eminent of the old Reformers, Gillespie, writes:[1] "As Church officers they [the ministers] are to be kept within the bounds of their calling, and compelled, if need be, by the Magistrate, to do those duties which, by the clear Word of God and received principles of religion, and by the received ecclesiastical constitutions of that Church they ought to do. The Magistrate is neither to administer Word, nor sacrament, nor Church discipline, but he is to take care that all these things be done by those whom God hath called thereunto. He may command Church officers to suspend or excommunicate obstinate and scandalous persons. *He may command them to ordain able and godly ministers.*" The other great Reformers held the same language.

In the face of these authorities the Free Church party, in their Claim of Right, asserted that in pronouncing this decree, requiring the Presbytery to fulfil a duty incumbent on them by statute as well as by ecclesiastical law, in a matter involving important civil rights, the Court of Session had "stepped beyond the province allotted to them by the Constitution, and in which alone their decisions can be held to declare the law, deciding causes spiritual and ecclesiastical, and had invaded the jurisdiction and encroached upon the spiritual privileges of the Courts of the Church, in violation of the Constitution of the Country, in defiance of the statutes, and in contempt of the laws of the kingdom." By such wild and indecent charges, repeated by the Non-intrusion

[1] "Aaron's Rod," 176.

ministers from their pulpits, their hearers were bewildered, and their minds unfitted to discern between right and wrong.

The majority of the Presbytery of Strathbogie proceeded accordingly to do their duty, and they ordained Mr. Edwards. As might be expected this brought upon them a storm of abuse from the real wrongdoers. They were charged with "a determination to violate the laws of the Church—a gross and insulting act of rebellion against her laws and government." They were held up to public execration, and were called to the bar of the General Assembly. In vain did Dr. Cook represent that they had done nothing but "yield obedience to the supreme civil tribunals of the kingdom in a matter declared by the tribunals to relate to civil rights." The violent counsels of the predominant party prevailed, and every one of the majority of the Presbytery was deposed from the office of the ministry. We need scarcely add that this sentence proved eventually a mere *brutum fulmen.*

It is unnecessary to notice the other cases arising out of the exercise of rights of patronage. They were all decided on the same principles as those which ruled the decision in the first Auchterarder case.

But before the last of that class of cases had been decided another action had been raised, in which the powers assumed by the dominant party in the General Assembly were to be further tested. This was the Stewarton case, and here, as in the other leading case, the question at issue was whether the Church had gone out of its own jurisdiction, and whether Church-made law was to prevail over Statute law in a matter involving the gravest civil interests. It was a case which was regarded by many Free Churchmen as having had "a more conclusive influence on the result latterly than Patronage had."[1]

The facts were these:—In 1834 and 1835 there were passed by the Assembly certain Acts known as the Chapel Acts, the effect of which was that ministers of *quoad sacra* churches were admitted to seats in presbyteries, and had districts set apart and placed under their cure *quoad sacra*. It was, like the Veto Act, new legislation, and it was strenuously opposed by the Constitutional party in the Assembly, but it was carried by a majority. In

[1] "Law of Creeds," by Mr. A. Taylor Innes.

terms of these Acts, and of an Act passed by the Assembly in 1839 regarding communion with Seceders, the Presbytery of Irvine admitted a Mr. Clelland, a minister of the Associate Synod, to be the minister of an Established chapel in the parish of Stewarton. They added his name to the roll of the Presbytery, and thereafter proceeded to take steps for allocating a parochial district to his church *quoad sacra*. The patron and several of the heritors of the parish objected to this. They objected to any *quoad sacra* minister sitting and voting as a member of a court which exercised jurisdiction in matters affecting their civil rights, and generally they objected to any innovation upon the existing parochial state of the parish. They accordingly applied to the Court for interim interdict, which was granted. The case was heard before the whole Court. It was exhaustively debated, and in January, 1843, the Court decided that the proposed action of the Church was *ultra vires* and illegal.

In this case, as in that of Auchterarder, the Presbytery rested their whole plea on the Statutes, which, they contended, gave them power to do what was proposed; but while they admitted this, they repeated the extraordinary plea that although the Court should find that their action was in violation of the Statutes, the Court of Session had no power to declare the illegality, or prevent the commission of the wrong. We give their plea in the words of the Lord Justice-Clerk when pronouncing judgment—the italics being his Lordship's in the printed report revised by him. He said:—"The leading counsel for the respondents (the Presbytery), in his argument at the bar, *expressly disclaimed* the notion that the jurisdiction claimed by the Church *could rest on any other foundation than on the Statute law of the land*." And again:—"He (the counsel for the Presbytery) anxiously declared that he rested the powers contended for solely on the authority of the Acts of the Legislature in reference to the Church." And then, referring to the plea that whatever the Statutes might enact the Civil court could not interfere, his Lordship went on to say:—"The plea of the Presbytery—that although the power is claimed in virtue of Statute alone, yet whatever violation of Statute may be committed, whatever civil wrong done, whatever may be the assumption of power, and however fundamental the changes made in the constitution of the Church, still the Supreme

Court cannot declare the illegality and prevent the wrong—is a proposition to which assent cannot, on legal principles, be seriously claimed." The same plea had, as we have said, been put forward in the Auchterarder case, and of course disregarded.

But the Free Church party asserted, and still assert, that in this case of Stewarton the Court invaded the jurisdiction of the Church, and acted "in defiance of the Statutes and in contempt of the laws of the kingdom." It had granted interdict, they said, "against the establishment of additional ministers to meet the wants of an increasing population, as uninterruptedly practised from the Reformation to this day."[1] But for that statement there was no foundation. The Chapel Acts were a novelty in the history of the Church, and no such attempt to alter the constitution of Presbyteries had ever before been attempted. The heritors did not object to the erection of any number of chapels, or to the ordination of any number of ministers to meet the wants of the population in the way this had always been done before, but they objected to its being done in a way that was as illegal as it was novel. They objected to the parish of Stewarton being divided; and they specially objected to plead, in matters affecting their civil interests, before a court illegally constituted. The Lord President said :—" It is clear that the Church, by its own authority, cannot authorize the ministers of what are called *quoad sacra* parishes to perform those duties which, *as directly concerning civil rights*, the law has only devolved upon the legally constituted ministers of the Presbyteries of the Church. This species of parish," his Lordship said, "was unknown to law. The erection of new parishes could only take place in virtue of authority flowing from Statute; and the whole history of the applications to Parliament for the erection of parishes before 1621 and 1633 serves to prove that the Presbyteries of the Church are composed of parish ministers and elders from legal Kirk Sessions."

"It was claimed," said the Lord Justice-Clerk, "that parties admitted as Mr. Clelland was, shall enjoy all the rights and privileges of ordained ministers and elders of the Church of Scotland—shall be parochial ministers to all intents and purposes. This procedure," his Lordship continued, "if it has any

[1] 'Claim of Right."

meaning at all, gives to the new minister and to the new Kirk Session, and to them exclusively, *the whole authority* over the district which any minister and Kirk Session can have, and withdraws the inhabitants generally from the jurisdiction and discipline of the parish minister and Kirk Session proper. These new ministers and elders are all brought into Church Courts—they have received the power of government in the Established Church. Presentations are to be presented to them. They receive the power of judging upon the same—a statutory function and a statutory duty. They claim the right conferred by Statute on the proper members of Presbytery. They claim to sit and act under special statutes, both as to schoolmasters and as to churches, manses, and glebes"—all which, of course, are matters essentially affecting civil rights.

Lord Wood said:—"The Church of Scotland is, in its constitution, as finally settled down and recognized by the State, a parochial Church; and its clerical members—with the exception of the Professors of Theology in the Universities—consist of ministers who are the ministers of the parishes forming the territorial divisions into which the country is distributed. It is such persons only who, by its constitution, are entitled to the rights and privileges of parish ministers, and who alone, more especially, have a right, as clerical members, to a seat, and to vote in the Church Courts, to which the powers and jurisdiction given to the Church have been confided, and by which its government is carried on. The elders, again, who are entitled to a seat and to vote are the elders of the Kirk Sessions in which the ministers preside. If I am right," added Lord Wood, "in regard to the constitution of the Church, I apprehend that it follows that the Presbytery of Irvine had no power to proceed in the erection of a *quoad sacra* parish in the manner proposed, and simply for this reason, that *it involves a change in the constitution of the Church*, which, be the act ecclesiastical or not, and whether it touches civil rights or not, no Court of the Church has power to make under the authority of any jurisdiction to which they can lay claim."

Looking at the matter in its practical bearings as a question of Church polity, the Chapel Act was, apart from its incompetency, legislation of a very crude and injudicious kind. The anomalous character of the parishes proposed to be erected was well pointed out by the Lord Justice-Clerk. "Look," he said, "at the character of this alleged parish, which is the title or foundation on which the minister and his Kirk Session have been recognized and allowed to sit in Presbytery. It is a parish *without any provision for permanency.* There is no security for maintaining the fabric of the Church. There is no endowment for any successor in the cure. *There is no security even for the continuance of the parish itself,* such as it is. If the people tire of the burden, on the death or removal of the minister, there will be no successor at all. The parish will not be kept up. And then this supposed parish drops wholly out of the Church; and while the alleged decree of Presbytery stands, making it a parish *quoad sacra,* the people are left just as they were—the parishioners of the original parish. This really renders the notion of a separate parish ludicrous."

There could be no answer to this. The Presbytery could not deny that parochial ministers sitting in Church Courts exercised important civil functions, but they represented that in allocating the new parish it was intended "that no civil right of these parties (the heritors) shall be affected by the allocation, and that the effect of the allocation is limited to matters of spiritual discipline and government." The Lord President effectually disposed of this truly silly plea. "Neither the law of the State," he said, "nor the law of the Church, at any period of its history, can be shown to have acknowledged so anomalous a class of parochial ministers as those who, when certain most important duties are about to be discharged by Presbyteries, must invariably either be required to withdraw, and have their names expunged from the sederunt, or be prohibited from taking any part in the proceedings then before the Court. The attempt to constitute any such nondescript class of ministers is in itself fundamentally opposed to the principle of Presbyterian parity, so essential a character of the establishment of the Church. They must either be qualified to act as constituted members in all respects or none." And the Lord Justice-Clerk quoted an authority which all Free Churchmen must respect. He said: "It is justly stated by Sir Henry Moncrieff that the erection of a parish *quoad sacra tantum* is altogether without precedent. It appears to me very plain that there *cannot* be such a parish. The parochial division of the country is a matter of public and constitutional arrangement. It subsisted before the Reformation. When Presbytery was established it was by means of a Church of parish ministers. Its government was vested in Kirk Sessions, Presbyteries, and other Courts. The only members recognized by the law were the ministers of parishes. And a parish, again, was a division and apportionment of a part of the country already subsisting, and subsisting for other purposes as well as for ecclesiastical arrangements."

These were the circumstances under which the Stewarton case was decided. Yet, as we have said, the Non-intrusion party asserted then, and the Free Church asserts to this day, that in pronouncing that decision the Judges of the Supreme Court acted in defiance of the statutes and in contempt of law. Indeed, it was made the ground of their secession even more than the decision in the Auchterarder case. By these decisions, and the others following on them, which were decided on precisely the same principles, there had been—so they put it in their final protest—"interference with conscience, dishonour done to Christ's crown, and rejection of His sole and supreme authority as King in His Church." They treated the judgment with contempt, and the Assembly declared its determination to maintain the status given to the *quoad sacra* ministers without regard to any decision of the Civil Court.[1]

Before leaving the Stewarton case it may be stated here, that the General Assembly of 1843, which repealed the Chapel Acts after the Seceders had left, was not insensible to the importance of erecting new parishes and giving their ministers seats in the Church Courts, where they could sit on equal terms with their fellow-presbyters. The constitutional party in the Church was as keenly alive as those who seceded, to the necessity of meeting the religious wants of the people, but they knew that this could be effectually done only by an endowed territorial system, and that the machinery necessary for that purpose could only be obtained by statutory enactment. The Rescissory Act bears that the Assembly being "deeply impressed

---

[1] Lord Cockburn's "Life," i. 235.

with the vast benefits which have been obtained for the people of this country by the extension of the blessings of religious instruction by means of the services of the *quoad sacra* ministers, and feeling most anxious that their great and useful services should be secured to the country on a proper and permanent basis, desires to express a sincere hope that measures will be taken to have the unendowed districts erected, legally and properly, into parishes, and endowments granted to their ministers." At the same time a committee was appointed to prepare an address to the Queen on the subject. The response of the State was prompt. The Chapel Acts were repealed by the General Assembly on 23rd May, 1843, and on 19th July in the following year, there was passed the Act 7 & 8 Victoria, c. 44, an Act which has worked so admirably—which has secured to the Church all the machinery she required for Church extension, and which forms the foundation of that system of endowed territorial work by which the country is being covered, and by which alone spiritual destitution can be met.

Equally prompt, too, was the response of the people to the appeal made to them to provide the funds necessary to endow the newly erected parishes. The result, as we have already stated, has been that up to 1889 inclusive, there have been added to the Church no less than 366 new parishes, each with a church, many with manses, and all with a perpetual endowment to the incumbents. Including the forty Parliamentary churches already mentioned, there have been in all 406 new parishes added to the Church. Each minister has a seat in the Church Courts; he has a defined district under his charge, and he enjoys the *status* and all the rights and privileges of a parish minister —the temporalities of the old parishes being left untouched.

No question can again arise such as that which was decided in the case of Stewarton, and the abolition of Patronage renders it impossible that any dispute should ever again occur such as that which was raised and settled in the case of Auchterarder. Neither is it likely that in the future history of the Church any other great constitutional question should arise—none at all events equal in importance to what was settled in these leading cases—for the position of the Church towards the law and the State was then discussed so thoroughly as to leave little room for further misunderstanding.

In looking back on all that vexatious litigation, one satisfactory thing is noticeable—namely, that they involved no question of doctrine. It was the same, as we have seen, in all the troubles which occurred before the Revolution. There had been conflicts, many and bitter, between the Church and the State, and between parties within the Church—questions of Church government and Church polity, the alternate setting up and pulling down of Presbyterianism and Episcopacy, but then, as in recent times, no question of doctrine was touched. Protestantism as embodied in the Confession of Faith is the one thing which all have held, and to which all have professed a common allegiance.[1] Another matter equally satisfactory is, that as regards jurisdiction and spiritual independence, the Church came out of the contest unscathed. Her absolute independence within her own sphere was recognized, and defined, and confirmed, in a manner more clear and satisfactory than it had ever been in any previous period of her history. The Non-intrusionists, however, as will be seen further on, imagined that, when out of the Establishment, they would enjoy a jurisdiction, and an independence in ecclesiastical matters, greater than what was to be found within it. How startling was the awakening they had from that delusion, in a litigation with one of their own members before the Court of Session, will be seen presently.

As regards the State, on every occasion when an opportunity occurred, the Government made it clear that in no case where the Church confined its action to its own domain could it be interfered with, and that only in cases in which that domain was overstepped, and civil rights assailed, would its action be disallowed. Sir James Graham, the principal Secretary of State for the Home Department, in the important State paper addressed by him to the Moderator of the General Assembly in January, 1843—in answer to the application of the Non-intrusionists to have their claim recognized, and the decisions of the Courts of law set aside—pointed out that the applicants had placed themselves in a wrong position, by an open resist-

[1] "Law of Creeds," 24.

ance to law in a matter concerning civil interests, which did not fall within the jurisdiction of the Church. "The Assembly," he said, "submitted the question at issue to the judgment of the Court of Session; they were dissatisfied with the decision. They had their legal remedy, and they used it. They carried the judgment by appeal to the bar of the House of Lords, and in that last resort the judgment of the Scotch Court was confirmed, and the Veto Act was pronounced to be illegal. This solemn decision fixed the principle of law which rules all the minor cases which have since arisen. The judgment in the second Auchterarder case, which found the patron and the presentee entitled to redress in the form of pecuniary compensation *for a civil wrong*, was a legal sequence of the former judgment; and here again the Assembly was content to plead before the Civil tribunal, and again the Assembly refuses to submit to the compulsion of an adverse decision. I am also compelled reluctantly to remark that the Church [the Non-intrusion majority], not content with disobeying the decrees of the Civil courts, has inflicted the severities of her discipline, as in the case of the Strathbogie Presbytery, on ministers whose only crime has been obedience to what has been declared to be the law of the land. All the other cases complained of in the Memorial and Declaration of Right, which relate to the settlement of ministers, have arisen from the determination of the Church to enforce the Veto Act in defiance of law." And putting the question of the jurisdiction conferred by the Statutes in its proper light, Sir James Graham said:—"Whether a particular matter in dispute *is so entirely spiritual as to fall exclusively within the jurisdiction of the Church courts*, may often be a difficult question, *but it is a question of law*, and questions of law are decided in the Courts of law; and questions of jurisdiction are also decided there—all subject to an appeal to the House of Lords, which includes within itself the highest judicial authorities, and which is able to command the opinion of those who are trusted with the power of deciding on the civil rights, the liberties, and the lives of their fellow-subjects." And Lord Aberdeen, speaking afterwards for the Government in his place in the House of Lords, said:—"The truth, my Lords, is that so far as Her

Majesty's government is concerned, and I believe I may say the Legislature, we are prepared to recognize to the utmost all the rights, privileges, and powers which the people and the Church have ever possessed by law, at any period of its history, in the matter of collation."

But we are not left to seek for the true spiritual independence of the Church either in the declarations of statesmen or in the *obiter dicta* of judges—not to speak of the very plain language of the Statutes. The question of her exclusive jurisdiction in matters falling within her own domain has, since 1843, been repeatedly raised and decided in cases before the Supreme Court in Scotland. For the proper understanding of the law as to the Church's powers it is desirable to look at these decisions.

A case occurred in 1849, where a schoolmaster complained to the Court of Session that in a process of discipline he had been treated with injustice by the Kirk Session of Blairgowrie. He also alleged irregularity in the proceedings, and averred that the sentence had been pronounced maliciously and without probable cause. But having ascertained that the Kirk Session had acted "within their competent duty and authority as a Church court," the Court of Session refused to review the judgment. "To any party alleging wrong by the Church courts," said Lord Justice-Clerk Hope, "the answer is plain. If these Courts were acting wholly within the matter committed to them they are distinct and supreme, and the authority under which they sit excludes any inquiry into their motives by the Civil courts." And he added:—"No one need be, unless he chooses, a member of the Church of Scotland, or of any other particular sect, in the constitution of which there are things to which he objects; but if he joins the same, he must take its constitution as he finds it." And having pointed out that the procedure complained of was founded on the authority of the Confession of Faith, which he characterized as Statute law, he said:—"I am not afraid of any hazardous results from the protection which I think the Church Courts possess from any inquiry into their motives, when exercising, in the matters falling within Church discipline, that separate government recognized in the Church as of Divine appointment." Lord Medwyn, in concurring, said:—"Wherever the matter clearly falls within the proper province of the

Church courts, its proceedings cannot be questioned in the Civil court."

In another case in 1850, in the parish of Kirkpatrick-Durham, in which the Court was asked to interpose on the ground of irregularity in the authentication of the records of the Church court—a plea which the Lord President characterized as "a really formidable objection"—his Lordship, in giving judgment against the complainer, said that as what had been done "was in accordance with the law and usage of the Church, we have no right to interfere, whether we approve of the sentence or not."

In the case of Lockhart, in the Presbytery of Deer, in 1851,[1] a minister who had been deposed by the General Assembly presented a Note of Suspension to the Court of Session, on the ground of the procedure having been irregular and oppressive. The Court, on the complainer's own statement, and without calling on the counsel for the Church to reply, refused to interfere. Lord President Boyle, in giving judgment, took occasion to say:— "Although we may form a different opinion in regard to matters of form, or even of substantial justice, in my opinion we cannot interfere to quash the sentence." And his Lordship added:— "Although I had the misfortune to differ with my brethren on the right hand—Lords Fullarton and Ivory—in the memorable cases of Auchterarder and Strathbogie, I did so on the ground that these cases *involved matter of civil right*, and that the decisions of the General Assembly involved a departure not only from the Statutes of the realm, but from the constitution of the Church itself." Lord Fullarton, one of the judges thus referred to as having been in the minority in these cases, said:—"In some of the cases which have been referred to—as, for instance, in that of Marnoch—there was no doubt a direct interference by the Civil court with a sentence of deposition pronounced by the Church courts. But these were very special cases, and, as I understand, were decided on that speciality. The offence for which the parties were deposed was contumacy, no doubt, against the Church judicatures, but the contumacy was obedience to the law of the land, as declared by this Court, and these sentences were treated not so much as the just exercise of ecclesiastical discipline, *as an alleged encroachment on the civil.*"

[1] 5th July, 1851, 13 D. 1296.

Equally important were the views expressed by Lord Ivory on that occasion:—"Even when a matter is properly within the province of the Civil court," he said, "and when we are interfering with an inferior civil judicatory, whose jurisdiction in that matter has been declared exclusive, and not subject to review, our right to control its proceedings arises from the fact that the inferior judicatory has exceeded its powers. We interfere *because the inferior court has gone beyond its province, and has by doing so lost the protection of the Statute under which it possesses exclusive jurisdiction.* I should no more think of disturbing a decision of the Ecclesiastical court in an ecclesiastical matter, than I should think of disturbing the decisions of the courts of Justiciary or Exchequer in a matter falling under their respective provinces. We cannot look," his Lordship added, "into the merits of the objections in this case. If these questions were ill decided, that is one of the inconveniences of having two separate tribunals, *each independent and supreme in its own province.* The law has entrusted all these questions to the Church courts. The proper court has heard these questions pleaded, and has pronounced judgment upon them, and I do not think it is competent for us to interfere." After alluding to the fact that, like Lord Fullarton, he had differed from the majority of the Court in the Auchterarder and Strathbogie cases, Lord Ivory added:—"I am bound to hold that these cases were rightly decided; but what was the ground on which the Court interposed? *It was not because they thought themselves entitled to interfere with the proper ecclesiastical jurisdiction of the Church courts,* but because they held *that the Ecclesiastical courts were going out of their province, and were touching matters which were properly questions of civil right.*"

We shall mention only one other case—that of Auchtergaven, decided in 1870.[1] It was a case where an accused party sought interdict against the Presbytery of Dunkeld from re-opening certain proceedings against him. The case was a strong one for the complainer, and if the Court of Session had had jurisdiction, he would in all probability have prevailed; but the Court held that they were precluded from interfering. The Lord Justice-Clerk, in giving judgment, said:—"If this were a

---

[1] Wight v. Presbytery of Dunkeld, 27th June, 1870.

case in which we were called upon to review the proceedings of an inferior court, I should have thought a strong case had been made out for our interference, but whatever inconsiderate *dicta* to that effect may have been thrown out, that is not the law of Scotland. The jurisdiction of the Church courts, as recognized judicatories of this realm, rests on a similar statutory foundation to that under which we administer justice within these walls. *Within their spiritual province the Church courts are as supreme as we are within the Civil*, and as this is a matter relating to the discipline of the Church, and solely within the cognizance of the Church courts, I think we have no power whatever to interfere." Lord Cowan said:—" I repudiate the idea of a Civil court being entitled to overrule a deliverance of the Assembly in matters of this kind. I think the Assembly is supreme in questions legitimately and regularly before them, just as much as the Court of Justiciary." And, referring to the plea that the case involved civil consequences to the complainer, Lord Cowan added:—" It may be that incidentally, and necessarily, the civil interests of the clergyman, or those subject to the procedure, may be affected. Every judgment pronounced by the Assembly in reference to a *fama* against a minister has necessarily that effect, but because the civil interests of the man found guilty of an offence may be affected, is that any reason for the Court interfering? By no means." Lord Benholme and Lord Neaves concurred.

The exclusive jurisdiction and absolute spiritual independence thus recognized in the Church of Scotland exist in no other Church. It is certainly not enjoyed by the courts of the Church of England. "From all these courts," Blackstone says, "an appeal lies to the king in the last resort."[1] And this has been construed as giving the right of ordinary appeal from all ecclesiastical or spiritual decisions.

In the face of all the decisions we have quoted, affirming the independence of the courts of the Church of Scotland in their own sphere, and the powerlessness of the Civil courts to interfere with them, the leaders of the Free Church continued to maintain, as indeed they still maintain, that they were obliged to leave the Church because she was coerced by the Civil courts

---
[1] Henry VIII., c. 19, § 4.

in matters purely spiritual. And four years after the last of these decisions had been pronounced, one of the ablest and most prominent among them, Dr. Robert Buchanan, in moving an overture in the Free Church Presbytery of Glasgow,[1] averred, as matter of fact, that "in *all* matters, *even the most purely spiritual*, the Church of Scotland is bound to take her guidance in the last resort from the Courts, not of Christ's Church, but of Cæsar's crown."

It was pending the trial of the Stewarton Case that the Non-intrusion party laid on the table of the General Assembly of 1842 the well-known document which is now known as "the Claim of Right." As a legal document it calls for our attention here, apart from the effect it had in exciting and misleading not the people only, but the great bulk of the ministers who seceded. The terms in which it is conceived, the procedure of the party consequent upon it, and its reception by the Government and by Parliament, illustrate still further the position of the Church towards the law and the State.

The proper title of this extraordinary document—that by which it was called when it was laid on the table of the General Assembly, and by which it is still called in the Standards of the Free Church—is, "Claim, Declaration, and Protest anent the Encroachments of the Court of Session." It consists almost entirely of an attack on the Judges of that Court.

The opening sentence—the preamble—on which all that follows rests, sets forth that notwithstanding "the securities for the liberties, government, jurisdiction, discipline, rights, and privileges" of the Church and its Courts, "provided by the statutes of the realm, and by the Constitution of the country, these have been of late assailed by the very Courts to which the Church was authorized to look for assistance and protection, to an extent that threatens their entire subversion." It then proceeds to set forth the several statutes, and it bears expressly that the only "exclusive jurisdiction" claimed by the Church is that which has been "by divers and repeated Acts of Parliament recognized, ratified, and confirmed." We quote these passages in order to call attention to the fact, that what was claimed was rested not on any inherent spiritual independence

[1] 1st April, 1874.

in the Church itself, but solely on the rights conferred on her "by statute," and "by the constitution of this country." And further, that the Court of Session was the tribunal "authorized" to assist and protect the Church if her legal rights were assailed. It is an important admission, repeating and confirming as it does the admission made by the counsel of the Non-intrusionists at the bar of the Civil court, that they rested their case on the Statutes, and that they recognized the jurisdiction of the Civil court to interpret them.

The Claim goes on to notice the different decisions—the first group being those which were pronounced before the time of the Non-intrusion controversy, and in regard to these it is averred that in all of them the Court of Session had decided on principles the opposite of those by which they were guided in the later cases. In regard to some of these earlier decisions we have already pointed out how untrue this statement in the Claim is: we cannot detain the reader by noticing the others in detail. We dismiss them with the observation that *in not one of them did the Court do what this Claim avers it did.*

This is a strong statement, but it is made advisedly. The Auchterarder case had been previously recited in the Claim, and it is to be noted that, unlike the others, no complaint is made that in that leading case the Courts of law acted oppressively or illegally. On the contrary, it recognizes the judgment of the House of Lords in that case as fixing the law that it was "illegal to refuse to take on trials, and to reject the presentee of a patron," in respect of the dissent of the people; and it states that "to the authority of that judgment so far as disposing of civil interests the Church implicitly bowed." How very much the reverse was their treatment of that judgment, and how persistently they defied the law as declared by it, we have seen. But they were obliged to recognize that it did settle the law, and the Claim goes on to complain that "*pending the efforts of the Church to accomplish the desired alteration of the law,*" the Judges of the Court of Session had pronounced a series of decisions adverse to the Church, in which they had disregarded both law and statute. The statement is, we need not say, unfounded. As regards those decisions which were connected with the Veto, or arising out of its enforcement, every one of them was decided on precisely the same principles as the first case. On this point the reader will probably be content to accept the testimony of a Free Church lawyer as conclusive. Mr. Taylor Innes says that each of the decisions in question "was based on the principle carefully laid down in the first case, and repeated in the others—in each after protracted deliberation."[1]

But no one would discover from the Claim of Right that any one of them was decided on that principle, or had the remotest connection with the decision of the House of Lords. Take one example. It is that of Culsalmond, in which, as in the other cases, the Judges are charged with tyrannically interfering to subvert the government of the Church, and with a violation of Statute law, when in point of fact they were only applying the decision in the Auchterarder case. The assertion in the Claim is that the Court in this case "interdicted the execution of the sentence of a Church judicatory prohibiting a minister from officiating or administering ordinances within a particular parish, pending the discussion of a cause in the Church courts as to the validity of his settlement therein." No explanation is given, and it is left to be inferred that the Court had arbitrarily interfered in a purely spiritual question depending in the Church courts, in which these Courts were acting in a legal and constitutional manner. The fact is withheld that the act complained of was the extraordinary attempt of the Commission of Assembly to suspend from his functions an ordained minister, and to prohibit the administration of ordinances in his parish, on the mere allegation of certain individuals that his settlement had been irregular. And there is also withheld the fact that the Commission had done this without hearing parties, and before they had even been cited. The whole matter arose out of the continued determination of the Non-intrusion party to enforce the Veto Act after it had been declared illegal.

The facts were, shortly, these:—An ordained minister had received a presentation to a parish, and the Presbytery, in fulfilment of their ministerial duty, sustained the call and admitted him. A minority of the Presbytery, however, and some of the parishioners, presented a petition to the Commission complaining of the settlement, on the ground, *inter alia*, and "more especially,"

---

[1] "Mr. Finlay's Bill and the Law of 1843," by A. Taylor Innes, p. 13.

that, in their proceedings in the settlement, the Presbytery had disregarded the Veto Act. The Presbytery *had* disregarded it, and they had done so for the simple reason that it was a nullity, having been declared *ultra vires* and illegal by the judgment of the House of Lords. The Commission, however, ordered the parties to be cited before them, and in the meantime took the unwarrantable step of prohibiting the minister from officiating or administering ordinances in the parish until the Commission should hear the case. It was in these circumstances that the minister applied to the Court for protection and got it. The Lord President said: "The attempt to arrest the settlement being founded principally, if not solely, on the application of the Veto law, and that law, as a legislative act of the Church, having been declared wholly abortive, the right of those aggrieved by the extraordinary and unprecedented interference of the Commission of the General Assembly, to apply for protection, flows directly from the solemn determination of the law promulgated by the judgment of the House of Lords in the case of Auchterarder. Any attempt," his Lordship added, "to use the Veto law as a bar to the taking on trials and admission of a presentee *is a direct invasion of civil right*. The Church is utterly powerless to subvert, by its own authority, the law of Patronage, which is a matter regulated by the statutory law of the land, and to which, until altered by the legislature, implicit obedience must be given." In such circumstances it was obviously the function, as it was the duty of the Court, to uphold the statute law, and to give effect to the decision of the House of Lords. It had no alternative. Yet all this is disingenuously kept back, and without a word of explanation the case is cited as one in which the Judges had tyrannically and lawlessly interfered to subvert the government of the Church and to violate statute law.

In the same way the Claim of Right misrepresents those decisions which proceeded on the same principles as those involved in the Stewarton case. Here, again, one example may suffice. It is characteristic of all the rest.

The reader will recollect that in the Stewarton case it was decided that it was illegal and *ultra vires* of the Church to alter the ancient and legal arrangement of parishes, and to change the constitution of Presbyteries, by introducing as a member there, having all the powers of a judge, any one who was not a parish minister; and that to do so was a civil wrong which the Civil courts had jurisdiction to redress. While that case was pending, certain cases of discipline against ministers occurred, and the accused parties, on being cited before the Presbytery, found *quoad sacra* ministers sitting there as members of the Court. They objected to this, and applied to the Court of Session for protection. They admitted that the crimes of which they were accused fell under the legitimate jurisdiction of the Church courts, but they demanded to be tried by competent judges. They objected to their cases being tried, or any sentence pronounced, by persons who had no legal right to sit as members of Presbytery. It was a legitimate plea, and the Civil court gave effect to it, and granted the interdicts asked. Yet, again, the Claim of Right, without any explanation, asserts that in these cases the Court of Session had gone out of its province, for no reason but to protect wrongdoers. The Court is accused of "interdicting the General Assembly and inferior Church judicatories from inflicting Church censures; as, *inter alia*, in a case where a Presbytery was interdicted from proceeding in the trial of a minister accused of fraud and swindling, and in another where a Presbytery was interdicted from proceeding with a libel against a licentiate for drunkenness, obscenity, and profane swearing." The facts essential to the understanding of the questions at issue are withheld. No explanation is given as to the unanswerable plea stated by the accused against the constitution of the Court before which they were cited, and the incompetency of the Presbytery, as constituted, to judge in the cases at all. The only inference left to be drawn is that in questions of legitimate discipline, which from the beginning of the Church's history have been recognized as falling within the exclusive jurisdiction of the Church Courts, the Court of Session had, without any ground or reason, and "in contempt of the laws of the kingdom," interfered to shield from the Church's discipline a swindler and a drunkard. It was a monstrous charge—as all the charges against the Judges are in this ill-advised document. The Lord President, in one of the cases referred to, emphatically declared:— "No one must suppose that it is our wish to interfere with the ecclesiastical functions of the Presbytery, but we have the assertion made, and there is no doubt of it, that an individual sits as a member of the Presbytery who is not entitled to enter the door, and that therefore any sentence pronounced by the Presbytery must be null and void *quoad* its execution." The accused party might be all that was bad, but he was entitled, the Court held, to be tried by the judges who, according to the law of the land and the law of the Church, were alone competent to try him, and in each case important civil and patrimonial rights were involved. All this is disingenuously kept back in the Claim of Right, and the people who read it were misled and deceived. Had the simple facts been stated how entirely would they have disposed of the false imputation against the Judges, that they had gone out of their way, and interfered with the legitimate functions of the Church Courts, in order to shield wrongdoers from discipline.

It is unnecessary to notice the other cases. Those we have mentioned are characteristic of the whole.

The Claim does not, as we have said, complain of the law. It does not ask for the Church any power or privilege which it did not already possess by Statute or by the law of the land. On the contrary, all that it asks is that the Church "shall freely possess her liberties, government, right, and privileges *according to law*." Neither does it say that the Court had, in any of the cases cited, erred in judgment when interpreting the law. Incredible as it may appear, the only complaint is one against the Judges personally. It is a charge which amounts to wilful corruption and a criminal subversion of justice. It is so unprecedented that we give it here entire as a historical curiosity.

The charge is, that the Judges of the Court of Session "not confining themselves to the determination of 'civil actions,' have, in numerous and repeated instances, stepped beyond the province allotted to them by the Constitution, and within which alone their decisions can be held to declare the law, or to have the force of law, deciding not only 'actions civil,' but causes 'spiritual and ecclesiastical,' and that, too, even where these had no connection with the exercise of the right of patronage, and have thus invaded the jurisdiction and encroached upon the spiritual privileges of the Courts of this Church;" that they had "assumed to themselves the regulation of the preaching of the Word, and administration of the sacraments;" that they had "reponed ministers, suspended from their office, to the power of preaching, thus assuming to themselves the 'power of the keys;'" that they had "interfered with the constitution of the chief court of the Church, and violated her freedom in the holding of General Assemblies;" and had "exercised powers not conferred on them by the Constitution." Further, that the Judges had "illegally attempted to coerce Church courts in the exercise of their purely spiritual functions;" "had wrongfully acclaimed, as the subject of their civil jurisdiction to be regulated by their decrees, ordination of laymen to the office of the holy ministry, admission to the cure of souls, Church censures, the preaching of the Word, and the administration of the sacraments; and had employed the means entrusted to them for enforcing submission to their lawful authority, in compelling submission to that which they have usurped, in opposition to the doctrines of God's Word, in violation of the Constitution, in breach of the Treaty of Union, in defiance of the Statutes, and in contempt of the laws of the kingdom."

And the framers of the Claim go on to declare that they cannot, " in accordance with the Word of God and the dictates of their consciences, carry on the government of Christ's Church, subject to the coercion attempted by the Court of Session as above set forth."

It was a serious charge to make against gentlemen occupying the high position of Judges in the Supreme Court, and it involved a grave responsibility. Coming as it did from their spiritual leaders, it could not fail seriously to shake the confidence of the people in the administration of justice. It recalls the solemn words of the Lord Chief-Justice of England on a similar occasion :—" One of the great safeguards of the Constitution has been the confidence of the people in the purity and integrity of the administration of justice. Woe to those who seek to undermine that confidence — to those who, by calumny and vituperation, seek to shake the confidence of the people in the administration of the justice of the country."

The document containing the "calumnious and vituperative" charges which we have quoted was adopted by the dominant party in the General Assembly of 1842. It is a document which even an experienced lawyer, with access to the law books and the voluminous law reports, could not test without a large expenditure of time, and few laymen could be capable of forming an intelligent judgment on it. It is safe to say that not half-a-dozen members of that Assembly attempted to bestow a critical examination on it. Yet after having been only once read, a motion was adopted "declaring in general in terms thereof." They went through the form of remitting it to a Committee to revise it, and to report any "verbal emendations" they might think necessary, and a few days afterwards it was finally adopted without being even read again. It was accepted on trust by all the members of the party, and, as a rule, the congregations accepted it on the word of their pastors. They were told that every statement in it was true, and they believed it. It is not to be wondered at that they did. Great excitement prevailed throughout Scotland at the time, and the people would naturally think that unless it were true, language so strong would not be used by men who professed to be fighting only for "the headship of Christ." The document was sent to the Presbyterian Church in England, and that body accepted it on trust, and believing everything in it to be true, virtually excommunicated the Church of Scotland. It was sent to the missionaries in India, and coming from men to whom they had been accustomed to look for guidance in ecclesiastical matters, the missionaries also took it on trust, and believing it, left the Church of Scotland.

But the missionaries had, besides the Claim of Right, other guidance by which they were influenced. It is proper to call attention to this, not only as it explains the course taken by the missionaries—a course which has often excited surprise—but also because it illustrates forcibly, if not the unscrupulousness, at all events the ignorance, which characterized the statements of the Non-intrusionists, including in their number men holding a very high place among them. In his work called "A Vindication of the Free Church Claim of Right," the late Sir Henry Wellwood Moncrieff, after admitting that the missionaries in India were influenced by that document, says that besides the Claim of Right they had an instructor on the spot, eminently qualified for the task of giving them the needful information—namely, Dr. Duff; and he refers to a

work by Dr. Duff, "Lectures delivered at Calcutta," as showing the "intelligence" with which he treated the subject, and the "popular and telling manner" in which he instructed the missionaries in India. The book is scarce, but it will repay a perusal by any one who desires to study the question. Probably Sir Henry Moncrieff, when he referred to it, had forgotten some of its contents. In misstatement of the facts, in reckless assertion, and intemperate language, it is quite on a par with the Claim of Right. Here is a passage which Dr. Duff, in the Lectures referred to, says "tersely represents the frightful effects" of the decisions of the Court of Session:—
"'If any man that is called a brother be a drunkard, &c., with such an one no not to eat.' The Court of Session says:— 'Though a man come staggering drunk into your Church courts, we shall force you to eat with him—we shall thrust him back to your Communion table, and force the ministers of Christ to break the sacred bread, and to give it into his polluted hands.' Christ says:—'A man that is a heretic after the first and second admonition reject.' The Civil courts say:—'No matter how heretical a man may be, both in theory and practice, ye shall not be suffered to reject him; we shall keep the convicted thieves, and drunkards, and debauchees, and profane swearers and heretics in their pulpits, in defiance of you.' And though God says unto the wicked:—'What hast thou to do to declare My statutes or that thou shouldest take My covenant in thy mouth,' 'we shall supply an answer by interposing our authority as that in virtue of which he shall still desecrate the sacred office.'"[1] This was said to the missionaries, and, coming from such an authority, they believed it. Dr. Duff, of course, believed it himself. He was misled by false information.

But Dr. Duff said to them more than this. The learned and upright judges who formed the majority of the Court, whose ermine was stainless, and never had been assailed until the framers of the Claim of Right thought fit to attack them, are characterized by Dr. Duff as men incapable of giving an impartial judgment, "deeply prejudiced," "deeply committed by many previous overt acts to the maintenance and support of Moderate ascendency," their judgment "pre-

[1] "Lectures on the Church of Scotland," p. 159, by the Rev. A. Duff, D.D., Calcutta, 1844.

occupied and foreclosed, yea, hermetically sealed, against all conviction."[1]

But Sir Henry Moncrieff says, further, that there will be found in the Lectures which Dr. Duff delivered in India an "exact examination of the history and legal bearings of the matter," by which he "instructed his audience," and a "spirit of impartial appreciation" which, Sir Henry says, must command acquiescence "in the reliability of his statements."[2] Here is an example, and it is an instructive one. Our readers will recollect that *the whole question* in the Auchterarder case arose from the refusal of the Presbytery to adopt the initiatory step of taking the presentee on trials. Speaking of the action of the Civil Courts, and arguing that the Act of Queen Anne, bad as it was, did not take away the right and liberty for which the Church contended, but which, he said, the Court of Session refused to recognize, Dr. Duff quoted to his Indian audience, and endorsed a statement of a high authority at home—Dr. Buchanan—as explaining what the liberty asked by the Church, and refused, was:—"The question is, were they at liberty, when a patron placed a man before them, to say, *we consent to examine this man* whether he has gifts for the ministry and whether he has gifts for that parish, but if we are not satisfied we will refuse to go on with the settlement. *This was what the Presbyteries of the Church claimed under that law of patronage*, and they conceived that there was nothing in that law or in any other laws of the Church to deprive them *of that liberty*."[3] Nor, of course, was there. On the words which we have put in italics the whole question turned—"*we consent to examine this man.*" That is what Dr. Duff told the missionaries and the other Presbyterians in India the Non-intrusionists had been always willing to do! The reader knows that it was just *because they refused to examine him*, and only because of that, that all the trouble arose.

Dr. Duff also told his hearers in India that "the proceedings against the Presbytery by the rejected presentee in the Auchterarder case were uncalled for and unjustifiable, because, although not ordained, he would suffer no civil wrong, as he would enjoy for life the temporal fruits of the benefice."[4] We

[1] "Lectures," 126. [2] "Vindication," 269. [3] "Lectures," 120. [4] Ibid. 131.

need not remind the reader that it was just because the illegal action of the Presbytery made it impossible for the presentee to get the fruits of the benefice that he was obliged to resort to the alternative of asking damages against them. And Dr. Duff goes on to make a still more astounding statement. He said that this "new action" was raised "to find not merely that an obnoxious presentee, rejected on the ground of the people's dissent, is still entitled to the temporalities of the benefice, but also that he is *additionally entitled to be admitted, however unworthy, to the spiritualities of the cure.*"[1] The italics are Dr. Duff's. We need not say that in every particular this statement is untrue. But the missionaries believed it, as they believed the other statements by Dr. Duff which we have quoted, and they left a Church in which they were told such things had been done, and which might every day be repeated, without remedy or redress.

And it was the same at home. The "clerical agitation" threatened at the meeting in Edinburgh, referred to by Lord Aberdeen, was carried out. Non-intrusion ministers went through the country repeating to the people the language of the Claim of Right. No one, they said, could now remain in the Church of Scotland except at a sacrifice of his Christian liberty, and of his most valued religious privileges, and without a practical "denial of the Headship of Christ." The ministers remaining in the Church, Dr. Candlish said, "are guilty of the very sin which would hand over the Lord of the Church bound and fettered into the hands of His enemies." And, ignoring the Church of Scotland as not a Christian Church at all, he added: "We are to make provision as if the Established Church had no existence." The language of the other leaders—Dr. Cunningham, Dr. Macdonald, Dr. Guthrie, and others—was even stronger than this. Dr. Macdonald pronounced the Church of Scotland to be "a God-dishonouring, Christ-denying, and soul-destroying Church." And the *Witness* newspaper, the organ of the party—professing to be a religious paper—told the people to regard the parish minister "as the one excommunicated man of the district; the man with whom no one is to join in prayer; whose church is to be avoided

[1] "Lectures," 132.

as an impure and unholy place; who is everywhere to be put under the ban of the community."[1] The congregations of the Seceding clergymen, looking up to their ministers as spiritual guides whom they had been accustomed to trust, believed all this, and, following the ministers, they left the Church—not one in a thousand of them having any intelligent idea where the truth lay, or what it was all about. What they were told to believe was that the Church of Scotland was no longer a Church of Christ; that its independence had been unjustly assailed, and its most valued spiritual liberties subverted; and that this had been done by the Judges of the Supreme Court, to whom they ascribed conduct so corrupt and oppressive that (if true) it made them a disgrace to the Bench. They were told, moreover, that the State had approved the action of the Judges, and refused to give redress, and that all this had been connived at, approved, and acquiesced in by the ministers who remained in the Church, and who thereby openly denied the "Headship of Christ."

The effect of all this on an excitable people may be imagined. They were not content with leaving the Church, but in many places in the northern counties they broke out into open violence. Many of the most respectable of the inhabitants were subjected to personal ill-usage for no reasons but that they adhered to the Church. In multiplied instances exclusive dealing—boycotting—was resorted to. In one instance an amiable and respected parish minister in the Highlands was dragged from his manse and brutally ill-treated.

Nor did the State escape denunciation. In an address by the "Convocation"—a meeting of the ministers of the party held in Edinburgh in November, 1842—and published to all Scotland, they declared that unless Her Majesty's Government conceded what they, the Non-intrusionists, asked, they would be guilty of "the heinous national offence of not only breaking the national faith, but of disowning the authority of Christ." It was thus that the people were excited and misled, and "educated" up to the point to which the leaders sought to bring them. The campaign was skilfully organized. It was conducted, Dr. Cunningham frankly admitted, by men "gifted

[1] "Facts not Falsehoods," by a Parish Minister, Edinburgh, 1843.

with the power of interesting, moving, and moulding public audiences, who spoke," he said, "at meetings regularly organized and held up and down the country." And Dr. Cunningham adds this striking admission: "It was thus we were *educated for the Disruption, which had otherwise been a great failure.*"[1]

With the facts now before the reader it is unnecessary to say anything in defence of the distinguished Judges thus held up, and still held up in the Claim of Right, to the contempt and detestation of the people of Scotland; but there is one testimony in their favour which it may be well to cite. It is by the Free Church lawyer already quoted—a gentleman in every way competent to form a correct judgment, who was familiar with all the decisions, and who had very carefully studied the whole subject. After narrating all the decisions assailed in the Claim of Right, Mr. Taylor Innes says: "I have never been able to join in the condemnation launched against the Judges who laid down this solid mass of our existing law. I believe that they dealt with a great constitutional question, which was forced upon them, and that they did so with immense deliberation as well as firmness, and that all the decisions from first to last depended upon that one principle of subjection and subordination, which, whether true or not, has never since been even called in question"[2]—the principle to which Mr. Taylor Innes refers being the very simple one that a law made by the Church affecting matters of civil right cannot prevail against a law made by Parliament. Elsewhere Mr. Taylor Innes writes:—"The decisions of the Church courts in all ordinary ecclesiastical matters have, for hundreds of years, been final and conclusive. Even in the controversy of 1843 the Court never denied the finality, in the Church's province, of the Church courts."[3] Had the people been told this by an influential Free Churchman thirty years earlier, Dr. Cunningham's "plan of campaign" would not have been so successful.

Having got their Claim and Protest adopted by the General Assembly, the leaders of the party carried it to the Government, accompanied by an Address to the Queen. In this document, again, they asked for the Church no new power or right or

---

[1] "Life of Dr. Cunningham," ii. 2.   [2] "Mr. Finlay's Bill and the Law of 1843," 34.
[3] "The Church of Scotland Crisis," 32 (Edinburgh, 1874).

privilege. The only wrong of which they complained was that the Church had been "coerced" by the Court of Session, and that the invasions of her rights and privileges of which they complained had been made, not by any existing law or statute, but solely by the corrupt and unconstitutional conduct of the Judges; and, practically, they demanded that the Legislature should disown the decisions of the Judges, and declare them to have been "in excess of their jurisdiction, subversive of statute law, and a violation of the constitution of the kingdom." The answer of the State was dignified, but couched in terms of forbearance. No Government, they were told, could listen to parties who came in an attitude of open defiance to the law as declared by the highest judicial tribunal. The Veto law, they were reminded, had been declared illegal, "but it has not yet been rescinded by the Assembly. When it does rescind it, it may safely confide in the wisdom of Parliament." At the same time they were assured that both the Government and Parliament were prepared to support the Church in all her just rights and privileges. "The faith of our Crown," the Queen declared, "is pledged to uphold you in the full enjoyment of every privilege which you can justly claim." Her Majesty reminded them of their own admission, in their Claim, that the constitution of the Church was settled by Acts of Parliament, and she added:—"The settlement thus fixed cannot be altered by the will of any number of individuals. The Church of Scotland, occupying its true position, in friendly alliance with the State, is justly entitled to expect the aid of Parliament in removing any doubts which may have arisen with respect to the right construction of the statutes relating to the admission of ministers. You may safely confide in Parliament, and we shall readily give our assent to any measure which the Legislature may pass *for the purpose of securing to the people the full privilege of objection, and to the Church judicatures the exclusive right of judgment.*"

Not satisfied with this, the Non-intrusionists had their Claim brought before Parliament, and from that High Court they received the same answer. The Prime Minister reminded them that when the Veto Act was passed, not only did the Government not interfere, but he, Sir Robert Peel, had, after that, recommended a vote of public money to facilitate the extension of the Church of Scotland. "But," continued Sir Robert, "when the House of Lords affirmed the Veto Act to be illegal, and the Church put itself in opposition to that decision, then the case assumed a different phase; and we must remember, when we are discussing this Claim of Right in Parliament, that we are not debating on some mere speculative opinion of right, but that the Veto Act, although declared to be illegal by the highest authority, nevertheless remains in force and continues to be acted on by the Church."

The memorial in which the Non-intrusionists brought their case before the Government was adopted at the important meeting already referred to, known as the Convocation, and was signed by almost every minister of the Free Church party. It contains the following important statement: "It has always appeared to the Church of Scotland," these gentlemen said, "that so far from having received or holding her emoluments and other immunities of her establishment, under condition of being subject on any act of her spiritual government to secular control, *she has by the very act of her establishment obtained the most explicit recognition of her absolute spiritual freedom*, and that her religious principle upon this head, recognized in that character of it by the State, has been secured to her for ever by the fundamental laws of the United Kingdom." Nothing could express more truly than this the function and rights of the Church, and it is very important to note that it was unreservedly accepted by the Government. "*No one*," Sir Robert Peel said, "*contends against the jurisdiction of the Ecclesiastical courts in spiritual cases*." And, speaking for the Government, he added in terms still more emphatic: "We admit that to the Church belongs *the exclusive jurisdiction in ecclesiastical matters*. If, indeed, an attempt were made on the part of the Civil courts to interfere with such jurisdiction, there can scarcely be a question, I think, that Parliament would step in, and confirm the authority of the Courts spiritual."

On the rights and claims of the Church therefore—all that the Free Church party asked, namely, "her absolute spiritual freedom," as expressed in the words of the Free Church party themselves—that party and the State were at one!

But still the Non-intrusionists, with unaccountable obstinacy, refused to repeal the Veto Act. It could not be a question of conscience with them. It had been made plain that it was a measure for which the Church had never, during all her previous history, contended. In the greatest heat of the controversy, Dr. Chalmers had never regarded it otherwise than as a matter of ecclesiastical polity, the object of which could be obtained by some other method than this which interfered with a civil right secured by Statute. The Veto Act, he said, had been "a blunder," and he earnestly advised its repeal. It was not worth contending for, he said, if it involved "the loss of the temporalities." They had been assured by the Queen and by Parliament, not to speak of the repeated declarations of the Judges in all the cases decided, that the jurisdiction of the Church in spiritual matters was not in question, and they were told by the Ministry that any measure proposed for making more clear the reasonable wishes of the people in the settlement of ministers, and the exclusive right of the Church in judging of them, would receive the favourable consideration of Parliament. Only let them repeal this Veto Act, which was out of their domain, because directly affecting a Statutory civil right. Lord Cockburn, always a friend of the Free Church— "a distinguished man," Sir Henry Moncrieff calls him, "for whose memory the Free Church has a great regard"—gave them the same advice that Dr. Chalmers had given them. They were suffering, Lord Cockburn said, "suffering severely and justly, for the folly of adhering to the Veto Act after the House of Lords declared it to be illegal. Giving it up would not have been inconsistent with any of their constitutional principles, however inconvenient it might have been to their policy, or however galling to their pride." But no. They would not repeal the Veto Act. It might be true that it affected civil rights; but if so, the civil right and the Civil courts ought to give way, and not the Church. Sir Henry Moncrieff, in his "Vindication of the Claim of Right" (p. 39), makes this very plain. "The Church held," he says, "that her allegiance to Christ prevented her from being diverted from the course she judged most expedient in disposing of questions on the subjects referred to, by any consideration of how civil rights,

real or imaginary, might be thereby affected." Again he says:—
"The Church had nothing to do with the question of what civil rights or advantages might or might not follow, but had simply to consider what was for the honour of Christ and the edification of His people."[1] And once again:—"They were ready to disregard any question of civil right which might arise out of their line of action in what *they* looked upon as their exclusive sphere."[2] This is plain speaking. It is the voice of the Church of Rome: the sacerdotal element asserting itself above and against law. The civil right is to be disregarded, the Statute law is to be set aside, and the sentences of Civil courts, adjudicating in matters affecting the civil rights of subjects, is to be defied—as we have seen it was defied—if any dominant majority in the Church shall simply choose to assert that Christ's honour, as declared and defined by them, required them so to act. Cardinal Manning was right when he said, "The powers which the Free Church claim are the same which I claim for my Church."[3]

But the State declined to surrender its civil functions to any subject—ecclesiastical or other—and it refused to disown the action of Judges who had only faithfully done their duty. It refused this because it knew that in every one of the cases a civil right was involved, and that its Courts had never intruded on the spiritual jurisdiction of the Church, and had disclaimed all right to do so. It knew that the Courts had only maintained the supremacy of the Statutes in civil matters, and were enforcing that and nothing else, and therefore it refused. And then came the Secession.

The General Assembly of 1843, freed now from the pressure which had paralysed its constitutional action, repealed the Veto Act and the Chapel Acts. At the same time it made to the people of Scotland, in a Pastoral Address, this declaration of what had guided and would always guide the Church of Scotland: "It is our firm determination," they said, "ever to maintain that in all questions purely spiritual the judicatures of the Church have the sole right of judging. Whatever the authoritative books of the Church assert as to the rights and duties of the Civil Magistrate, they never fail to combine with

[1] "Vindication," 36.   [2] Ibid. 31.   [3] *Contemporary Review*, April, 1870.

these declarations the doctrine of the supremacy of the King and Head of the Church, and of the perpetuity of the government which He has instituted in the hands of Church officers distinct from the Civil Magistrate. By these principles we are determined to abide."

Within three months after the secession of the Free Church party, there was passed by Parliament what is known as Lord Aberdeen's Act. It was not new legislation. It was a Declaratory Act—its object, as declared in its preamble, being "to remove any doubt that may remain as to the power and jurisdiction of the Church;" and it made very clear what had always been the law of the Church—namely, that in the settlement of ministers the people possessed the fullest right of objection, and the Church judicatories the exclusive right of judgment. It is unnecessary to notice the provisions of this Act, as it has been superseded by the later Statute of 1874 abolishing patronage, and conferring on the people the right of choosing their own ministers.

Notwithstanding the threats held out at the meeting in Edinburgh, referred to by Lord Aberdeen, the Non-intrusionists continued to maintain the principle of an Established Church, and when they seceded they made it one of the principles on which their new organization was founded. In the memorial already referred to, adopted at the meeting of the "Convocation," held a few months before the Secession, they stated that they felt it their duty "to make a solemn representation to her Majesty's Government," setting forth, among other things, "the inestimable value of the benefits which the Establishment confers upon the country;" and calling upon the rulers of the nation "to maintain the Constitution of the Kingdom inviolate, and to uphold a true establishment of religion in the land." This solemn declaration was signed, as we have said, by nearly every one of the ministers of the Free Church party; and in the following year, when they left the Church, their sentiments on this subject remained unchanged. Dr. Chalmers, their first Moderator, speaking for the newly founded Church, said: "Though we quit the Establishment we go out on the Establishment principle. *We are the advocates of a national recognition and national support of religion,* and we are not Voluntaries." And long after 1843 another of their leaders—Dr. William Cunningham—in his published writings continued to denounce the voluntary principle, and to maintain the principle of a national recognition of religion. The same sentiments are expressed in the Claim of Right, which sets forth "the high value" which the party placed on the connection of the Church with the State, and how deeply they would "deplore and deprecate" any separation. The adoption of the voluntary principle by a large party in the Free Church was a matter of later date. It found prominent expression in the proposal of a union of the Free Church with the United Presbyterian Church; but the movement was opposed by Dr. Begg and others of the constitutional party who adhered to Free Church principles. These gentlemen obtained the opinion of eminent counsel that the Establishment principle was a fundamental one in the constitution of the Free Church, and that no majority, however large, could alter it. The result was that the promoters of the union were compelled to abandon it. Had they persisted in consummating it, they would have forfeited their status as members of the Free Church, leaving the temporalities in the hands of the constitutional party.

There remains little more to be said; but the exceptional position of the Church of Scotland as regards her jurisdiction, and the powers of her judicatories as Courts recognized by the Constitution of the kingdom, will be further illustrated, and perhaps still better understood, if we shortly state, in contrast, what has been decided as to the position of Nonconformist churches in these respects. It will not be necessary to cite more than one case. It arose within the Free Church in 1859, and it is instructive because the position of that body towards the law, and the claims they asserted, were very fully discussed in it and authoritatively settled.

The facts were shortly these:—The minister of the Free Church at Cardross—Mr. MacMillan—complained that a sentence of deposition pronounced against him by their General Assembly was illegal, because contrary to the constitution of their Church, and he asked the protection of the Court of Session. It was pleaded for the Free Church that it was an ecclesiastical question in which a Civil court could not interfere. The grounds on which they urged this showed how entirely they had misunderstood the pre-disruption decisions. "The Civil courts of the country," they said—we quote from the judicial report of the case—"had held that the patrimonial interest which, in the Established Church, the State had connected with the clerical office, gave them a right to interfere with and stay the execution of sentences of the Church courts, and they did so. *To prevent this interference—to secure what they regarded as necessary to their spiritual independence—the adherents of the Free Church renounced the benefits of the Establishment,* giving up their patrimonial interests, in the existence of which, and their legal connection with the clerical office, the right or obligation of the Civil courts to interfere had been placed and justified." The decision of the Court undeceived them. They were told, in effect, that the relative positions of themselves and the Established Church were just the reverse of what they supposed. Were a case such as this to occur in the Established Church, they were told, the Civil courts *could not* interfere, because that Church had an independent jurisdiction recognized by law, but that in the Free Church *they could* interfere, because it was a body which had no jurisdiction at all. "It must be kept in mind," Lord Ivory said, "that the Established Church and its judicatories form a recognized institution of the land; that the judicatories are of the description which exercise jurisdiction by the authority of the country; that their courts are supreme and independent courts in ecclesiastical matters; that they are just as much supreme as the Justiciary Court is in regard to criminal questions, or this Court in regard to civil questions; and therefore, as every independent judicatory has, inherent within itself, the power of doing all that is necessary to follow out its proper jurisdiction, they may make their own forms of proceedings, and no other Court can interfere, because no other Court is more independent than themselves, and while they are proceeding within their proper functions, they are as supreme as this Court. But there is this important distinction in the present case, which is too much overlooked by these defenders (the Free Church), that even in the matter of process they have no jurisdiction. In the proper sense of the term they have none, but in the matter of process they have no power and no jurisdiction, and no right to make rules; and these rules when made have no other authority than, by the constitution, consented to by all the parties, and made effectual in consequence of the agreement of the individuals composing that body. Anything that goes against what is set down in the constitution is an infringement of the contract."

"If anything is clear in the case," Lord Deas said, "it is that the defenders are vested with no jurisdiction whatever, ecclesiastical or civil. The Statute law of the land conferred on the Church of Scotland jurisdiction to be exercised by Kirk Sessions, Presbyteries, Provincial Synods, and General Assemblies, but there is no such Statute law applicable to the association called the Free Church. When the defenders left the Establishment they left all jurisdiction behind them. If they meant to carry it with them, as some expressions in the deeds and writings produced would seem to indicate, it is enough to say that this could not be done. The constituent members of these presbyteries, synods, and assemblies of the Free Church are not judges in any legal sense. They sit, and act, and vote solely in virtue of private contract regulating their proceedings among themselves." "The question to be tried was, whether the contract be of the import alleged, and whether it was duly acted on," and of that question, they were told, the Court of Session, and not their General Assembly, were the judges. The Lord President (Colonsay) said: "If the office-bearers, or the governing authorities of the body, go altogether beyond the sphere of the constitution of the association; if they deal with a member in a way they are not authorized by their constitution to deal with him; if they attempt to exercise over him a power or authority which he, by becoming a member, did not give them, and if by so acting they have done him injury, he will not be precluded from seeking redress, nor will the Courts of Law hold themselves precluded from giving him redress."

Thus was the exclusive jurisdiction and spiritual independence of the Church of Scotland again recognized, and thus did the Free Church party learn that in leaving the Establishment they had left behind them a jurisdiction which would have proved an effectual bar to Mr. MacMillan's claim, and that they were now firmly under the jurisdiction of the Court of Session, a position in which the Church of Scotland was not, and never had been, in any period of her history.

The law on which the Court proceeded in this case applies to all dissenting bodies, and it is the same in England.

One of the most profound thinkers of modern times—the late Sir William Hamilton—made a careful investigation into the case of the Non-intrusionists, and in 1843 he published the result of his inquiry. Addressing the party he said:—"The result of my researches has satisfied me that in the position you are taking you are completely, unambiguously, notoriously wrong, and that the grounds on which certain of your party have attempted to support their own views, and succeeded in persuading you, are perhaps—I speak it advisedly—the most signal and melancholy perversion of truth to be found in the whole annals of religious controversy." Referring to the sacrifices they were making, he said they were "martyrs by mistake."

In the Cardross case the words of Sir William Hamilton found practical verification. Let us repeat their own words:— "To prevent the interference of the Court of Session—to secure what they regarded as necessary to their spiritual independence—the adherents of the Free Church renounced the benefits of the Establishment." That is their own judicial statement—the reason they assigned for their separation—the reason for founding the Free Church. If so, then with the decision in the Cardross case the Free Church ceased to have a *raison d'être*.

This is as much as to say that, except in the all-important point of the exclusive jurisdiction of the Church of Scotland in spiritual matters, there is between that Church and the Free Church no difference in principle, as there is none in doctrine, discipline, or ritual. Each holds the principle of a State established Church—the Free Church so firmly that no section of it, no majority however large, could abandon that principle without forfeiting its property and endowments. And as regards the other great section of Presbyterianism in Scotland—the United Presbyterian Church—while it has been voluntary in practice, there is nothing in its standards inconsistent with the principles of the national Church.

What we have said of the position of the Church towards the law and the State may be summed up in a few sentences.

The Church is for all the people. It was not established to favour one particular sect over another. By missionary enterprise, in very early times, it secured for itself a position in the remotest verge of the country, and in the same spirit of beneficent aggression it gradually extended its influence. From the first it was with a view to the welfare of the State itself, and of the whole population, that those in authority recognized the Church, and gave her jurisdiction, and protected her in her property. And at the Reformation the Church received its present constitution and its more formal establishment, in order—to use the words of the Act of Security—"that the true Protestant religion, and the worship, discipline, and government of the Church, should continue, without any alteration, to the people of this land in all succeeding generations."

From the earliest times to the present the endowments of the Church have consisted of donations from the private means of the donors, gifted for the religious instruction of the people. Practically the Church has never derived any endowment from the State, and no one in the kingdom is taxed for its support. In law, the property of the Church belongs to it, by a title as indefeasible as that of any other corporation or individual in the kingdom.

The State, in its legislation, has never encroached on the proper province of the Church. Its only stipulation has been that the Church, in its legislation, should not touch civil rights, which must be ever within the province of the State.

As regards the civil courts, they have only—when applied to by parties having an interest, and only then—interpreted the Statutes by which the limits and conditions of the Church's jurisdiction have been defined, and its privileges secured, and given protection to subjects who complained that the Church was encroaching on their civil rights. In all their decisions the Courts of Law have recognized in the Church that exclusive jurisdiction in spiritual matters which she possesses by statute, and with which the civil courts are powerless to interfere.

What the State expects from the Church, in return for her establishment and protection in her property, is that she shall faithfully make provision for the spiritual needs of the people.

THE DOCTRINE

OF

THE CHURCH OF SCOTLAND.

BY

REV. ADAM MILROY, D.D.

THE DOCTRINE

OF

THE CHURCH OF SCOTLAND.

INTRODUCTION.

In the present day the assertion is frequently made by Christian writers and preachers that Christianity is not a system of doctrines, but a life. The statement is true so far as it goes, but it is one-sided and incomplete. Christianity is a life, but it is a life which is animated by Christian motives, and these motives are based on Christian doctrines. Doctrine and duty are, in the teaching of our Saviour and in the writings of the apostles, inseparably united; and it is from Christian doctrine that Christian morality derives its new authority, exalted position, and transforming power.

If this vital connection be disregarded in Christian teaching, the vigour and life of practical religion disappear. Morality existed before Christianity appeared, and would continue to preserve an existence should Christianity be discarded. But the existence thus preserved would, as experience has shown, be one in which the powers of life were weak, flickering, and partial. Morality cannot maintain a healthy and vigorous life apart from the religious truths which minister to it support and nourishment; and the inculcation of practical duties which is not based on Christian truths must, from its nature, lack strength and substance, and however elegant it may be in outward form, it is in reality but wordy drivel.

Ritual also, in so far as it expresses or symbolizes a belief, has its foundation in doctrine. The adoration of the Host in the Roman Catholic service, the prostration of the worshippers, the clouds of incense, and all the ceremonies of the mass are only significant expressions of the belief which lies at the basis of the worship; and the simple Presbyterian communion-service is also the right and fitting expression of a creed in which there neither is nor can be room for sacrificing priest or visible sacrifices, or for the ritual which may fittingly accompany a sacrificial offering. Hence it follows that when doctrine and ritual are severed, when a ceremony is adopted simply because it is thought to be becoming or beautiful in itself, it may be not only incongruous in the worship, but, as the symbol of a belief which is not entertained, it may cause, in the solemn service of God, truth to be sacrificed to fanciful prettiness.

There may or may not be a vital connection between doctrine and Church government. The presence or absence of such a connection depends upon the view which is held with regard to the ground on which the government is based. If any particular form, be it Episcopal, Presbyterian, or Independent, be regarded as being of Divine appointment, then it takes its place in the category of doctrines; but if it be regarded as in itself a matter of indifference, then the particular form is not a doctrine, but a matter of expediency.

HISTORY OF DOCTRINE IN SCOTLAND TILL 1560.

The claims which England made of supremacy over Scotland were opposed not only by the swords of warriors in the battlefield, but by the pens of monks in the cloister. If England claimed Scotland as a fief, a genealogy of kings was produced which showed that Scotland had been an independent kingdom under her own monarchs for a period reaching back nearly to the confusion of tongues at the tower of Babel. When the English Church claimed supremacy over the Scottish Church, documents were ready to prove that the Church had been established in Scotland, if not by the apostles, at least by their immediate successors, and had existed as an independent church for many centuries before such a claim was advanced. The story is pleasingly told by John Fordoun. The Scots, who had settled in Scotland long before the birth of Christ, had been converted to the Christian faith under King Donald, about the year 203 A.D., and to this faith they had constantly and faithfully adhered. But a tradition concerning Palladius interrupted the smooth course of his history. It was to the effect that, in the year 430 A.D., Palladius was sent by the Pope to Scotland as its first bishop. Then the question naturally suggested itself, in what state had the Church been in Scotland during the interval. Fordoun, with admirable boldness, confronts and settles the question. Palladius was the first bishop, but during the two centuries before his arrival the Church had only presbyters or monks as teachers of the people and celebrants of the sacraments, according to the rite of the primitive Church.[1] Hector Boece supplements the statement of Fordoun by adding that the presbyters or monks who preached and dispensed the sacraments in Scotland before the arrival of Palladius were Culdees. In this way the belief arose that for more than two centuries before the first bishop arrived from Rome, the primitive Culdee Church had existed in Scotland, which was Presbyterian in government and virtually Protestant in doctrine. This primitive Church was afterwards gradually corrupted by the emissaries of Rome, though she never lacked some faithful witnesses for the truth, but she was restored at the Reformation, and perfected in 1638 at the Glasgow Assembly. This fair vision, as has been shown in a previous section of this work, vanishes when brought into contact with the facts of history.

In the fictitious narrative of an early Culdee Church we have one plain fact presented to us, and it is about the only fact connected with it; that fact is that John Fordoun, a zealous and learned monk, and Hector Boece, the first principal of the University of Aberdeen, calmly entertained and taught the belief that a church had existed and flourished in Scotland for two centuries without a bishop, and had no misgivings about it. That church was founded in 203 A.D., and it was not till 430 A.D. that the first bishop, Palladius, came.

[1] Fordoun, lib. iii. c. 8.

During that period presbyters had preached, administered the sacraments, and governed the Church; and these two historians, able, scholarly, and faithful Scottish Catholics, do not express by a single word their suspicion that this church was no church, or that the sacraments were not duly administered because there was no bishop. They contemplated the absence of that dignitary in a church with an equanimity which some modern Episcopal writers would do well to possess.

ST. NINIAN.

The earliest authentic account of Christianity in Scotland takes us, as has been pointed out in our first volume, to Galloway towards the close of the fourth century. Some of the native population had been converted to Christianity. Among these native Christians the name of St. Ninian stands prominent.

We may form a tolerably correct notion of the doctrines which Ninian preached, and the worship which he established, from a consideration of the training which he received and the spirit of the age in which he lived. As the son of a native Christian prince, he had been trained in the Christian Church which existed in Britain while the great Roman empire still maintained its sway. He went to Rome to prosecute his studies, and resided there from 370 to about 395. We possess full accounts of the theology which was taught in the schools, of the preaching from the pulpits, and of the ritual and worship in which the Christian doctrines were embodied. When he first went to Rome, the Arian heresy was triumphant. It was during his residence there that Theodosius ascended the throne, and under his patronage the Arians were condemned and orthodoxy was finally victorious. Jerome was busily engaged in writing his Latin version of the Scriptures, which is still known as the Vulgate. Ninian may have studied rhetoric under Augustine, when, still unconverted and unbaptized, he taught in Rome; and he may have seen and heard the same Augustine when he returned to Rome a converted and baptized Christian. Rome in the earlier part of his residence was only partially Christian. The party which adhered to the worship of Jupiter and the other ancient deities was still numerous and powerful.

It was only in 388 that the Senate by a majority acquiesced in the view of the emperor, forbade the worship of idols, and accepted Christianity as the religion of the Romans. Paganism had been sorely wounded, but it still retained much of its vigour and popular favour when Ninian first studied at Rome.

During his residence there the man who wielded most power in the Church, who guided its policy and compelled obedience even from the Roman emperor, was not the Bishop of Rome, but Ambrose, bishop of Milan. He was the leading churchman in Italy. The Christianity of his day, the Christianity taught in the schools in which Ninian was trained, is well known. The Nicene creed was restored, and belief in the doctrine that the Son was of the same essence as the Father, and equal to Him, was declared and enforced as the only orthodox opinion, to be received and held by all the faithful. At the second Council of Constantinople, held in 381, the orthodox creed was further amplified by the doctrine that the Holy Spirit was on an equality with the Father and the Son, and entitled to the same honours and worship. The canon of Scripture was settled at the Council of Hippo (393), and included not only the several books of the Old and New Testaments, but the Apocryphal books of the Old Testament as well. These were the Scriptures which Ninian regarded as the Word of God. Three great feasts of the Church, at least, were universally observed—Christmas, Easter, and Pentecost—by which the work of Christ in the redemption of man was indicated from its beginning to its completion. The worship of Mary had not, indeed, been fully developed, but it was rapidly advancing. More than fourteen centuries had to elapse before the immaculate conception was decreed to be an article of faith, but already the opinion that she was altogether without sin was gaining ground. The worship offered to her by some enthusiastic female votaries, who seemed to have transferred to her the honours which had been paid to Ceres, was indeed condemned by the Church; but the language employed, and the legend to which that language gave birth, ended in a short time in the Mariolatry which has become so deeply rooted in the Catholic Church. Saints were invoked, and special days were dedicated to their commemoration. Images and pictures were placed in churches, at first solely for the purpose of instructing the ignorant; but already the danger was felt lest the ignorant should pay reverence not to the Saviour or the saint who was represented, but to the image or picture itself.

Relics of saints and martyrs were held in high esteem. The legend that Helena, the mother of Constantine, had found the true cross in 326, though it had been unknown to her contemporaries, was now attested by men such as Ambrose and Chrysostom, and was devoutly believed. Fragments were borne by pious pilgrims into all countries. The Catacombs of Rome furnished relics of the saints in quantities sufficient to supply the ever-increasing demand. It was while Ninian was in Rome that Theodosius was obliged to stop the sale of relics from the Catacombs. By these relics the usual miracles were performed: the sick were cured, devils were cast out, the dead were restored to life, and all the various wonders with which legends usually abound were plenteously wrought.

Pilgrimages to holy places were also very popular. We see the estimation in which they were held from the fact that the greatest teachers of the time warn the people against them. Jerome, for example, reminds them that in Britain as well as in Jerusalem, the gate of heaven stands open to us; and Gregory of Nyssa, writing to Ambrose, says, "Change of place brings God no nearer."

Ninian returned to Galloway, orthodox in creed, with the Bible including the Apocrypha; familiar with the ritual observed in the churches of Italy and Gaul—a ritual which in its main features exists still in the Roman Missal; trained in the observance of the great Christian festivals; accustomed to observe saints' days; believing in the intercession of saints; and very likely trained to reverence their relics and bow in reverence before their statues or pictures. He entered upon his labours in Galloway at a favourable period. Rome was making her last effort to establish order in her Scottish province, and to curb the native tribes which had assailed her possessions; and the effort for a time had been successful. When Ninian founded his church in 397, the Roman legions sent by Stilicho had vanquished the assailants. For a period of thirteen years comparative tranquillity prevailed, but then the legions were withdrawn, the Roman government ceased, the country was invaded, and whatever the success of Ninian may have been, it is only too apparent that the people among whom he laboured speedily relapsed almost altogether into paganism.

ST. COLUMBA.

The next period is that which witnessed the labours of St. Columba and his immediate followers. We are separated by nearly two centuries from the former period. A Christian colony from Ireland has settled in some of the Hebrides and on the western coasts of Argyllshire, and has founded there the kingdom of Dalriada; excluding this small portion, the rest of Scotland from the Pentland Firth to the Forth is inhabited by the Picts. The western portion, from the Forth to the Solway Firth, forms a part of the territory still retained by the native British, and is known as the kingdom of Strathclyde. On the eastern side, the country from the Firth of Forth to the mouth of the Tweed forms a part of the kingdom of the Angles of Bernicia. Omitting Dalriada and the small settlements of Picts in Galloway, there were three separate kingdoms in Scotland, inhabited by peoples different in race and in language—Pictland by Picts, Strathclyde by Britons, and Bernicia by a Saxon race. The people were, practically speaking, pagan. They were converted to Christianity in little more than a century (Columba came to Iona in 563, and St. Cuthbert died in 687). The question which lies before us is, What was the nature of that Christianity which was preached to them, and which they embraced?

Pictland was converted by means of St. Columba, his fellow-labourers, and immediate followers; the apostle of Strathclyde was St. Kentigern; the apostle of Northumbria was St. Cuthbert. Of the first and last of these we possess authentic records, and are therefore in a position to know the general nature of their doctrinal opinions. With regard to Columba we possess the Life written by his successor, Adamnan. It cannot have been written much later than a hundred years after the death of Columba, and the writer had conversed with men who knew Columba. In the Life the notices of beliefs and worship are altogether incidental, but they are on that very account the more valuable and trustworthy. They at least give material for ascertaining the state of the early Columban Church.

The controversy between Presbytery and Episcopacy does not fall to be considered here, unless the one or the other claims to have been alone instituted by Divine authority. It is now almost invariably acknowledged that in the apostolic age at any rate bishop and presbyter were identical, and that apart from the apostles only two orders existed—the presbyter, who was also called the bishop, and the deacon; how soon the presbyter and bishop came to be separated into two orders, and by what authority the separation was made, are subjects with which we have here no concern. Long before the time of Columba a distinction had been made, and three orders existed—bishops, presbyters, and deacons. These three orders are found in the Columban Church. The bishop, however, occupied a peculiar position. The Columban mission consisted of monks presided over by an abbot. This abbot was a presbyter. The monks were by their vows pledged to render to their abbot unquestioning and prompt obedience, and thence it followed that though one or more of the monks had episcopal orders, yet they had to render implicit conventual obedience to their abbot, though he, as regards orders, was inferior to them. It has been strenuously asserted, and as strenuously denied, that the presbyter-monk of Iona consecrated the first bishop of Lindisfarne. We do not possess materials to enable us to pronounce definitely on the point. If we adhere strictly to the words of Bede,[1] then we must acknowledge that there is no mention of bishops having any share in the consecration of Aidan. Bede simply says that the presbyters of Iona were impressed by the good common sense shown by Aidan, and so ordaining him sent him to preach. On the other hand it must be granted that the primitive identity of bishops and presbyters had long disappeared; it had been the exclusive privilege of the bishops to ordain presbyters and deacons. A bishop could only be consecrated by bishops. In the Irish Church, indeed, it was held that the presence of only one bishop was necessary, but that a presbyter could be ever ordained a bishop by his fellow-presbyters was opposed to Bede's training

[1] III. 5.

and convictions. If the presbyters of Iona had themselves consecrated Aidan, it is almost certain that Bede would not have simply stated the fact, but would have remarked on the unusual and invalid procedure. There still lingers in the Alexandrine Church a tradition that in early times even the Bishop of Alexandria was consecrated by the presbyters. The tradition was very probably founded on primitive practice, but that practice had ceased centuries before the first bishop of Lindisfarne was consecrated in Iona. On the whole it must be acknowledged to be most unlikely that in the early Columban Church presbyters ordained bishops, for when we have a fuller account of an episcopal consecration, we find three bishops taking part in it.[1] But while the three orders of bishops, presbyters, and deacons existed in the Columban Church, diocesan episcopacy was unknown. The presbyter-abbot of Iona was supreme.

The eucharistic service was known in the Church of Columba, as in the other churches, as the Mass. In the language of the people it was Aiffrin (from *offerendum*), a name which appears in Inchaffray. The service is conducted at the altar, before which the officiating priest stands. The Eucharist is an offering presented to God.[2] This expression would not, of itself, imply that any propitiatory character was attached to the rite, for the alms contributed by the people were laid on the altar, and are called an offering, but are not regarded as being of a propitiatory nature. There can, however, be no doubt that such a meaning was attached to the service of the mass in the Columban Church. It is expressly called the sacrificial mystery, or the mystery of the sacrifice—words embodying the belief which had long been universal in the Christian Church, that there was in that sacrament a sacrifice offered unto God.[3] Between this conception of the Eucharist in the Columban Church and the modern Protestant conceptions of the same rite, there is a wide gulf reaching down to the very foundation of Christian theology. In the Protestant view, which it is maintained is the view taught by Christ and his apostles, and according to which the sacrament was administered in the earliest and

---

[1] Bede, lib. iii. cap. 22.   [2] "Col. Vita," i. 32.
[3] II. 1, *sacrificiale mysterium, vel sacrificii mysterium.*

purest age of the Church, we have the table of the Lord and not an altar, we have a presiding minister and not a sacrificing priest, we have the Lord's Supper and not the sacrifice of the mass. In the Columban Church there were the altar, the priest, and the sacrifice.

It has been maintained by Roman Catholic writers[1] that the doctrine of the real presence, or transubstantiation, was also a tenet of the Columban Church. It is true that Adamnan uses expressions which, if used after the real presence had been declared to be a dogma of the Church, might fairly be regarded as implying a belief in that doctrine. It may even be granted that no one who believed in the real presence could readily find stronger or more appropriate language to express such a belief than that employed by Adamnan. He habitually speaks of the consecrated elements as the body and blood of Christ, and of the act of consecration as a making of the body of Christ;[2] but it is very unsafe to deduce from these and similar expressions a belief in transubstantiation as now defined by the Roman Church. Catholics, Lutherans, and Calvinists are all agreed that in the sacrament of the Lord's Supper worthy receivers are made partakers of the body and blood of Christ; but it is in attempting to answer the question as to the manner in which the body and blood of Christ are present in the sacrament and partaken of by the worthy receivers that widely divergent and even conflicting views have arisen. In the days of Adamnan the question had not yet been agitated in the Church. It was not till more than a century after his death that an attempt was made to give a clear notion of the manner in which Christ was present in the Eucharist,[3] and it was not till the Lateran Council, in 1215 A.D., more than 500 years after the death of Adamnan, that, not the fact, but the nature, of the real presence in the Eucharist was formally shaped and defined as an article of faith. The language of the early Columban Church, just as the original words used by the Saviour at the institution of the sacrament, may be interpreted in harmony with the doctrine

---

[1] *E.g.* Montalembert, "Monks of the West," iii. 284. [2] "Col. Vita," i. 35.
[3] Paschasius Radbert, 831 A.D.

of transubstantiation; but it by no means follows that Columba or his followers believed in that dogma because they employed language which, read in the light of long-subsequent ages, could be applied to a belief then entertained. At any rate the work which Columba and his fellow-labourers had before them was to teach the heathen Picts to believe in God and in Jesus Christ, and not to discuss with them the question regarding the manner in which the Lord was present in the sacrament.

Baptism was of course regularly administered. Some writers have attached importance to the fact that in the administration of this sacrament no mention is made of the chrism or sign of the cross or any such observances. These things are not mentioned; but it should be remembered, on the other hand, that the object of Adamnan, in the "Life of Columba," is not to give a full and particular account of the manner in which Christian rites were practised, for the rites themselves are only mentioned incidentally. If there is no mention of the sign of the cross in baptism, there is abundant proof afforded that the sign of the cross was in common use, and that supernatural power was attached to it in common belief. Columba makes the sign of the cross over a milk-pail, and the demon that lurked in the bottom of the pail is immediately expelled, and the milk which he had spilled is miraculously restored.[1] In his first visit to King Brude, at Inverness, he finds the gate of the palace barred and bolted against him. He makes the sign of the cross on the gate, and the bolts are violently driven back, and the folding doors of themselves fly open.[2] When it is thus plain that the sign of the cross was in common use, and was in popular belief of such miraculous efficacy, it is superfluous to inquire whether, in accordance with the universal practice of the Christian Church at the time, it was also used in baptism by Columba and his followers.

Of extreme unction there is no trace. The practice of anointing the sick as a means of restoring them to bodily health had prevailed from apostolic times. It had, before the time of Columba, been represented as a sacrament, intended

[1] II. 15.   [2] II. 36.

not for the bodily, but for the spiritual benefit of the sick; but centuries had still to elapse before anointing the dying took its place as the sacrament of extreme unction.

Stress has been laid on some incidents in order to prove that auricular confession, as now known, prevailed in the Columban Church. The mother of Colca, a disciple of Columba, is living secretly in grievous and unconfessed sin. The saint, knowing this fact, instructs Colca to visit his mother, to deal strictly and closely with her, and get her to acknowledge her sin. Colca obeys, and with some difficulty gets his mother to confess the sin which she thought had been unknown to any one. She then does penance according to the judgment of the saint, and is afterwards absolved.[1] On another day a man named Libran came to Columba. He had come from Connaught, and had performed the long and toilsome pilgrimage to Iona in order thereby to atone for his sins. After a conference with the saint he confessed his sins to him, and submitted to the penance enjoined.[2]

In both these cases we are at a great distance from auricular confession as demanded by the Church of Rome in the sacrament of penance. If we look at these narratives simply as they are presented to us, and do not seek to force into them a meaning which shall support an opinion already formed, they afford no ground for the arbitrary conclusions which have been extorted from them. To awaken a feeling of guilt in one who is living contentedly in secret and grievous sin—to assure a sincere and stricken penitent that God doth not despise a humble and contrite heart—to hear the confession of a man who had committed many gross sins, and to assign him a lengthened period of discipline and probation before admitting him to the holy communion, are actions which have no necessary connection with the Romish sacrament of penance, but may be performed, and are performed, alike by Roman Catholic priest and Protestant minister. We may find a nearer approach to confession in the *Amchara*, or soul-friend, whom we find in the Columban Church, sometimes attached to an individual, sometimes as the official of a monastic community. But here, again, we are apt to be led astray by attributing modern

[1] I. 10. [2] II. 40.

notious to an ancient expression. In mediæval or modern times the presence of a spiritual director or confessor in a religious community implies auricular confession, penance, and absolution; but it does not follow that the same conclusions must be drawn from the existence of a soul-friend or spiritual adviser in the early Church. Confession of sin has always been regarded as a necessary part of repentance, both in the Hebrew and the Christian Church; but confession of sin to a priest, though it was gradually becoming a common practice, was not regarded as essential in the Christian Church till a period more than 500 years after the time of Columba. It was not till the Lateran Council, in 1215, that the practice was enjoined as an article of faith, and every Christian became bound, under heavy penalties both in this life and the life to come, to confess his sins to a priest, and perform the penance imposed. That decree seems to have been greatly neglected in Scotland, notwithstanding the penalties which its neglect involved. In a visitation of the diocese of Dunkeld, held nearly three centuries after the Lateran Council, it was found that none in the Highland districts had confessed their sins for thirty years. If auricular confession had been a tenet of the Columban Church, that Church must have stood alone in holding the dogma, and have anticipated by centuries the decision which was ultimately arrived at. There is no incident recorded in the life of Columba which, read in the light of his times, would lead us to adopt this view, which is in itself strange and improbable.

There is a close connection between the opinion which may be entertained regarding the state in which departed Christians exist, and the efficacy of prayers offered by the living on their behalf, or offered by the departed on behalf of those still living on earth. If it be believed that at the moment of death man's doom is irrevocably pronounced, and he enters either into a state of bliss from which it is impossible to fall, or a state of pain and torture from which through eternity there is no escape, prayers for the departed are utterly out of place. If it be believed that the spirit when released from the body loses all love and sympathy for those whom it loved on earth, and ceases to have any concern or even knowledge regarding them, it would be in vain for man here to ask that he should be remembered in the prayers of those who, oblivious of all earthly love and affection, live in the bliss of heaven. No such belief entered into the creed of the ancient church. In the early days of Christianity, when the second coming of the Lord and the end of the world were regarded as events which might happen at any moment, and in any case were expected to happen speedily, there was no room for speculations regarding the state in which the departed existed before that coming should take place. But when time showed that the second advent was not to take place speedily, speculations began and doctrines were formulated. The ablest and boldest leader in these, as in other speculations, was Origen. Borrowing several ideas regarding the state of the departed from the old Aryan religions, he taught that the souls of all men, righteous and unrighteous, must in the day of judgment pass through the fire of purification, and that sooner or later all without exception should come out of that fire thoroughly cleansed from every stain of evil. The purifying process was not confined to sinful men. All the fallen angels, too, must pass through that fire, and after long ages of chastening and cleansing suffering would, without excepting even Satan himself, eventually become pure and meet to dwell in God's holy household.[1] No modern universalist has equalled Origen in the boldness and breadth of his views on this subject, but bold and broad as they were, they were adopted by some of his most eminent followers, and for a considerable period maintained a position in speculative theology. In the Western Church they were not so favourably received. The purifying fire was transferred to the period before the day of judgment; the souls of believers only, and not of all God's fallen creatures, were to pass through it, and come out only after having made personal satisfaction for personal sins. But when Columba came to Scotland purgatory had not been fully admitted into dogmatic theology. Its outlines sometimes loomed in the hazy distance, and again faded out of view. A long time had yet to intervene before that region was clearly descried, surveyed, and annexed as a valuable possession to the Christian system.

[1] Hom. 3. Ps. xxxvi.: Hom. 8, Num.; "De Principiis," lib. ii. cap. 6, &c.

In the preaching of Columba purgatory is unknown. Two states only after death are recognized, heaven and hell. The souls of just men pass at death to heaven, to be with Christ; the souls of unrepentant sinners pass at death to hell and torment.[1] This was the doctrine which prevailed in the Western Church while Britain was still a Roman colony. In the sermons, for instance, which St. Ambrose preached on the death of the Emperors Valentinian and Theodosius—sermons which St. Ninian may have heard while studying in Italy—the deceased are spoken of as being in heaven with Christ, and there blessed in the enjoyment of life eternal. His contemporary Jerome, in comforting a husband on the death of his wife, speaks of her as being now in heaven with the Lord; while Augustine, even when praying for his deceased mother Monica, expresses his belief that God has already granted her the boons which he is asking. It was this belief which was cherished in the early Columban Church. The cessation of intercourse with Rome had kept them almost two centuries behind in the development of doctrine on this subject, or two centuries nearer to the primitive truth.

For many ages prayers for the dead have been regarded in Western Christianity as prayers for souls in purgatory; prayers to saints are regarded as addressed to those who have been canonized by a decree. Both notions are comparatively modern. The ancient belief knew nothing of purgatory or formal canonization, but yet from very early times prayers were offered for those who had ceased to live here, and holy men who were believed to be in heaven were asked to pray to God on behalf of those on earth. The phrase "prayers to the dead," or "prayers for the dead," conveys not merely a repulsive, but an erroneous notion of the belief on which the practice was founded. Never was the conviction more intensely cherished than in those early times, that physical death had no power to weaken, much less to destroy, that life which alone was real. They whose prayers were invoked, or for whom blessings were asked, were not dead; they were living with a fuller measure of life than they ever had possessed before, and nearer to God than they had ever been. The

[1] Lib. i. 1, 24, 31; iii. 7, 8, 10, 11, 13.

Columban Church, in common with the rest of Christendom, spoke of the day on which a pious man died as his birthday;[1] physical death was only the portal through which the soul passed into a higher life. Prayers for the departed no more implied the belief that they were in a state of suffering than prayers for the health and happiness of the living imply that they must be in a state of sickness and misery. In the liturgy of Chrysostom, which is the liturgy of the Greek Church at the present day, the Eucharist is offered on behalf, among others, of the apostles, martyrs, and specially the Holy Mother of God, Mary ever virgin. These are not regarded by the Eastern Church as being in a state of suffering. In the Roman Mass a very early prayer is still retained in which God is entreated to remember all His servants and handmaidens who sleep in the sleep of peace and are at rest in Christ. Surely those who are at rest in Christ are not tormented in the flames of purgatory. Prayers for the departed were customary in the Christian Church long before purgatory had been discovered. They were the result of a lively belief in the communion of saints, a communion which death was powerless to sever. The love which had found an outlet in intercessions for friends while they lived on earth continued still to find expression in prayer for their welfare after they had passed through death into the life beyond.

Belief in the communion of saints led the living to seek an interest in the prayers of good and holy men who had entered within the veil. There has in all ages of the Church been cherished a belief in the efficacy of prayers offered by one Christian on behalf of another; in the belief of the early Church the efficacy of such intercessory prayer was not confined to earth. It was not thought that the love to man which animated the soul on earth was cast aside when that soul entered into glory, or that the prayer of the righteous man for others, which had power with God when the man lived here, ceased to be offered or had lost its efficacy in heaven. Here, again, we must be on our guard against allowing comparatively late ideas to be imported into early times by the use of current phrases. "Saints" and "invocation of

[1] *Dies natalis.*

saints" have now a settled meaning in theology. The canonized saints who may be invoked by men on earth now form a peculiar order, admission to which in Western Europe is granted only by the Pope; in early days, and in the Columban Church, saints were simply holy men, and as holy men they had power with God in this world, and greater power when they passed into the next world.

What was the belief of the Columban Church in these particulars? Mass was celebrated for departed souls. When Brendan died in Ireland the news of his death was miraculously communicated to Columba in Iona, and Columba immediately orders the solemnities of the mass to be prepared, "for to-day," says he, "is the birthday of blessed Brendan."[1] A still more striking instance is recorded. One morning while the monks were preparing to engage in their ordinary labours, Columba suddenly commanded them to prepare for the celebration of the Eucharist out of reverence to a soul that, the night before, had gone to paradise. In obedience to the command of their abbot, the monks put on their white robes as on a festival, went into the church, and began the service. While they were chanting "that customary intercessory prayer"[2] in which St. Martin's name is commemorated, and when they had uttered the name of that saint, Columba bade them add the name of Columban, who had passed to the Lord the previous evening, and whose death in Leinster had been miraculously announced in Iona.[3] Here mass is celebrated on the decease of a friend, and out of reverence to him the monks, robed in white garments, chant the service. In chanting the offices they come to the customary prayer. The word rendered *prayer* (*deprecatio*) has a definite meaning in the service for departed souls: it is the part embodying the petitions that God would not enter into judgment with them, nor cast them away from His presence, nor deliver them to the power of Satan. A peculiar interest is attached to the fact that Columban's name is introduced immediately after that of St. Martin. In the most ancient Gallican liturgy, which was closely followed by the Irish Church, there occurred the name of Martin, bishop and confessor, not in the number of the deceased for whom prayers were offered, but in

---

[1] Lib. iii. 12. [2] *Dum . . . illa consueta decantaretur deprecatio.* [3] Lib. iii. 13.

the number of those through whose intercessions and merits God was entreated to hear the prayers of the suppliants. If this or a similar liturgy was used in the Church of Iona on that day, then the fact that Columban's name was mentioned immediately after that of Martin would show that in the opinion of Columba, his friend, who had passed to the Lord the night before, had still a living interest in the welfare of his friends on earth, that he prayed for them, and that his prayers had power with God. The belief and practice of Columba in this case would be repudiated by both Protestants and Catholics. No Protestant minister would celebrate mass for a departed friend or pray that God would be merciful to his soul, while Protestant ministers and Catholic priests would shrink from the thought of adding the name of a friend who had died but yesterday to those of the Blessed Virgin, the apostles and martyrs, through whose intercessions and merits they hoped to obtain the boons of pardon and peace. We have here, as in many other instances, a belief existing in a form in which it can be claimed by neither Romanist nor Protestant.

Kindred to this belief in the efficacy of prayer offered for departed souls was the belief that holy men who had passed into the fuller life above heard the prayers addressed to them by suppliants on earth, and interceded with God on behalf of those who asked their aid. The men of the early Columban Church believed thoroughly in the power of prayer. Through the prayers of Columba while he lived some kings had been victorious in battle and others had been vanquished. Distance formed no obstacle to the power of prayer. There was a sure conviction in those days that the call of one Christian man to another for his prayer in the hour of peril would make itself audible however great the distance which separated them. Columba is caught in a storm off the Hebrides, and asks the prayers of Cainnech, who is at that moment in his monastery in Ireland. Cainnech feels an irresistible impulse to hasten to the Church and pray for the safety of Columba and his friends. His prayer was heard: "the storm immediately ceased, and the sea became very calm."[1] It was but a step further to invoke the prayers of a holy friend who had gone to God. Eternity

---

[1] Lib. ii. 12.

was very near to the men of that age. They did not think that their friends who had died in the Lord were so far away that they could not hear their cry, nor so unsympathetic that they had no concern for the sufferings or welfare of those left behind.

Immediately after the death of Columba his intercession was invoked, and belief in its efficacy was prevalent. Adamnan, indeed, laments that there were very many people so stupid that they did not recognize that they owed their safety in the midst of pestilence to the prayers of Columba, whose monasteries lay within their territories; but thankfully acknowledges that he and the inhabitants of the Western Isles recognized the patron to whom they owed immunity from the plague.[1] One particular incident out of many may be adduced. On one occasion Adamnan was sailing from Ireland to celebrate in Iona the vigil and feast of Columba. On the day before the feast he was detained by a contrary wind at the island of Shuna. He thereupon prayed to Columba to send a fair wind that so he might be able to celebrate mass on the morrow in the church of Iona. After the saint had been invoked the wind shifted, and Adamnan reached Iona in ample time for the service.[2] Whatever opinion may be held regarding the cause of the change of wind, there can be no doubt that Adamnan prayed to Columba, and saw an answer to his prayer in the change of wind which ensued. At other times the saint is sarcastically taunted rather than invoked, just as the fetish is reproached, and even beaten, when the expected boon has not been obtained. The monks were once bringing oak trees from Lorn to Iona to repair their monastery. An adverse wind obliged them to take shelter in Kerrera. They ask Columba if their detention in Kerrera is pleasing to him, and tell him that they had thought once that he had been honoured and powerful in the sight of God. The wind immediately shifted, "and then," Adamnan adds, "the chiding with the holy man, slight though it was, in that complaint assisted us not a little.[3] It matters nothing whether we accept or reject the miraculous element in these narratives, in either case the narratives themselves bear clear and incontrovertible testimony to the belief and practice of the Columban Church in its earliest and purest days.

[1] Lib. ii. 47.   [2] Lib. ii. 46.   [3] Ibid.

The belief in the intercession of saints which prevailed in the age of Columba was diametrically opposed to that which was entertained in the Protestant Church after the Reformation. A narrative belonging to each period respectively places this opposition in the clearest light. In the year 597 A.D., Columba died. On his deathbed he gave his farewell instructions to the brethren. "These, O my children, are the last words I address to you—that ye be at peace and have unfeigned charity among yourselves; and if you thus follow the example of the holy fathers, God, the Comforter of the good, will be your Helper, *and I abiding with Him will intercede for you.*"[1] In the year 1599 A.D., another man, holy, able, pious, and learned, who had done great and good work in his day, Robert Rollock, the first professor and principal of the University of Edinburgh, lay on his deathbed. One of his relatives visited him and asked that when Rollock had been received into heaven he should intercede with God for him and other friends. The indignation of the dying man was aroused by the request. Weak and almost breathless though he was, he raised his body and said, "I renounce that office, Christ is the only Mediator."[2] Columba in his last moments promises when he has been received into heaven to intercede with God on behalf of his brethren; Rollock rejects the request for intercession with utter abhorrence. Those two narratives shed a flood of light on the belief in the intercession of the saints held in the early Columban Church and in the Scottish Church of the Reformation period and of the present day.

In common with the whole of Christendom, Columba and his followers observed the stated festivals of the Church. At that early period these were not so numerous as they afterwards became, but the observance of the feasts of Christmas, Easter, and Pentecost, commemorative of the incarnation and resurrection of our Lord, and of the descent of the Holy Ghost, are proved by unmistakable evidence, which is all the more valuable in that it is merely incidental. Adamnan does not give a formal list of the festivals kept, but he mentions occurrences which he says happened at these festivals. Wednesday is a day of fasting.[3] The feast of the Nativity is mentioned.[4] The forty days

---

[1] Lib. iii. 24. [2] Rollock's Works; Wodrow Society, I., lxxxv. [3] Lib. i. 20. [4] Lib. ii. 8.

of Lent precede Easter,[1] and Easter itself, with all the paschal solemnities, is duly observed.[2] When the monks of St. Augustine met the monks of Iona a fierce controversy arose, not about the keeping of Easter, but regarding the Sunday on which Easter should be kept. In itself the question rested on a matter comparatively insignificant. The computation for determining the Sunday on which Easter should fall which had been used by both the Irish and British Churches, and had been followed by Columba, was based on the cycle of eighty-four years. This method of computation had been introduced into Britain while it was a province of the Roman empire. The Roman legions were withdrawn in 410 A.D., and intercourse with Rome was almost suspended till 597 A.D., when Augustine arrived in Kent on his mission to convert the heathen Saxons. During this interval an improved method of computation for determining the Sunday on which the festival of Easter should fall had been adopted in other countries, and was introduced into England by Augustine. According as the one or other calculation was followed it frequently happened that the Easter Sunday observed by the one party was separated from the Easter Sunday observed by the other party by an interval amounting sometimes to four weeks. The one party was fasting in Lent at the very time that the other was fasting in the Easter weeks, a result which caused confusion both in the sacred services of the Church and the culinary arrangements of households. The controversy was decided in 664 A.D., in the synod held at Whitby. The Columban missionaries were defeated, but refused to acquiesce in the adverse decision, and returned to Iona.

This controversy, though trivial in itself, establishes two points. It shows that the Columban Church knew nothing of that doctrine which was at a distant period to prevail in Scotland, according to which Easter and Christmas, and all such festivals, were abolished as superstitious observances of human invention. That was not a controversy as to whether Easter should or should not be observed, but as to the Sunday on which it should be observed. The suggestion not to keep Easter would have been rejected with indignation and abhorrence by the combatants on either side. Both parties kept

[1] Lib. ii. 10.   [2] Lib. iii. 24.

Easter and the preceding forty days of Lent. The principle that festivals such as Easter and Christmas should not be observed since the observance of them is not expressly enjoined in the New Testament, not only lacks even a shadow of support in the creed and practice of the Columban Church, but is in direct opposition to the ancient practices in which Columba himself had been trained before he entered upon his mission to heathen Scotland.

But another inference also is clearly established. The refusal of the Columban Church to conform to the Roman usage in determining the Sunday on which Easter was to be observed shows how far that Church then stood from the implicit obedience to Rome which Roman Catholics now deem essential. In the synod at Whitby, Wilfrid, the advocate for the Roman custom, referred his opponents to the decrees of the Apostolic see, and maintained that it would be sinful if, knowing these decrees, they should refuse obedience.[1] About thirty years before the Whitby Council, Pope Honorius had himself written to the Irish Church, in which Columba was born and educated, exhorting them not to esteem their small number, placed in the utmost bounds of the earth, wiser in this matter than all the other churches of Christ and all the bishops upon earth.[2] This letter, which produced the desired effect in the south of Ireland, could not have remained unknown in the north; yet though the Columban clergy were thus confronted with the papal authority and with the general practice of other Christian countries, they still refused to yield obedience. The refusal tacitly involved a claim on their part to the right of private judgment. There was, on the one side, the authority of papal decrees, the Pope's letter, and the common practice; on the other, the authority of the old custom which prevailed in the Irish Church and had been followed by Columba and his immediate successors; and weighing the reasons for and against, they resolved to resist the innovation. It is, however, only fair to bear in mind that Rome itself did not regard the change as a matter affecting faith or morals, but only as a more correct method of computation; therefore the extreme conclusions sometimes drawn from this occurrence, according to which the

---

[1] Bede. iii. 25.   [2] Ibid. 3.

clergy of Iona are represented as protesting here against the doctrinal teaching of Rome and maintaining the purity of the ancient faith, have no foundations of fact on which to rest. The opposition was not an instance of fidelity in maintaining truth against error, but rather an instance of the extreme tenacity with which good men sometimes adhere to a practice because it is old, and resist a better because it is new.

Besides the tenets now enumerated as held by the Columban Church, the doctrines which had been definitely settled by the general councils, and which formed the common property of Eastern and Western Christianity, were also received. Five hundred years of church history lay behind Columba, and in these centuries many doctrines regarded as essential had been authoritatively established and universally accepted. Bede, than whom there can be no more competent witness, both from his knowledge of the Columban Church and his adherence to the Catholic faith, testifies to the orthodoxy of the preachers from Iona in every point save their unfortunate mistake in regard to Easter Sunday — a mistake which he charitably ascribes to ignorance arising from their isolated position.[1] It was by men from Iona, or by men belonging to a kindred school, that the rest of pagan Scotland was Christianized; and of their teaching we shall now take a rapid view.

ST. KENTIGERN AND ST. CUTHBERT.

While Columba was engaged in conducting that mission from the Irish Church which eventually succeeded in converting the kingdom of the Picts, a similar work was proceeding in the kingdom of Strathclyde, a district comprising the modern counties of Stirling, Dunbarton, Lanark, Ayr, and Dumfries. The population was Cymric, descended from the ancient British race. The work of conversion was conducted by Kentigern. The Life of this saint which we possess was written to order about 500 years after his death by Jocelino, a monk of Furness Abbey.[2] It is valuable as bringing into clear light the opinions which were popularly entertained in the latter part of the twelfth century regarding the characteristics and labours of a saint, but as a record of the life of St. Kentigern it is of little

---
[1] Bede, iii. 1–4. [2] "The Historians of Scotland," vol. v. ("Vit. S. Kent.")

worth. The miracles recorded, while showing sometimes originality and even a sense of humour on the part of their inventors, go beyond the furthest stretch of which modern belief is capable. If we compare some incidents given in its mass of fables with notices in other records, Kentigern emerges as an historical personage from the halo of glory with which monkish legend invests him. He is living at the time when the Britons, under the leadership of Arthur, are with varying fortunes striving to stem the advancing tide of Teutonic pagan invaders. He is a prominent figure among the British ecclesiastics, marked by his piety, prudence, and courage as the fit person for the dangerous task of conducting a Christian mission among the heathen people of Strathclyde: but it is in Wales that we first find him on sure historical ground. There, as we have seen, he is the companion of St. David, he founds a monastery, and for years presides over it. Thence, on the invitation of the Cymric king Rhydderch, he journeys northward to prosecute a Christian mission in the newly acquired kingdom, and finally settles at Glasgow, where he died in 603, after thirty years' faithful and successful work in the Cymric kingdom of Strathclyde.

The main facts with which we here are concerned are the following:—Kentigern and his monks belonged to the ancient British Church, just as Columba and his monks belonged to the Irish Church. The two Churches were essentially the same in doctrine and usages. The tenets of the Christian faith taught by Kentigern in Strathclyde, and the rites used, did not differ from the tenets taught and the worship celebrated by Columba in Pictland. The meeting between Kentigern and Columba, which Joceline describes, whether historical or not, at any rate embodies in narrative form a fact of which there can be no doubt—their loving agreement regarding "the things of God and what concerned the salvation of souls."[1]

There remained still one portion of Scotland to be converted from paganism to Christianity, the district on the eastern side extending from the Firth of Forth to the Tweed. It formed a part of the Anglican kingdom of Bernicia, which was bounded on the north by the Forth and on the south by the Humber.

[1] "Vit. S. Kent." c. 39.

The people were of Anglican origin and speech, belonging to the Teutonic invaders, who had dispossessed the Celtic inhabitants and settled in their place. They differed thus in race and language from the people who inhabited Dalriada, Pictland, and Strathclyde, who belonged to the Celtic race and spoke Celtic dialects. There are indications of a mission having been conducted among them at an early period by the British Church, but the main agents in converting Northumbria to the Christian faith were missionaries from Iona. The work was effectually begun in 635, thirty-eight years after the death of Columba, and thirty-two after the death of Kentigern. The missionary monks were presided over by a bishop-abbot, as in Strathclyde, and not a presbyter-abbot, as in Iona. There is no great interval of time between Aidan, who virtually began, in 635, the work of converting the heathen Angles in Northumbria, and Cuthbert, who was the chief agent in carrying on the work of conversion in Tweeddale and Lothian. Aidan had founded a monastery at Melrose. On the night on which he died, in 651, Cuthbert, who was keeping his flock in Lauderdale, saw in vision the soul of the departed saint carried by angels into heaven, and thereupon resolved to become a monk. He was received into the monastery of Melrose by Eata, the abbot, who had himself been educated by Aidan. With his subsequent history we have here no concern. It may suffice to state that ten years later he became provost of Melrose, and that when the great controversy regarding the Sunday on which Easter should be held was decided at Whitby, in 664, Cuthbert adhered to the party which adopted the Roman usage.

In the matters relating to the doctrines and worship of the Church established among the Anglican inhabitants of Lothian and Tweeddale, we are again on firm historical ground. We possess the "Life of St. Cuthbert," written by Bede, who was born while the saint was still alive, and who submitted his manuscript to the revision of some who had been associated with the saint in his labours. We also have, from the same author, the history of the Northumbrian mission, which was founded by Aidan and extended by Cuthbert. It would be an easy task, had space allowed, to show from the writings of Bede the doctrines which were preached, and the worship in which these doctrines were expressed, but the following facts may suffice for our present purpose. The Church was founded by Columban monks from Iona, and built up by them or by men whom they had trained. We find in it, as might have been expected, what we found in the Columban Church—altars, sacrificing priests, masses, prayers for the departed and prayers addressed to them, the stated festivals and fasts, monasteries and monks, bishop, priest, and deacon. We find also nunneries, to which holy women retire. The esteem in which holy men were held is passing into veneration for their relics. The Church becomes zealous for the Roman usages. Cuthbert, on his deathbed, enjoins his monks "to have no communion with those that err from the unity of Catholic peace by not celebrating Easter at the proper time." What would he have said of those who do not celebrate Easter at the proper time, or at any other? His death, as described by an eye-witness, Herefrid, abbot of Lindisfarne, was the death of a faithful soldier of Jesus Christ, who had fought a good fight and kept the faith, and looked for the crown of righteousness which the Lord should give him, but yet there was much in that affecting scene to clash with the tenets of Protestant theology. "Now, when the time of nocturn prayers was come, having received the salutary sacraments at my hands, he fortified his departure, which he knew had now come, by the communion of the body and blood of our Lord; and, having lifted up his eyes to heaven and extended his hands on high, his soul, intent on heavenly praises, departed to the joys of the kingdom of heaven."[1]

The passage just quoted, as well as others in the writings of Bede, shows that in the Northumbrian Church at that time, as in the Church of Iona in the time of Columba, belief in purgatory was not an article of faith. Cuthbert had seen in vision the soul of Aidan carried to heaven on the night on which he died. The Abbot of Lindisfarne has no doubt that Cuthbert himself departed to heavenly joy. Hilda, abbess of Hartlepool, a member of the royal family, who had been one of Aidan's scholars, is at her death conveyed by angelic hosts

[1] Bede, "Vit. S. Cuth." c. 39.

THE DOCTRINE OF THE CHURCH. 159

to the goodly fellowship of the saints above, and when the tidings of her death reach another convent, the sisters assemble in their church and pass the remainder of the night in prayers for the soul of her who had gone to glory.[1] It is interesting to notice here that in the Anglican Church of Northumbria, just as in its mother Church of Iona, prayers are offered for departed souls though they are believed to be in heaven.

We have now taken a survey, in so far as our present purpose is concerned, of the work of those men who were the principal agents in converting pagan Scotland to the Christian religion. We have allowed the authentic documents, written shortly after the time in which these missionaries lived, to tell of the doctrines which they preached and the worship which they practised. The state of matters thus disclosed is very different from the accounts promulgated in popular lectures and treatises, and generally accepted in common belief. In this department of history, as in so many others, partisans have come to the documents not to learn from them fairly and honestly the information which they give, but to find in them the opinions which they themselves bring. Hence the early church of Scotland has been claimed by modern Romanist and modern Protestant as having been identical with them in doctrine and worship. Both err from the truth. To estimate aright its position it must be borne in mind that in its day the Catholic Church was as yet undivided. Some centuries had to elapse before the Roman legates laid on the altar of St. Sophia the anathema pronounced by the Pope against the Greek patriarch and all his adherents, and the Greek patriarch replied by a like anathema against the Pope and all his followers. A thousand years separate the church of Columba from the church as defined by the Council of Trent. During that long period there was, according to one view, a development of Christian truths under the guidance of the Spirit of truth; according to another view, a development of errors under the guidance of the spirit of error. In either case the fact remains that there was development. The Church of Rome as it is at the present day

[1] Bede, "Hist." iv. 23.

is not the Church as it was in the time of Columba and the other men who converted Scotland. That early Scottish Church in its beliefs was not even fully abreast of the age in which it lived. It was rather two centuries behind the age. It taught the Christian doctrines which were received when Britain was still a Roman colony, but had not adopted some opinions which had acquired currency during the period of its isolation, and which were rapidly crystallizing into authoritative dogmas. To assimilate that early church to the present Roman Catholic, would require the addition to its creed of many doctrines deemed important and essential, but as regards the tenets which it held there would be found little to alter.

On the other hand, no Protestant Church in Scotland can fairly claim to be the lineal descendant of that church which was first planted in the land. The reformers in Scotland did not present their system of doctrine as being a restoration of the doctrine adopted by Columba, Kentigern, and Cuthbert. They went in their antiquarian researches 500 years further back, and presented their system as being the authoritative teaching of Jesus Christ and his apostles. Even supposing that the Church first founded in Scotland by Columba, Kentigern, Cuthbert, and their fellow-labourers, had continued absolutely the same, preserving her original doctrines and worship uncontaminated by any foreign corruption, there would have been, in the opinion of the reformers, much to discard, and in what was retained much to purify. In that reformation the altar is abolished and the communion table is restored; the sacrificing priest officiating before the altar is expelled, and in his stead there is the minister presiding at the head of the table around which the communicants are seated; the Eucharist is not an offering of the body and blood of Christ to God on behalf of the living and the dead, but an ordinance in which the sacrifice on the Cross is commemorated and worthy receivers spiritually feed upon Christ crucified; prayers to holy men who have died in the Lord are rejected as blasphemous, and prayers for the departed are forbidden as unscriptural and superstitious. Christmas, Lent, Easter, the stated fasts and festivals, are all abolished as having no warrant in God's word. All these practices and observances, which existed in the early Scottish

Church, were founded on doctrines, and at the Reformation the rites and observances, with the doctrines from which they sprang, were all swept away. The Columban Church has been called sometimes a Presbyterian Church from the fact that it was governed by a presbyter-abbot, to whose jurisdiction even bishops were subject. This unusual submission of the bishop to the presbyter finds indeed a faint parallel, not in Presbyterian church government, but in those early years of the Scottish Reformed Church when the tulchan bishop had to give an account of his conduct to the General Assembly, and humbly submit to the rebukes of the presbyter who presided as moderator; but with the exception of that shadowy likeness all similarity in church government disappears.

The holy heroes who were instrumental in converting Scotland gave themselves to reading the Scriptures, to solitary meditation, and to fasting and prayer. They were men of strong faith, of much charity, of abundant labours, of self-denial, and of dauntless courage. Saintlier lives than those described in the pages of Adamnan and Bede are nowhere found in the records of ecclesiastical history; but we err altogether if, as has sometimes been done, we infer from the holiness of their lives the orthodoxy of their faith when tested by our standards. The inference to be drawn from the saintliness of those men of God is not that therefore their faith and worship must have been the same as ours, but that the operations of the Spirit of God, and the holy and beneficial fruits thereby produced, are not limited by the boundaries within which man's narrow and limited views of Christian faith and doctrine would fain endeavour to confine them.

The opposition to the Roman usages gradually became weaker in Scotland. Adamnan, abbot of Iona, adopted the Catholic computation, and succeeded in getting some at least of his monks to follow his example. Strathclyde had already conformed. The contention was finally settled by Nectan, king of the Picts, who in the year 710 summoned a meeting of the nobility and clergy, explained to them the grounds on which he had become convinced that the Roman usage as regards Easter should be observed, and decreed that the clergy should keep the proper Easter Sunday and adopt the coronal tonsure. A few of the clergy lifted up their testimony against this defection from ancient practice, and were for some years tolerated in their nonconformity; but as they showed no signs of yielding, they were finally, in 717, expelled from the kingdom, and this miserable dispute regarding cycles and shaving came to an end.

At this point darkness, as we have already seen, settles over the history of the Scottish Church for a period of three centuries, and we must pursue our journey by the aid of such light as may be derived from legend and from notices in brief and scattered records. All the information gleaned from these sources shows the Church emerging from the state of isolation and becoming more closely connected with Rome. The legends of Serf and Boniface refer to the early part of the eighth century. Stripping these legends from the husks of miracle and fiction with which they are surrounded, discarding even the statement that these men came from Rome to Scotland, we find this kernel of fact, that they belonged to the party which had conformed to the Roman usages, that whether they came from Ireland or elsewhere, they came to Scotland bringing with them Roman clergy of the various minor orders, and that they exercised a great and decisive influence on the fortunes of the Scottish Church. They gained the favour of the Pictish monarch, and not many years after their arrival the Pictish Church conformed, and the recusant Columban monks were expelled.

THE CULDEES.

It is at this time, and in these circumstances, that we first find mention made of the Culdees in Scotland. They were the outcome of an influence which, from a very early period, had existed and worked within the Church. Men longing to reach a high spiritual life and maintain a close communion with God deemed that these objects could be gained only by solitary contemplation and secret silence, and therefore withdrew themselves from the world and lived alone in desert and sequestered places. Monks forsook their monasteries, and laymen forsook their business and their homes, that by solitary discipline they might rise nearer to God. Christian Scotland in its very earliest period, as well as all other

Christian lands, furnishes numerous instances of such solitaries. The hermits gradually became communities, living separately in rudely constructed cells clustered around the church. It is as communities that they appear in Scotland, and are known as Culdees. They are not peculiar to Scotland; but are found in England and Ireland, and on the Continent. In Scotland they are clerics, they settle at Dunkeld, at St. Andrews, Lochleven, and numerous other places, and there perform their clerical functions. We pass over their history;[1] our business with them is only in so far as doctrine is concerned. There is a poverty of facts connected with the period of the Culdees, and some Protestant writers, supplementing the poverty of facts from the riches of their own imagination, have drawn pleasing and beauteous pictures of the Culdees as holy men who preached only the pure Gospel faith, until gradually and slowly the Culdee faith, along with the Culdees themselves, became corrupted through their contact with Rome. There can be no doubt as to their general purity of life. Ample testimony is borne to their piety and godliness, even by those who came in their room. But with regard to the Culdees, as we have just seen to be the case with regard to Columba and other early Christian missionaries, we shall be led to utterly false conclusions, if we infer from the simplicity and purity of their lives the simplicity and purity of their faith, as judged by Protestant orthodoxy.

With regard to them, and the time in which they flourished in Scotland, we have the following plain facts:—Instead of resisting the influence of Rome and protesting against her errors, they do not appear in Scotland until the struggle against the Roman usages has been terminated, and the few Columban clergy who still remained faithful to ancient practices have been banished. They come as adherents of the Romanizing party, and take the place of the monks who, for their resistance to that party, have been driven away. No sooner do they appear than the connection with Rome becomes closer. That assembly of

---

[1] For the Culdees see Jamieson's "History of the Culdees," which, however, was written before many sources of information had been investigated; Dr. Reeves' "British Culdees;" Dr. Skene's "Celtic Scotland," vol. ii. pp. 236-277. Dr. Bellesheim's account of the Culdees, given in his "History of the Catholic Church in Scotland," is mainly Dr. Skene's account translated into German, and then retranslated into English.

nobles and clergy, called by King Nectan in 710, which resolved to adopt the Roman usages and expelled the protesting remnant, placed the kingdom under the protection of St. Peter, and in a short time numerous churches are dedicated to the same saint. Then we find that two ecclesiastics, Sedulius, bishop of Strathclyde, and Fergus, who afterwards preached and converted from Perthshire to Caithness, were both present at the council held at Rome in the year 721, and subscribed the canons then enacted. That does not look like holding aloof from Rome and testifying against her erroneous teaching. Further, we have the undoubted fact that during the period in which the Culdees were in honour and power, reverence for the relics of saints increased greatly, and reverence became adoration. A portion of the body of St. Columba was brought to Dunkeld, was there enshrined, and became famous for the miracles which it wrought. Three fingers, part of an arm, a knee-pan, and a tooth of St. Andrew were brought to Kilrymont, and the place was dedicated to God and the saint, and became known as St. Andrews. The estimation in which the relics were held appears from the fact that the kingdom, which in 710 had been dedicated to St. Peter, is dedicated to St. Andrew as its patron saint by King Angus, who reigned 736–61. Scotland had no relics of St. Peter; it now had obtained a large and precious store of the relics of St. Andrew, and therefore was placed under the protection of that saint, whose fingers, arm, knee-pan, and tooth could always be had recourse to for ensuring discomfiture of foes and spiritual and temporal blessings for itself. The Culdees were the custodians of the relics.

In the reign of Malcolm Canmore the Scottish Church emerges into clearer light. In the year 1069 Malcolm married the Saxon Princess Margaret, and in the Life of the queen written by her confessor, Turgot, we have some definite information regarding the state of the Scottish Church at that time. A conference is held with the Scottish clergy, including Culdees. It is acknowledged first of all by Queen Margaret and the English ecclesiastics who accompanied her that "the Church in Scotland is at one with the Catholic Church in worshipping one God in one faith." She finds there are some things which ought to be amended; but the corrections which she suggests and effects are in no way connected with doctrine. It is not the faith, but some practices of the Culdee Church which she seeks to change. It was the practice to begin the observance of Lent, not on Ash Wednesday, but on the Monday of the following week—a practice which had formerly been universal in the Catholic Church. She wished them to begin the fast on Ash Wednesday, and they consented. The people had a superstitious dread of partaking of the sacrament of the Lord's Supper, and neglected that holy rite. Queen Margaret's reasoning against this superstitious fear, which the Culdees seem to have encouraged, was clear, cogent, and scriptural. She found that the Lord's day was profaned by ordinary labour, while Saturday was observed as a day of rest. Here, too, she convinced the Scots of their error. Another abuse which she succeeded in abolishing related to marriage within the forbidden degrees. She found that the Scottish Church allowed a man to marry his deceased brother's wife, or even his step-mother, and this practice she prevailed upon them to abandon. Such were the main abuses which Margaret found in the Culdee Church. Surely not even the most zealous Protestant can dream of asserting that these practices were the marks and fruits of a pure and simple faith, and that the changes effected by the queen were Romish corruptions. He might of course object, not to the observance of Lent beginning on Ash Wednesday, but to Lent being observed at all; but Margaret found that the Culdees observed Lent, and merely proposed a change of day for its commencement—Wednesday instead of Monday. By all these changes she brought them, indeed, into closer conformity with Roman practices, but surely every one, unless hopelessly blinded by prejudice, must acknowledge that the closer conformity thus effected led to a more scriptural view of the duty of communicating and of the preparation needed for the due observance of that holy ordinance, to a more scriptural view of the Lord's day and of the sanctity of marriage and the purity of marriage relationships.

An observation made by Turgot concerning the Scottish Church has, from its very indefiniteness, afforded ample room for the play of imagination. He says that there were in some places in Scotland certain of the clergy who were wont to celebrate mass in some barbarous rite or other; what it was he knew not. The Prior of Durham speaks here in a tone approaching as near to supercilious indifference and contempt as is possible for such a holy man. He did not know, nor did he care to know, what the barbarous rites were; but though he did not know, some writers have conjectured that they consisted in the simple and primitive administration of the Lord's Supper, as opposed to the ceremonies used in the celebration of mass. The conjecture rests on no evidence. At the first introduction of Christianity into Scotland the priest celebrated mass standing before the altar, and there is not the slightest tittle of evidence to show that any change was made until the Reformation. It has also been suggested that the barbarous rite consisted in the priest saying mass in the vernacular. This suggestion also has no evidence to support it, and is besides, in itself, strangely improbable. The use of the native language in the service of the altar would not have separated the Celtic from the Catholic Church. Even the Council of Trent, held 500 years after the time of Queen Margaret, did not condemn the celebration of mass in the vernacular, but only declared that it did not seem expedient to the fathers that mass should be everywhere celebrated in the vulgar tongue, and pronounced *anathema* on those who maintained that mass should be celebrated in the common language of the people, and in no other.[1] So great a change as the substitution of Latin for Celtic in the public services of the Church could hardly have been made without encountering some opposition, but we read of none, nor of anything to warrant the conjecture that such a change had ever been made. We still possess very ancient Celtic liturgies, but they are so called not because they are Celtic in language, but because they were used in the Celtic Church. The Celtic liturgies are all written in Latin. In the time of Malcolm Canmore there was no prescribed Missal of universal authority. Forms slightly differing from each other were used in different countries. In Scotland, so far removed from Rome and a century or two behind the age in ecclesiastical observances,

---

[1] Sess. xxii. c. 8; Canon ix.

there must have been rites in the service of the altar which, to Turgot, fresh from the services in Durham Cathedral, seemed strange and even barbarous. Of the irregularities in Scottish ministrations we have a striking instance in the fact that long after the time of Turgot, in the year 1242, the Synod at Musselburgh found it necessary to forbid the elevation of the Eucharist by the priest before he had pronounced the words of consecration.[1] The prohibition shows that such a practice must have been in use; and the elevation of the Eucharist for the adoration of the people, before the words of consecration had been spoken, was a rite not only barbarous, but idolatrous.

Another statement regarding the Culdees found in the legend of St. Andrew has been considered to furnish evidence that they did not conform to the Catholic Church, but cherished a simpler and purer faith. There were two churches in St. Andrews, a greater and a smaller. In the greater church was the altar of the patron saint, and at that altar mass was said only when the king or bishop happened to be present. The Culdees, however, were wont to say their office after their own fashion in a corner of the smaller church.[2] On this slight foundation a vast superstructure of pure Culdee doctrine has been reared. As to what this office of the Culdees in St. Andrews may have been, and in what fashion they said it, there is absolutely nothing known. The time referred to in that part of the legend was a period when the possessions of the Church in St. Andrews were mainly in the hands of laymen and the services of the church were greatly neglected. It is a time of religious declension which the legend there describes. We are further informed in the legend that the same Culdees appointed one of their number to be an *amchara*, soul-friend, or confessor, who should hear confession, enjoin penance, and give absolution. Confession, penance, and absolution do not savour of the pure faith of Protestantism. The truth is, that in this instance, as in the others regarding the Lord's day and marriage relationships, when the Culdee practices differed from the Catholic they differed for the worse.

But we are not left merely to form conjectures regarding the usual form of worship in Culdee monasteries; we have an inven-

[1] Bellesheim's "History," i. 353. [2] Dr. Skene's "Celtic Scotland," ii. 350-360.

tory of the books which belonged to the monastery of Lochleven. Robert, who was Bishop of St. Andrews from 1122 to 1159, granted the possessions of the Culdees in Lochleven to the canons-regular of St. Andrews, and among the books thus granted were a Lectionary, a Missal, and a Gradual. The Lectionary is a book which contains the Scripture lessons read in the Church service; the Missal contains the prayers, canon, and ceremonies of the mass; the Gradual, the passages to be chanted. These books were, in fact, the ordinary service-books of the Church, and they indicate unmistakably that mass was celebrated in the Culdee monasteries.

Marriage was not uncommon among the Culdee clergy; marriage is prohibited to Roman Catholic clergy, therefore the Culdees were not Roman Catholics: such is the sum of the argument which seeks to prove the purity of faith in the Celtic Church from marriage being permitted to the priests. That some at least of the officiating Culdee clergy had wives is very probable. A tradition that such had been the case had come down to the early part of the sixteenth century. Dean Mylne, rector of Moneydie and Prebendary of Dunkeld,[1] who communicates it, says truly that in this instance they were merely following the practice which existed in the Eastern Church. Such a tradition could not have originated among a celibate clergy such as then officiated in Dunkeld Cathedral, but must have had some foundation on which to rest. In Ireland at the same time the clergy were not all celibates. There are instances of bishops having been succeeded by their sons, and monastery-readers by their sons for successive generations. It has been strenuously maintained by the advocates of celibacy that in such cases the men had, while laymen, married and begotten sons and daughters, that their wives had died, and only on becoming widowers had they taken orders. Such an explanation might be admitted if the instances of son succeeding father had been rare; but when the cases are numerous, and are found continuing from generation to generation, it must be abandoned as untenable. It could not happen then any more than now that a wife would conveniently die at the same time as her husband's father so as to allow her mourning widower

---

[1] "Vitæ Dunkeld. Ecc. Epis."

to find consolation and emolument by entering holy orders, and succeeding to the office just vacated by his deceased parent, and that these opportune deaths should regularly happen generation after generation. The plain truth is that we are confronted with only two alternatives—marriage or immorality; we must choose the one or the other. We need not hesitate to adopt, with Dean Mylne, the more charitable view.

The period of the Culdees lies from 1100 to 700 years behind us, and in order to judge fairly and honestly of the relation in which they stood to the Catholic Church of their day, we must look at the Church as it then was, and not at the Roman Catholic Church as it now is. At that time the celibacy of the clergy had not been enforced. Marriage was allowed, though celibacy was reckoned better. At the Council of Nice, in 325, a proposal to enforce clerical celibacy was unsuccessful. The attempt to enforce the rule was never abandoned. Ordinances in its favour were repeatedly made, but not obeyed. In 1074, that is, some years after the marriage of Malcolm Canmore and Princess Margaret, and after the consequent reformation of practices and morals in Scotland, Hildebrand resuscitated the old ordinances in favour of celibacy, but even his iron will and despotic rule failed to enforce universal obedience in the portion of the Catholic Church which acknowledged his supremacy. In the Oriental Church the celibacy of the clergy has never been enforced. The ordinance of Hildebrand, after encountering much opposition, became in course of time the universal rule throughout Western Europe; but the state of the clergy showed only too plainly that while the vow of celibacy was observed, the seventh commandment was disregarded. There is no need to deny or excuse the fact that some of the Culdees had wives, nor did the marriage relationship interfere with the due discharge of their clerical duties; for, as Dean Mylne testifies, when called on to minister in the order of their course, and to live observing profound silence in their cells, the married Culdees left their wives at home.

The Culdees' striving after a higher spiritual life and a closer communion with God produced its results in purity and true holiness; and their Christian graces and virtues were borne witness to by the tradition which lingered in the land for ages after they themselves had disappeared. Even Turgot, who did not find himself at home among the Scottish clerics, and was by no means prejudiced in their favour, speaking of the Culdees of Scotland as he actually saw them in Fifeshire, tells us that in his time "there were many in the kingdom of the Scots who, in different places, inclosed in separate cells, led lives of great strictness, in the flesh, but not according to the flesh; for even on the earth they led the life of angels. These the queen often visited and talked with, for in them she strove to love and venerate Christ; she was wont to commend herself to their prayers, and as they would take no earthly gift from her, she would earnestly request them to prescribe for her some work of charity or mercy, and whatever they prescribed she devoutly fulfilled."[1]

The Culdees differed widely and essentially in doctrine from modern Protestantism. The sacrifice of the mass for the living and the dead, the intercession of saints, the adoration of their relics, pilgrimages to their shrines, severe penances to mortify the flesh and win Divine favour, priestly absolution, conformity to Roman usages in the service of the altar, and reverence for the authority of Rome itself—all these are found in the Church of the Culdees, and all these practices, and the tenets on which they were based, were eventually rejected as gross superstitions and deadly doctrinal errors; but the life of self-denial, purity, and charity which they led in this faith, though it be now but dimly seen through the mist of ages, should still win reverence, and give them a title to stand high in the roll of Scotland's Christian worthies.

The period between the death of Malcolm Canmore and the Reformation, 1093–1560, however important in itself, has not, till we reach its close, much connection with the further development of doctrine. Instead of the pure doctrines of the Scottish Church having, as is sometimes represented, become corrupted during that space, these doctrines were at its close essentially the same as when it began. They had developed in some directions, but they had not radically changed. The manner in which Christ was present in the Eucharist was in 1215

[1] "Vit. S. Margaretæ," cap. ix.

declared to be by transubstantiation; and the same council which declared this tenet to be the doctrine of the Church also made auricular confession obligatory. Infant communion, which had been universal, was now abolished in the Western Church, though it is still retained in the Eastern. At a comparatively late period, in 1415, the cup was forbidden to the laity, and they were permitted to communicate only in one kind. The worship of the Virgin Mary greatly increased during this period, and new festivals in her honour were appointed. All these decrees, however, proceeded on lines which had already been laid down. The bread and wine in the Eucharist were, after the words of consecration had been spoken, regarded as the body and blood of Christ in the time of Columba: the Lateran Council merely defined in what sense they were to be so regarded. Auricular confession had from very ancient times been recommended: it was now enforced. The denial of the cup to the laity did not, according to the council which enacted it, involve imperfect communion, for the council maintained that Christ is present in body and blood, soul and divinity, as well under the species of bread as of wine. Infant communion, which was administered by the cup alone, ceased as a matter of course when the cup was forbidden save to the clergy.

The worship of the Virgin was also handed down from the Celtic Church. The legend which tells of the transference of the relics of St. Andrew to Kilrymont in the eighth century, tells also of a chapel which was erected there in honour of St. Mary the Virgin; and this dedication was made in one of the chief seats of the Culdees, shortly after they appeared in Scotland.[1] Churches and wells were dedicated to her. The worship existed when Queen Margaret came to Scotland. It afterwards developed in Scotland, as it did throughout Western Christendom, but it certainly was not introduced by her. The doctrine of indulgences received great enlargements. In theory, contrition, confession, and satisfaction were needed, and a gift of money for pious purposes might be substituted in room of penance; but in practice, contrition and satisfaction were often kept in the background, and the money contribution was the main condition of receiving the benefit. At a late period, in

[1] Skene's "Celtic Scotland," ii. 272.

1477, the inexhaustible treasure of the superfluous merits of Christ and his saints which was possessed by the Church and dispensed by the Pope, was declared to be available, for a remuneration, for the benefit of souls in purgatory. This development was new to the Scottish Church, as it was to all others.

Early in the twelfth century the Salisbury liturgy was used in public worship instead of the Celtic, and continued till the Reformation. The Celtic liturgies differed from those in general use elsewhere only in a few unimportant points. The Salisbury liturgy differed from the Roman Missal now used only in some slight particulars of ritual and order, but these variations in no case imply any difference of doctrine.[1]

Towards the close of the fourteenth century Rome was supreme, and though for a time there were rival Popes, each of whom claimed allegiance, Scotland, with the rest of Western Europe, owned the papal supremacy, though there was a difference of opinion as to which Pope was the real one. An opposition to the practices of the Romish Church, and to the tenets on which these practices were based, had long prevailed, and had found supporters in statesmen, poets, and preachers. This opposition at length found an exponent in Wickliffe, a priest of the Church in England. He asserted publicly in preaching and in writing that the Church of Christ consisted of all those who were, as sons and daughters of God, heirs of eternal life, and as such priests to God; that over this Church the apostle Peter had no more authority than any other apostle, and therefore the Bishop of Rome, or the Pope, had no more authority, as the alleged successor of Peter, than any other bishop; that the authority for faith and conduct among the members of this Church was, not the Bishop of Rome, but the Word of God as contained in the Scriptures; that this Word of God should be presented to the common people not in Latin, which they did not understand, but in their mother-tongue, which they did understand. Among other inferences which he drew from the Bible and taught to the people was the inference that in the Eucharist the bread and wine after the words of consecration had been pronounced, remained still plain bread

---

[1] Bellesheim, ii. 390–409, and the authorities quoted.

and wine. Such opinions, ably supported and widely and eagerly adopted, aroused horror and indignation. The Council of Constance, in 1415, pronounced anathema on Wickliffe's opinions, and on all who believed them, and further ordered his books to be destroyed and his bones to be burned. As many copies of his books as could be found were accordingly destroyed, and his bones were dug out of his grave and duly burned. The opinions of Wickliffe, however, still lived and flourished, and had been preached widely in Scotland before they were condemned by the Council of Constance. Prominent among the preachers was John Resby, an English priest, who was at length, in 1407, seized and brought before a council of clergy presided over by Laurence of Lindores. Two out of forty heretical opinions which he was accused of teaching are specified by Bower: the first, that the Pope was not really the vicar of Christ; the second, that no one could be pope or vicar of Christ unless he was a holy man—opinions which Bower characterizes as most dangerous. It is said that Resby was triumphantly refuted by Laurence, and that it was only through sheer obstinacy that he refused to acknowledge himself defeated.[1] The only account of the trial is written by a zealous defender of the faith which was attacked; if there had been an account of it by Resby himself or any of his followers, the triumphant arguments of Laurence of Lindores might appear in another light. At any rate they failed to convince Resby, who adhered to his own views, and suffered death by burning rather than renounce them. His death did not arrest the progress of the doctrines which he had preached. His writings were secretly preserved, and his followers, who were known by the name of Lollards, greatly increased. So great was the progress of these "most dangerous" opinions that the students in the newly erected University of St. Andrews were enjoined, on taking the degree of Master of Arts, to promise on oath to defend the Church against all Lollards and their supporters; and nine years afterwards, in 1425, the Scottish Parliament enacted that diligent inquiry should be made for Lollards by every bishop, and that due punishment should be inflicted according to the law of holy Church.

[1] Bellesheim, ii. 54, and translator's note.

It was not long till this law was put into execution. Paul Crawar, a disciple of Huss, came from Prague to St. Andrews, where he practised as a physician and disseminated his doctrines. He also was arraigned before the court of inquisition, over which Laurence of Lindores still presided. Bower gives a fuller account of the doctrines which he taught than he did in the case of Resby. He was accused of teaching that the laity had a right to read the Bible, that civil tribunals could try and punish clerical offenders, that purgatory was a fable, that pilgrimages were useless, that the power of the keys, priestly absolution, and transubstantiation were all human inventions; and of discarding the Missal and beginning the communion service with the Lord's Prayer, and then reading a passage from Scripture descriptive of the sufferings of the Saviour. He too was condemned as an obstinate heretic, and burned accordingly at St. Andrews in 1433. The religious movement in Bohemia, of which Huss and Jerome were the leaders, sprang from the teaching of Wickliffe. Crawar, though a Bohemian, belonged to the same school as Resby. The doctrines now enumerated show a movement against the teaching and authority of Rome, beginning in England, extending to Bohemia, and returning to Scotland. It is alleged by Bower that Crawar and his followers also denied the resurrection of the dead, preached community of goods, and led immoral lives; and Protestants have been taunted for expressing a doubt as to Bower's accuracy in making this allegation. The previous opinions are all in accordance with the doctrines of Wickliffe and Huss. The denial of the resurrection of the dead is never attributed to any of their followers save in this instance. The Council of Constance enumerated forty-five heretical opinions in the writings of Wickliffe, which they expressly condemned, and 260 dangerous inferences from these articles; they enumerated also thirty heretical doctrines taught by Huss,[1] and in all that long catalogue there is no mention whatever of a denial of the resurrection. If Crawar actually held such a view, he was singular in this respect. It seems strangely improbable that men who carried their lives in their hand, and who might any day be led to the stake, should have discarded

---

[1] These lists are given in the appendix to the decrees of the Council of Trent.

a belief in the resurrection—a belief held by none more strongly than by the teachers whom in all other points they so faithfully followed. There may have been some ground for the charge that they preached community of goods; at least it is certain that they preached against the wealth of the clergy. Among the deadly errors taught by the Wickliffites and condemned by the Council are found these—that it is contrary to Scripture that ecclesiastics should possess property; that it is contrary to the rule of Christ to enrich the clergy; that all, from the Pope to the lowest member of a religious order, are heretics in so far as they possess property.[1] Doctrines such as these were very likely preached by Crawar and the Lollards, and the teaching that churchmen should renounce all possessions and go forth to preach with neither purse nor scrip could not be regarded otherwise than most dangerous heresy by men who held richly endowed bishoprics, abbacies, or livings.

The doctrines of Wickliffe took firm root in Scotland, and were not extirpated by the burning of some of its prominent teachers. The above trials took place in the diocese of St. Andrews. In 1494 Lollardism is found to have many adherents in the diocese of Glasgow. Upwards of thirty suspected persons, men and women, some of them of high rank, were summoned by Archbishop Blackadder before King James IV. and his council to answer a charge of heresy. They were accused mainly of holding that transubstantiation was false, that the worship of images and relics of saints was unlawful, that indulgences were futile, that masses for souls in purgatory were vain and unprofitable, that prayer should be addressed to God alone, that priests might marry, that the Pope was the head of the church of antichrist, that Christ had abolished the power of princes, and that every man and woman who was a true Christian was as such a priest unto God. These charges show that the opinions taught by Resby and Crawar still prevailed. There was also an advance. Views were now held in Scotland regarding the nature of the Christian priesthood which contained the germs of an entire revolution in received dogma and practice. It is not merely the validity of the official acts of immoral priests, bishops, and popes that is now denied: such

[1] "Errores Wickliffi," 10, 32, 44.

a denial had often been made before; but it is asserted, on the other hand, that men are priests to God, not because of outward consecration or imposition of hands, but because of their union with Jesus Christ, the only high-priest over the house of God.

From the fact that the Lollards are represented as denying doctrines held by the Catholic Church, they are in danger of being regarded as simply protesting against received opinions. Such a view of them would be partial and one-sided. No religious movement can ever be carried on by means of mere negations. Much may require to be pulled down, but something esteemed better must be erected in its room. It can easily be seen from the charges made against them that they were not mere destructives. Prayer to the saints or the Virgin was condemned, but prayer to God alone took its place; instead of priestly absolution, there was Divine forgiveness; instead of the sacrament of the mass administered according to the Salisbury Missal, there was the sacrament of the Lord's Supper administered according to the primitive Gospel rite; instead of the clerical priestly order, there is universal Christian priesthood; and instead of the authority of tradition, council, or Pope, there is the supreme authority of the Word of God. Reading between the lines of the charges made against them, it is apparent that there was much that was positive in the teaching of the Lollards. The movement must also have been widely extended. The scattered notices which occur in Scottish history regarding it are concerned only with the few cases which attracted judicial notice, but they do not reveal, although they indicate, the extent and depth of the movement itself.

When Patrick Hamilton was, in 1527, condemned for heresy at St. Andrews, the reformation of the Church had for some years been actively prosecuted in Germany, and in the charges made against Hamilton we can see that the doctrines of the Reformation had extended to Scotland. These doctrines soon gained many converts among the clergy of the Scottish Church. This fact is apparent from the number of priests who were executed for heresy, from the number who had to seek refuge by flight, and from the number who eventually joined the Reformers and became preachers of the reformed faith. These doctrines spread rapidly among the people. At a later period, when the triumph of the Reformation seemed probable, many joined the movement in hope of sharing in the plunder of the fallen Church, but no such motive influenced those who embraced the cause when it was weak and the Church was so strong that it seemed secure. It was not at first so much the doctrines of the Church as the practices of churchmen which engendered a deep dissatisfaction in the minds of the people, and made them ready recipients of the tenets which the Reformers preached.

Efforts were made to avert the coming catastrophe, chiefly by means of the execution of the penal laws against heretics, the reformation of the clergy, and the instruction of the people. It is only fair to say that the penal laws were put into force in comparatively few cases. When Cardinal Beaton was in power we have seen a firm hand guiding the policy and directing the measures taken in defence of the old Church, but after he was removed we find tokens mainly of vacillation and weakness. The attempts to reform the clergy resulted in the passing of good resolutions never carried into practice. For the religious instruction of the people measures were adopted in the council held in 1552 which, if executed, might have greatly changed the position of affairs. Chief among these measures is the preparation and adoption of Hamilton's Catechism. This work contains an explanation of the ten commandments, of the seven sacraments, of the Lord's prayer, and of the angelic salutation. It was not to be put into the hands of the people, it was not meant to be a guide to the parish priest in the composition of his sermons, like the Tridentine Catechism, but was intended to serve the purpose which the Book of Homilies served in the English Church. The parish priest was on Sundays and holidays, if no preaching friar was present, to read to his parishioners for half-an-hour from the catechism, and was further enjoined to read the whole book consecutively. The work is an admirable exposition, from the Catholic point of view, of the subjects indicated. In matters of doctrine it may be regarded as sometimes diverging into subtle and useless disquisitions, and in matters of practical duty into the casuistry of the confessional;

but on the whole it is a clear, simple, and able work. The teaching is in accordance with that of the Catholic Church as it then existed. Within the latter half of the present century two questions which then were open have been finally decided: the immaculate conception of the Virgin and the supremacy of the Pope. On the former subject the catechism teaches the opinion which in 1854 was declared to be orthodox; on the latter, which was only settled in 1860, the catechism is silent. The work was admirably adapted for the purpose in view. If even at that late period the clergy had become exemplary in their conduct and faithful in the use of the means put into their hands for the instruction of the people in faith and duty, the Reformation movement in Scotland might have had a different result.

In 1559 the provincial general council of the Scottish Church again met. The usual good resolutions for the reformation of the lives of the clergy were again enacted, and this time it was resolved that they should be enforced. The parish priests were anew enjoined to read the catechism to their people—a duty which they seem to have neglected—and various other salutary measures were passed. But the effort to reform the Church from within came too late. In 1560 Parliament met, the Confession of Faith of the Reformed Church was laid before it, read over article by article, and after a feeble opposition by three bishops, one abbot, and two peers, was adopted as the established creed of Scotland.

THE SCOTTISH CONFESSION OF FAITH.

On the meeting of the Scottish Parliament in August, 1560, a petition, as has been stated in the earlier part of this work, was presented in name of "the barons, gentlemen, burgesses, and other true subjects of this realm, professing the Lord Jesus within the same," craving among other things that the false doctrine and idolatrous worship of the Popish Church should be abolished. Parliament wished to know what it was proposed to substitute in their room, and accordingly commanded the Reformers "to draw into plain and several heads the sum of that doctrine which they would maintain, and would desire the present Parliament to establish as wholesome truth, and only necessary to be believed and to be received within the realm." The task of drawing up such a document was committed to John Knox, John Winram, John Spotswood, John Willock, John Row, and John Douglas. They undertook the duty, and after four days they laid before the house "The Confession of the Faith and Doctrine believed and professed by the Protestants of the Realm of Scotland."

This Confession is so important as exhibiting the doctrines of the Reformers, and as laying down the lines to which Scottish theology has in its main features been conformed from that time to the present day, that it is necessary to give at least a summary of the document.

It consists of twenty-five articles :—

I. "We confess and acknowledge one only God, to whom only we must cleave, whom only we must serve, whom only we must worship, and in whom only we must put our trust." This God "is one in substance, and yet in three persons, the Father, the Son, and the Holy Ghost; by whom we confess and believe all things in heaven and earth, as well visible and invisible, to have been created, to be retained in their being, and to be ruled and guided by His inscrutable providence to such ends as His eternal wisdom, goodness, and justice hath appointed them, to the manifestation of His own glory."

II. *Of the Creation of Man.*—God created man in His own image, gave to him wisdom, lordship, justice, free-will, and clear knowledge of himself: "from which honour and perfection man and woman did both fall; the woman being deceived by the serpent, and man obeying the voice of the woman; both conspiring against the sovereign majesty of God."

III. *Of Original Sin.*—"By which transgression, commonly called original sin, was the image of God utterly defaced in man, and he and his posterity of nature became enemies to God, slaves to Satan, and servants to sin; insomuch that death everlasting hath had, and shall have, power and dominion over all that have not been, are not, or shall not be regenerated from above; which regeneration is wrought by the power of the Holy Ghost working in the hearts of the elect of God an assured faith in the promise of God revealed to us in His word; by which faith we apprehend Christ Jesus, with the graces and benefits promised in Him."

IV. *Of the Revelation of the Promise.*—After God had sought Adam again, had rebuked his sin and convicted him of the same, He "in the end made unto him a most joyful promise that the seed of the woman should break down the serpent's head; that is, he should destroy the work of the devil." This promise was repeated and made clearer from time to time, and was joyfully embraced and firmly received by all the faithful from Adam till the incarnation of Jesus Christ.

V. God preserved, instructed, multiplied, honoured, decored, and from death called to life His Church from Adam till the advent of Christ.

VI. *Of the Incarnation of Christ Jesus.*—When the fulness of time came, God sent His Son, His eternal wisdom, the substance of His own glory, into this world, who became incarnate, very God and very man, two perfect natures, united and joined in one person.

VII. *Why it behoved the Mediator to be very God and very man.*—This union of two natures in Christ proceeded "from the eternal and immutable decree of God, from which all our salvation springs and depends."

VIII. *Of Election.*—"That same eternal God and Father, who of mere grace elected us in Christ Jesus his Son, before the foundation of the world was laid, appointed Him to be our head, our brother, our pastor, and great shepherd of our souls; but, because that the enmity between the justice of God and our sins was such that no flesh by itself could or might have attained unto God, it behoved that the Son of God should descend unto us, and take to himself a body of our body, flesh of our flesh, and bone of our bones, and so become the Mediator between God and man; giving power to as many as believe in Him to be the sons of God, as himself doth witness, 'I pass up to my Father and unto your Father, to my God and your God;' by which most holy fraternity, whatsoever we have lost in Adam is restored to us again; and for this cause we are not afraid to call God our Father; not so much because He hath created us, which we have in common with the reprobates, as for that He hath given to us His only Son to be our brother, and given unto us grace to acknowledge and embrace Him for our only Mediator, as before is said. It behoved, further, the Messias and Redeemer to be very God and very man, because He was to underly the punishment due for our transgressions, and to present himself in the presence of his Father's judgment as in our person, to suffer for our transgressions and inobedience, by death to overcome him that was the author of death; but because the Godhead alone could not suffer death, neither could the manhead alone overcome the same, He joined both together in one person that the imbecility of the one should suffer and be subject to death, which we had deserved, and the infinite and invincible power of the other, to wit, of the Godhead, should triumph and purchase to us life, liberty, and perpetual victory; and so we confess and most undoubtedly believe."

IX. *Of Christ's Death, Passion, and Burial.*—"Our Lord Jesus offered himself a voluntary sacrifice unto his Father for us. He suffered not only the cruel death of the cross, but also, for a season, the wrath of his Father, which sinners had deserved; but yet we avow that He remained the only well-beloved and blessed Son of his Father, even in the midst of His anguish and torment, which He suffered in body and soul to make the full satisfaction for the sins of the people: after the which we confess and avow that there remaineth no other sacrifice for sin, which if any affirm, we nothing doubt to avow that they are blasphemous against Christ's death, and the everlasting purgation and satisfaction purchased to us by the same."

X. *Of His Resurrection.*—"We undoubtedly believe, that insomuch as it was impossible that the dolours of death should retain in bondage the Author of life, our Lord Jesus, crucified, dead, and buried, who descended into hell, did rise again for our justification; and destroying of him who was the author of death, brought life again to us that were subject to death and to the bondage of the same."

XI. *Of His Ascension.*—"We nothing doubt but the self-same body which was born of the Virgin was crucified, dead, and buried, and which did rise again, did ascend into the heavens for the accomplishment of all things, where, in our names, and for our comfort, He hath received all power in heaven and earth, where He sitteth at the right hand of the Father, inaugurate in His kingdom, Advocate and only Mediator for us; which glory, honour, and prerogative He alone amongst the brethren shall possess till that all His enemies be made His footstool; as that we undoubtedly believe that they shall be in the final judgment; to the execution whereof we certainly believe that the same our Lord Jesus shall as visibly return as that He was seen to ascend; and then we firmly believe that the time of refreshing and restitution of all things shall come, insomuch that these that from the beginning have suffered violence, injury, and wrong for righteousness' sake shall inherit that blessed immortality promised from the beginning; but contrariwise, the stubborn, inobedient, cruel oppressors, filthy persons, idolaters, and all such sorts of unfaithful shall be cast into the dungeon of utter darkness, where the worm shall not die, neither yet shall their fire be extinguished: the remembrance of which day, and of the judgment to be executed in the same, is not only to us a bridle whereby our carnal lusts are restrained, but also such inestimable comfort, that neither may the threatening of worldly princes, neither yet the fear of temporal death and present danger move us to renounce and forsake that blessed society which we, the members, have with our Head and only Mediator, Christ Jesus; whom we confess and avow to be the Messias promised, the only Head of his Kirk, our just Lawgiver, our only High Priest, Advocate and Mediator. In which honours and offices, if men or angels presume to intrude themselves, we utterly detest and abhor them, as blasphemous to our Sovereign and Supreme Governor, Jesus Christ."

XII. *Of Faith in the Holy Ghost.*—The Holy Ghost is equal with the Father and with the Son; faith and assurance of faith are inspired by Him. Without Him we should for ever remain enemies to God, and ignorant of his Son Christ Jesus. "And so we confess that as God the Father created us when we were not, as his Son our Lord Jesus redeemed us when we were enemies to Him, so also do we confess that the Holy Ghost doth sanctify and regenerate us, without all respect of any merit proceeding from us, be it before or be it after our regeneration."

XIII. *Of the Cause of Good Works.*—The cause of good works is not our own free-will, but the Lord Jesus who, dwelling in our hearts by true faith, bringeth forth such works as God hath prepared for us to walk in.

XIV. *What Works are reputed Good before God.*—In the holy law which God hath given to man all such works as displease and offend his godly Majesty are forbidden, and all such as please Him and as He hath promised to reward are commanded. These good works are of two sorts, those which are done to the honour of God, the works of the first table of the law—Commandments I.-IV., and those which are done to the profit of our neighbours, the works of the second table—Commandments V.-X. The contrary is sin most odious. Therefore "good works we affirm to be these only that are done in faith and at God's commandment, who in His law hath expressed what the things be that please Him; and evil works, we affirm, not only these that expressly are done against God's commandment, but these also that in matters of religion and worshipping of God have no other assurance but the invention and opinion of men."

XV. *Of the Perfection of the Law and the Imperfection of Man.*— "The law of God is most just, most equal, most holy, and most perfect." Obeyed perfectly it would give life and bring man to eternal felicity; but our nature is so corrupt, so weak, and so imperfect, that we are never able to fulfil the works of the law in perfection. . . . "And therefore whosoever boast themselves of merits of their own works, or put their trust in the works of supererogation, boast themselves in that which is nought, and put their trust in damnable idolatry."

XVI. *Of the Church.*—The Church has existed from the beginning and shall exist to the end of the world. It is a company of men chosen of God, who rightly worship and embrace Him by true faith in Christ Jesus. Of this Church, which is the body and spouse of Christ Jesus, Christ is the only head. This Church is Catholic, that is, universal, because it containeth the elect of all ages and nations who have communion with God the Father and with His Son Christ Jesus, through the sanctification of His Holy Spirit. Out of this Church there is neither life nor eternal felicity. This Church is invisible, known only to God, who alone knoweth whom He hath chosen, and comprehendeth as well the elect that be departed, commonly called the Church triumphant, as those that yet live and fight against sin and Satan, and shall live hereafter.

XVII. *Of the Immortality of the Soul.*—The elect departed are in peace, and rest from their labours; the reprobate and unfaithful departed have anguish, torment, and pain that cannot be expressed.

XVIII. *Of the Notes whereby the True Church is discerned from the False; and who shall judge of the Doctrine.*—The notes by which the true Church is discerned from the false are neither antiquity, title usurped, lineal descent, place appointed, nor multitude of men approving an error, but are these three—(1) The true preaching of the Word of God; (2) the right administration of the sacraments of Christ Jesus; and (3) ecclesiastical discipline uprightly administered as God's Word prescribeth, whereby vice is repressed and virtue nourished.

The interpretation of the doctrine contained in those books of the Old and New Testaments which the ancients have reputed canonical, and in which all things necessary to be believed for salvation are expressed, appertaineth neither to any private nor public person, nor to any church, but appertaineth to the Spirit of God, by whom also the Scripture was written. The Spirit of God is the spirit of unity, and in nothing contrary to himself. "If then the interpretation, determination, or sentence of any doctor, church, or council be repugnant to the plain Word of God written in any other place of Scripture, it is a thing most certain, that there is not the true understanding and meaning of the Holy Ghost, although that councils and realms and nations have approved and received the same. For we dare not admit any interpretation which repugneth to any principal point of our faith, or to any other plain text of Scripture, or yet unto the rule of charity."

XIX. *Of the Authority of the Scriptures.*—The authority of the Scriptures is of God, and "such as allege the Scriptures to have no other authority but that which they have received from the Church are blasphemous against God and injurious to the true Church, which always heareth and obeyeth the voice of her own Spouse and Pastor, but taketh not upon her to be mistress over the same."

XX. *Of General Councils, of their Power, Authority, and Cause of their Convention.*—There should, on the one hand, be no rash condemnation of decisions made by godly men assembled together in general councils lawfully called; but, on the other hand, decisions given in the name of general councils are not to be received without due examination, but are to be proved by the plain Word of God. The causes why general councils meet are to confute heresies, and to give public confession of their faith by the authority of God's written Word, and not by any opinion or prerogative that they could not err. Another cause was for good policy and order in the Church. "Not that we think that any policy or an order in ceremonies can be appointed for all ages, times, and places: for as ceremonies, such as men have devised, are but temporal, so may and ought they to be changed when they rather foster superstition than edify the Church."

XXI. *Of the Sacraments.*—There are only two sacraments, Baptism and the Lord's Supper. They were instituted (1) to make a visible difference between God's people and those without the league; (2) to exercise the faith of His children; and (3) to seal in their hearts the assurance of His promise and of that most blessed union which the elect have with their head Christ Jesus. The vanity of those who affirm that sacraments are only naked and bare signs is utterly condemned, and the belief is strongly avowed that by baptism we are engrafted into Christ Jesus to be made partakers of His justice whereby our sins are covered and remitted; and also in the Supper, rightly used, Christ Jesus is so joined with us that He becometh true nourishment and food to our souls. There is no transubstantiation of the bread and wine into Christ's natural body and blood; but the Holy Spirit carrieth us by true faith above all things that are visible, carnal, and earthly, and makes us feed on the body and blood of Christ Jesus which was once broken and shed for us, which now is in heaven and appeareth in the presence of His Father for us. The Holy Spirit can never be divided from the right institution of the Lord Jesus, nor fail to bestow on the faithful the fruit of that mystical action. But all the benefits bestowed come of true faith apprehending Christ Jesus, who only maketh His sacraments effectual to us. "But this liberally and frankly we confess, that we make a distinction between Christ Jesus in his eternal substance and the elements in the sacramental signs; so that we will neither worship the signs in place of that which is signified by them, neither yet do we despise and interpret them as unprofitable and vain, but do use them with all reverence, examining ourselves diligently before that we do so."

XXII. *Of the Right Administration of the Sacraments.*—That the sacraments may be rightly administered two things are necessary— (1) That they be ministered by lawful ministers; (2) that they be administered in such elements and in such a manner as God hath appointed. Lawful ministers are defined as those who (1) are appointed to the preaching of the Word, (2) into whose mouth God hath put some sermon of exhortation, and (3) who are lawfully chosen thereto by some church.

That the sacraments may be rightly used, it is required that the end and cause why the sacraments were instituted should be understood and observed by minister and receivers. The end for which the priests of the Papistical Church say their mass, and the opinion which they hold regarding it—viz. that they as mediators between God and his Church do offer unto God the Father a sacrifice propitiatory for the sins of the quick and the dead, is a doctrine which, "as blasphemous to Jesus Christ, and making derogation to the sufficiency of His only sacrifice, once offered, for purgation of all those that shall be sanctified, we utterly abhor, detest, and renounce."

XXIII. *To whom Sacraments appertain.*—Baptism appertains as well to the infants of the faithful as unto them of age and discretion; but the Lord's Supper appertains to such only as are of the household of faith, and can examine themselves both in their faith and in their duty towards their neighbours.

XXIV. *Of the Civil Magistrate.*—Kingdoms are marked out and ordained by God. The power and authority of civil rulers are God's holy ordinance, and are appointed by Him for manifestation of His own glory, and for the profit and welfare of mankind. The rulers themselves are to be loved, honoured, and feared as the lieutenants of God. To them appertain chiefly and most principally the conservation and purgation of religion. They are appointed not only for civil policy, but also for maintenance of the true religion, and for the suppression of all idolatry and superstition whatsoever. They who resist the supreme power in these matters resist God's ordinance, and they who deny aid, counsel, and comfort to princes and rulers vigilantly executing their office, "deny their help, support, and counsel to God, who by the presence of His lieutenant doth crave it of them."

XXV. *Of the Gifts freely given to the Church.*—Such as with heart unfeignedly believe and with mouth boldly confess the Lord Jesus shall most assuredly receive in this life remission of sins, and in the general judgment resurrection of the flesh, "glory, honour, and immortality, to reign for ever in life everlasting with Christ Jesus: to whose glorified body all His elect shall be made like when He shall appear again in judgment, and shall render up the kingdom to God his Father, who then shall be, and ever shall remain in all things, God blessed for ever: to whom with the Son, and with the Holy Ghost, be all honour and glory for now and ever. So be it."

"Arise, O Lord, and let thine enemies be confounded; let them flee from thy presence that hate thy godly name. Give thy servants strength to speak thy word in boldness, and let all nations cleave to thy true knowledge. Amen."

These articles having been approved by Parliament virtually became the "Confession of Faith of the Church of Scotland," although they did not formally receive this title till they were ratified by the Parliament, and by Regent Murray, in 1567. The men who adopted the articles did not regard them as infallible or final. In the preface to them addressed by the Estates and inhabitants of Scotland professing the holy gospel of Christ Jesus to their own countrymen and all other realms and nations professing the same Lord Jesus with them, they protest "that if any man will note in this our Confession any article or sentence repugning to God's Holy Word, that it would please him of his gentleness, and for Christian charity's sake, admonish us of the same in writing; and we upon our honour and fidelity do promise unto him satisfaction from the mouth of God—that is, from his Holy Scriptures—or else reformation of that which he shall prove to be amiss."

This Confession of Faith, unlike that of Westminster in the following century, was not drawn up at the command of an English Parliament by English divines, aided by a few Scottish commissioners, and adopted by the Church and Parliament of Scotland for the purpose of securing uniformity of religion throughout the whole empire. It was written by Scotchmen as a confession of the faith which they themselves held and proclaimed to their fellow-countrymen, and which the compilers desired them to embrace and maintain as the truth of God. It is no dry catalogue of theological dogmas prepared by recluses of the study, but it exhibits the living faith of men who had jeoparded their lives in proclaiming and defending the truths which they taught, who had frequently seen their comrades fall around them in the stern conflict which had been fought, and who knew that the issue of the struggle in Scotland was still uncertain, and that they might any day be required to lay down their own lives for adherence to the Confession which they now made. Hence it is uniformly earnest, and even sometimes stern in its tone.

It is Calvinistic, or more properly speaking, it exhibits the truths of God's absolute sovereignty and free grace, of which Calvin indeed was an able advocate, but which in the middle ages had been maintained by the Thomists against the Scotists, and at a period still more remote by Augustine against Pelagius, and before Augustine had been taught by St. Paul, and before St. Paul by the Hebrew prophets. It was no new doctrine, but a very old doctrine which had become obscured, which was now brought to light. The tenets peculiar to it are stated in a comparatively mild form, milder indeed than the form in which they are presented in the Thirty-nine Articles of the Church of England, which were finally adjusted in 1561. The Scottish Confession assumes election as an undoubted truth, but views it almost entirely on its practical side as regards the privileges and duties of the elect. From the first transgression of man, which it regards as original sin, it deduces the corruption of human nature with its results; but on the imputation of Adam's first sin to his posterity, and of the consequences which have been inferred from that imputation, it is altogether silent. Salvation from first to last is the gift of God. Man's merit as a procuring cause is utterly excluded. Whatever personal merit man may possess has been wrought by God's Spirit freely bestowed. Regarding the incarnation it fully adopts the doctrine which had been definitely settled by the early councils—Christ

Jesus very God and very man, with two distinct natures, the divine and the human, in one person; and it enumerates, and with the early councils condemns, the heresies opposed to these tenets. On the mediatorial work of Christ it is clear and definite. Christ Jesus voluntarily offered himself as a sacrifice unto the Father for us; He suffered to make full satisfaction for the sins of the people; He presented himself in the presence of his Father's judgment as in our person; but it deems it sufficient to state the fact in language taken from Scripture, without seeking curiously to explain its nature or to define its limits. In connection with this subject, the Confession assigns a prominent place to two cognate truths—the Fatherhood of God and the Brotherhood of Jesus Christ—which were afterwards allowed to fall greatly into the background. The neglect of them contributed to that sternness which characterizes much of subsequent Scottish theology. It is only of late years that these truths have been restored to the place which was rightfully assigned to them by the first Scottish Confession. Another instance of the practical nature of the document, and of its avoidance of subtle questions, may be seen in the article concerning faith in the Holy Ghost. The Thirty-nine Articles and the Westminster Confession both enunciate as a matter of faith the procession of the Holy Spirit from the Father and from the Son—a tenet which was promulgated by a council of the Western Church held so late as 809, and which was one of the causes that led to the rending of the united church in twain. The Scottish Confession falls back on the decree of the Council of Nice, and merely acknowledges the Holy Ghost to be God equal with the Father and with his Son; of the procession of the Spirit it says nothing, but proceeds to speak of the work of the Spirit in sanctifying man.

It takes high ground on the nature of sacraments. They are not merely signs, they are also seals of benefits actually conferred. Baptism is not a symbolical act signifying that as water cleanseth the body, so the blood of Christ cleanseth the soul. "By baptism we are engrafted into Christ." In the Lord's Supper "believers eat the body and drink the blood of the Lord Jesus, so that He remaineth in them and they in Him." This view of the sacraments, which is strongly insisted upon, was greatly lost sight of in after years, and the lower view of the sacraments had an important influence in modifying the theology of these years. Edward Irving declares that the teaching of the Confession on this point revolutionized his mind. "It delivered me from the infidelity of evangelicalism, which denies any gift of God either in the work of Christ, or in the sacraments, or anywhere, until we experience it to be within ourselves; making God a mere promiser until we become receivers—a religion of moods, and not of purposes and facts; having its reality in the creature, its proposal of reality only in God."[1]

The Confession seeks to restore primitive Christianity, not so much by directly attacking Romanism as by enunciating truths before which Romanism falls. It states that Christ is the only Mediator between God and man—there is no need for any other and there is no other, therefore the work assigned to angels and saints as mediators and intercessors with God is a vain imagination: that Christ has, once for all, offered himself as the only sacrifice, and so propitiatory sacrifices offered in the mass disappear along with priest and altar: that no man, not even the holiest, fulfils God's law perfectly; that when he has done all he must confess that he is an unprofitable servant; therefore there is no such thing as an inexhaustible treasury of superfluous merits of saints committed to the custody of the Church, and so all pardons and indulgences based on draughts on that treasury vanish with the source from which they spring: and if the elect departed are in peace, and the reprobate and unfaithful departed are in everlasting woe, there is no place found for purgatory.

The men who composed the Confession proceeded on the fundamental principle, that all things necessary to be believed for the salvation of mankind are sufficiently expressed in Scripture, and that Scripture derives its authority not from the Church but from God; and, according to them, the interpretation of Scripture did not belong to any private or public person, nor even to any Church, but only to the Spirit of God speaking in the writings which He himself had in-

---

[1] Preface to "The Confessions of Faith," xcix. c.

spired. From this principle the Confession quite logically denies the right of Pope, Church, or Council to prescribe articles of faith which, on that authority, are to be received as necessary to salvation. All articles of faith must be subjected to the test of Scripture, and adopted or rejected according as they agree or disagree with that standard. Hence, although the articles on the personality of Christ are in strict accordance with the decisions of early councils, they are not received on the authority of these councils, but because they, having been tested by the Word, have been found to be in agreement therewith. By proceeding on this principle our Reformers are not at all touched by the objection, which is legitimately urged, against those who accept implicitly the decisions of councils down to a certain point, and there stop. It has quite properly been asked of such—Why stop there? Where do you draw the line? and Why do you draw the line at that particular point? Why do you accept as authoritative the decrees of those councils which determined the doctrine concerning the person of the Saviour and the procession of the Holy Ghost, and reject the decrees of those which determined the immaculate conception of the Virgin and the infallibility of the Pope in faith and morals? Whatever difficulty some may find in answering these questions, our Reformers would have had none. According to them all doctrine must be tried by the Word. If it abide that test it is to be received; if it do not, it is to be rejected.

There was another conclusion which legitimately flowed from the position assumed by our Reformers which they neither drew, nor dreamed of drawing—the principle of universal toleration. If neither public nor private person, if neither Church nor council, has an authoritative right to interpret Scripture, and enjoin men to receive that interpretation as being alone true, then men must be convinced in their own minds that an interpretation is actually the mind of the Spirit, before they can receive it as necessary to be believed. Internal conviction, not outward compulsion, must be the condition on which they shall receive the teaching as true. Our Reformers themselves were sincerely and thoroughly persuaded that the doctrines which they proclaimed were the

Divine truths taught in the Word, and therefore they rightly claimed full liberty to hold and teach these truths, and sternly repudiated the right of Pope or Church or civil magistrate to compel them to keep silence or embrace dogmas opposed to those truths which they deemed Divine; but when other men as conscientiously arrived, according to their light, at different conclusions, and sought to hold and teach the opinions which they were sincerely persuaded God was revealing to them in his Word, they were branded and punished as holders and disseminators of false doctrine. The sincere convictions of the Scottish Reformers were to constitute not only the creed which they themselves professed, but the creed which those who did not share in their convictions should, by pains and penalties, be compelled to profess. Here, at the first establishment of the Reformed faith, we find that characteristic which a Pope in the seventh and Cromwell in the seventeenth century found and deplored—the incapacity of Scottish theologians to think it possible that they might be mistaken in the conclusions at which they had deliberately and conscientiously arrived. These conclusions were the truth, and what was truth for them must be truth for others. In adopting this method of enforcing belief they contradicted the principle which they had clearly enunciated in the eighteenth article of the Confession, and while claiming the advantage of that principle for themselves they firmly denied it to others.

A ready means of enforcing this intolerance is provided by the article concerning the civil magistrate. This article is said to have been specially revised by Lethington and Winram. If the hand of the statesman may be seen in the first part, which treats of the authority of kings and the Divine source from which that authority is derived, the hand of Winram, who had taken part in sending George Wishart and Walter Milne to the stake for holding the opinions which he himself now supported, may be detected in the latter part, which treats of the power of the civil magistrate in relation to religion. At any rate the doctrine which, in its practical application, had led to the persecution of Reformers was now bodily adopted by the Reformers themselves, and used for the persecution of their opponents. The excuse has been found in the position of affairs and in the opinions then almost universally entertained. Whatever the validity of the excuse may be, there can be no question of the fact. There is not in the Confession the faintest indication of the dogma that the civil magistrate, as such, has nothing to do with religion; but on the contrary it states plainly that it is chiefly and principally his duty to provide for the preservation and reformation of religion, and for the suppression of all idolatry and superstition. In countries acknowledging the Roman Catholic faith the task assigned to the civil magistrate was easy and simple. He had an infallible authority to guide him in deciding between the true and the false. The Church defined for him what was verity and what was falsehood; the tribunals of the Church pointed out to him the specific individuals who cherished heretical opinions, and all that he had to do was to execute judgment on the persons so specified. According to the Scottish Confession the mind of the Spirit was not to be ascertained by the mere authority of any man or of any church, but was to be revealed to men by the Spirit, through patient and prayerful investigation of the Word of God. Accepting this principle, the civil magistrate had a much more difficult task assigned to him in suppressing error than his brother magistrate had in those lands where an infallible church authoritatively indicated to him the error which he must extirpate. If a difference of opinion should arise between the Scottish civil magistrate and the Scottish Church regarding truth and error, the Confession in reality provided no umpire to decide between them. It has been asserted, indeed, that means were provided, and that the means were very simple. "Presbyterians do not ask anything of civil rulers but what they undertake to prove that Scripture requires of them, and what they are therefore bound to do, not as subordinate to the Church, but as subordinate to God's Word."[1] This is all very well when the civil ruler acknowledges the validity of the proof, but when the validity is denied, and the civil ruler believes and maintains that Scripture does not require him to do that which Presbyterians ask him to perform, the problem remains unsolved. In the Scottish Parliament of 1560 no such difficulty presented itself. The truth to be main-

---

[1] Cunningham's "Historical Theology," i. 410.

tained was the Confession which they had adopted; the idolatry and superstition to be suppressed were the doctrines and practices opposed to the Confession. So far all was easy for the civil magistrate; but the principles whereby the early Scottish Reformers claimed the right of private judgment for themselves but denied it to others unless it led to their conclusions—claimed supremacy for their own opinions and refused even toleration for opinions differing from theirs—and enforced conformity to their own views by the aid of the civil magistrate—were in after years adopted and carried into execution by whatever party secured the ascendency, and produced disastrous results in the history of the Church and the nation.

There is a golden rule for the interpretation of Scripture given in the Confession, attention to which would have made a great difference in Scottish history and theology. It does not find a place in the canons of ordinary biblical criticism, but it deserves to have a foremost place in the higher, or even the highest, department of that bewildering science—WHATEVER INTERPRETATION OF SCRIPTURE OPPOSETH THE RULE OF CHARITY SHOULD BE REJECTED AS FALSE. The application of this rule would now make havoc of many opinions and practices, but might not on that account be an unmixed evil. The Scottish Reformation itself destroyed many long-cherished and deeply-rooted religious beliefs and practices, but it gave in their stead beliefs and practices purer and more ennobling.

DOCTRINE OF THE CHURCH UNDER THE SCOTTISH CONFESSION, 1560-1617.

During the period between the adoption of the twenty-five articles as the Confession of the Faith of the Church of Scotland, and the approval, in 1647, of the Westminster Confession as "a common Confession of Faith for the three kingdoms," Presbytery and Prelacy were, with varying success, struggling for mastery; but unless when matters of doctrine were imported into the contest, we are not here concerned with that dispute. Throughout all those years the Confession adopted in 1560 remained unaltered, never having been affected by the changes of church government. It was on that Confession that the theology of Scotland was moulded. For three generations it was the standard for religious belief and teaching, and the Westminster Confession was adopted as being "in nothing contrary to the received doctrine of this Kirk."[1] In point of fact, it was not until the Presbyterian Church was re-established after the Revolution that the Westminster Confession was legally recognized as the only public and avowed Confession of the Church of Scotland. It was under the old Scottish Confession that Scottish theology was nurtured and grew to maturity.

The Reformation in Scotland had been conducted on the principle of taking Scripture as the only rule in doctrine and worship; and an opportunity soon occurred of showing how adherence to this principle led them to disapprove of some practices in a Church with which they were very closely connected. The second Helvetic Confession was published in 1566, and was immediately adopted by the Reformed Churches of Switzerland, Germany, and France. On its completion a copy was sent to some of the Scottish ministers in order to ascertain how far the Scottish Church agreed with the Reformed Churches in doctrine. The superintendents and a number of the most eminent ministers met in St. Andrews, and after due examination of the document, declared that they agreed on every point, save one, with the Confession which had been submitted to them. The one point on which they differed was with regard to festivals. The Helvetic Confession sanctioned the observance of Christmas, the Feast of Circumcision, Good Friday, Easter, Ascension, and Whitsunday. The observance of these festivals was repudiated by the Church of Scotland, on the ground that it had no warrant in Scripture. "For," said they, "we dare not religiously observe any other feast day than what the Divine oracles have prescribed."

The ground on which the Church disapproved of the observance of festivals should be particularly noticed. The reason assigned for its procedure in this instance guided its decisions in many other cases. There were many reasons why the Scottish Church should comply with the practices of the other Reformed Churches. The observance of the festivals

[1] Act of Assembly approving the Confession of Faith, 1647.

was expedient in itself, was practised by churches distinguished for their purity, and could be traced back to a remote antiquity; but all these reasons were of no avail. Experience had shown that some religious observances deemed expedient had ended in debasing Divine worship, and transforming it into idolatry; if other churches adopted measures not sanctioned by Scripture, there was all the more need for the Scottish Church to show an example of Scriptural purity; if antiquity was appealed to in defence of the practice, a still more remote antiquity could be appealed to when inspired apostles ruled the Church and such festivals were unknown. That decision was based on a doctrine which gives the key to much of the subsequent history of the Church—that neither expediency, nor the example of others, nor ancient practice, but Scripture warrant, is to be the only rule. It is this doctrine which explains the tenacity with which religious opinions and practices were maintained, and the dauntless courage and unflinching firmness with which measures that seemed to imperil it were resisted.

In the Assembly of 1580 the application of the principle which had led to the rejection of festivals as being mere human inventions, resulted in a unanimous finding that diocesan Episcopacy "had no warrant in Scripture, but had been introduced into the Church by the folly and corruption of man's invention." It was therefore discarded, and presbyterian parity was declared to be of Divine right. This was a development of doctrine. Hitherto the Church, though preferring Presbytery, had not declared Episcopacy to be unscriptural. That step was now taken. The leader in the movement was Andrew Melville. A presbyterian by conviction, he was from his intimate knowledge of the New Testament in the original—a rare accomplishment in Scotland at that time—from his acquaintance with patristic literature, and from his familiarity with the working of the presbyterian system in the churches of France and Switzerland, able to bring from all these sources arguments against Episcopacy which to those who heard them proved conclusive. He argued that in the New Testament the terms bishop and presbyter denoted the same individual—the presbyter was there a bishop, and the bishop was a presbyter. He adduced the authority of the early fathers to show that the superiority of bishops over presbyters originated not by Divine right, but by human appointment, and maintained that, in practice, presbyterian parity, which had been instituted by God, produced far more beneficial results than episcopal supremacy, which had been instituted by man. The arguments prevailed, and Episcopacy was condemned "as unlawful in itself, and as having neither foundation, ground, nor warrant in the Word of God." No one was to be a bishop of bishops, but every bishop was to be pastor of his own flock.

It must be acknowledged that the cause of diocesan Episcopacy in Protestant Scotland suffered greatly from the manner in which it was introduced, and from the grounds on which it was chiefly defended. The reason assigned for its introduction was not the preservation of three orders in the ministry, but the preservation of three orders in parliament. It was founded on political expediency, and not on Divine authority. Behind political expediency worked the selfish interests of statesmen. The bishoprics which became vacant by the death or forfeiture of the Roman Catholic incumbents were seized by nobles who could not, indeed, be bishops themselves, but who appointed ministers to enjoy the empty title, to draw the revenues of the see, and hand the greater portion over to their patrons. It was impossible that any enthusiasm could be aroused in defence of such an order, save among those who, from selfish motives, were interested in its preservation. On the other hand, there was the firm conviction that Presbyterian parity was taught in Scripture, while the supremacy of bishops was destitute of any such support. It was that belief which led Scotsmen to fight and to suffer in the cause which they believed to be the cause of God. A mere persuasion that Presbytery was better adapted than Episcopacy to the Scottish character, that it was to be preferred because the people had become accustomed to it, could never have sustained them in undertaking and prosecuting the contest, which at length they conducted to a successful issue. They were bold in action and firm in endurance because they believed that they were acting and suffering for God's own ordinance. Presbytery and Episcopacy are still contending, but there is a remarkable change in the weapons of attack and defence generally employed on each side. Episcopalians in Scotland no longer rest their cause on grounds of expediency, but on the Divine right of Episcopacy; many Presbyterians abandon entirely the claim of Divine right for Presbytery, and urge for it only arguments founded on expediency. The heavy artillery has recently, in many cases, been abandoned by the one party, while it has been seized and vigorously plied by the other. The result of this change remains to be seen. One thing is certain: it was not the belief that Presbytery was expedient for Scotland on grounds of custom or prejudice that endured the fight and gained the victory in former days, but the sincere belief that, taking the Word of God as the only rule, Episcopacy had no warrant, and Presbyterian parity was clearly enjoined. That principle was first formally recognized by the Assembly of 1580.

Under the guidance of Melville a marked development was also made in the doctrine regarding the Church, and especially regarding the ecclesiastical power of its office-bearers. Dr. Grub, to whom every student of Scottish ecclesiastical history owes a deep debt of gratitude, has perhaps viewed the doctrine regarding the Church laid down in the Confession and First Book of Discipline through a medium coloured by his own beliefs when he says—"The Church itself was held to exist, not in any virtue of any life of its own derived from its Lord through the apostles, but in consequence of the belief of its members in the system of doctrine laid down in the Scriptures. . . . All ecclesiastical power proceeded from the people; and from them directly, not from any Divine commission or descent, the office-bearers of the Church derived their authority."[1] The Confession clearly stated that the Catholic Church consisted of men chosen of God who rightly worshipped and embraced Him; that it existed not by the faith of its members in a system of doctrine, but by their "true faith in Christ Jesus, who is the only head of the same Church." That all ecclesiastical power proceeds from the people is the doctrine on which Independency is founded. Presbytery derives ecclesiastical

[1] "Ecclesiastical History of Scotland," vol. ii. pp. 98, 99.

power from a totally different source, and that source is explicitly declared in the Second Book of Discipline. According to that document, God the Father has through the Mediator Jesus Christ given ecclesiastical power to his Church; and this power is to be exercised by those "unto whom the spiritual government of the Church by lawful calling is committed;" or, as otherwise stated, "it is given immediately to the office-bearers, by whom it is exercised to the good of the whole body." Hence Christ is the only king in His Church, and it is His office to rule by the ministry of men duly appointed according to the Word. Such is the Presbyterian doctrine regarding the source and exercise of ecclesiastical power. The doctrine thus formulated by Melville and approved by the Church was in after years sometimes obscured and almost lost sight of, and the Church regarded as little more than a benevolent institution. Higher and more correct views again prevail; and where the Church is regarded as a living body, in which Christ rules by the ministry of men duly appointed, and by the administration of sacraments and ordinances, it is again regarded in that light in which it was at the first presented by Andrew Melville.

In the same year in which the Assembly adopted the resolution against Episcopacy, Scotland was agitated by a Popish scare. A Confession of Faith was drawn up and subscribed by the king and his household, and nine years afterwards was, at the request of the Assembly, ordered by the council to be subscribed by all subjects.[1] It was finally incorporated into the National Covenant of 1638, of which it forms the first part. It concerns us here only in so far as it shows the firm adherence of the people to the Confession of the Scottish Church, and their resolve to maintain it at all hazards. That Confession, as we saw, was mainly positive; it exhibited doctrines from the acceptance of which the rejection of the contrary Roman Catholic doctrines naturally followed. This Confession was mainly negative; it contained a long enumeration of erroneous doctrines and practices of "Papistry," which the subscribers declared they abhorred and detested. It was an evidence of

---

[1] It is called the King's Confession, as having been drawn up at first for the king and his household; Craig's Confession, as having been composed by John Craig; and the Negative Confession, as containing a long list of tenets which were denied.

zeal for the Reformed faith, and of bitter antagonism to the faith which it had supplanted.

When the General Assembly met in Aberdeen in 1616, James had for thirteen years been seated on the English throne, and had in some measure succeeded in his long-cherished project of bringing the Church of Scotland into conformity with that of England. Episcopal government had been restored, but much still remained to be accomplished. His object was to establish uniformity, or failing that, as close an agreement as possible between the two kingdoms in doctrine, worship, and discipline. For this end there were needed a new Confession of Faith, a new liturgy, and new canons. The new Confession was duly prepared, submitted to the Assembly, and approved. It is a document which possessed no authority, as it was never adopted as the Confession of the Church, but it is of importance as indicating the theological views of the period, and the modifications or development of doctrine which had taken place since 1560. The Confession itself had been drawn up by John Hall and John Adamson, for the purpose of superseding the old Confession. It was submitted to an Assembly held in Aberdeen, the stronghold of Episcopacy, and presided over by Spotswood, archbishop of St. Andrews, and which, as Calderwood tells us, "was decored with silks and satins" by a number of lords and barons. It was a time when a reaction against the doctrines of Calvin had begun, especially in Holland, and the influence of the new Dutch school of theology was felt in Scotland. The Synod of Dort did not meet till two years after the Aberdeen Assembly, but the opinions of Arminius, which were condemned by that synod, had already obtained wide currency. It might be thought therefore that a new Confession, introduced under such auspices and for such an end, would present the doctrines of Christianity at least in a more modified form than the old one. On the contrary the new was more rigidly orthodox. A strict Calvinist might truthfully describe it as being clearer and fuller on the fundamental points of the system.

There is a fuller orthodox statement of the doctrine of the Trinity. The eternal generation of the Son, and the procession of the Holy Spirit from the Father and the Son, are now affirmed. The decrees of God are absolute and from all eternity. "Before the foundation of the world, God according to the good pleasure of His will did predestinate and elect in Christ some men and angels unto eternal felicity, and others He did appoint for eternal condemnation, to the praise and glory of His justice." Here, not only the men predestinated to eternal life, but the angels also, are elected in Christ, which is an extension of the work of the Saviour unknown to the Scottish and the Westminster Confessions. All things were not only created by God, but created out of nothing. The story of the fallen angels which Milton, nearly half a century afterwards, told in "Paradise Lost," is anticipated and tersely and forcibly expressed. "Some of the angels of their own free motive sinned against God, left their original, forsook their habitation, and abode not in the truth, and thereby became damned devils." There is not only election mentioned, but its counterpart, reprobation; and reprobation is not merely a passing over of some, but an absolute appointment to eternal condemnation. Redemption is particular, limited to the elect alone, who in time are redeemed and restored, not of themselves or of their works, but only of the mercy of God through faith in Jesus Christ. The distinction between the active and the passive obedience of Christ is now recognized. The doctrine of substitution, that Christ fulfilled the law and suffered the penalty of the elect's sin in their room, is more clearly stated; the offices of Christ as prophet, priest, and king are specified and explained; and the imputation of Christ's righteousness to the believer is distinctly affirmed as an article of faith.

In this Confession there is an advance along the whole line, and it is an advance in strict Calvinistic orthodoxy. Opinions which could have been freely held under the Scottish Confession could not have been maintained under that of Aberdeen. It was designed to promote the closer union of the Scottish with the English Church—an object which had been diligently prosecuted by King James since his accession to the English throne, and which had been in some part already accomplished. It was discovered that the time had not yet come to effect conformity in creed, ritual, and discipline, and therefore the movement in its full compass was temporarily arrested. Five articles, seemingly concerning ritual alone, were sent down by the king to the Scottish bishops, with the royal command that they should be immediately enforced. The new Confession was therefore dropped, and was never again resuscitated; but it remains as an old neglected stone pillar on which there can still be read, inscribed in clear characters, the faith then professed, and is an unimpeachable witness to the significant fact that though the government of the Church had been changed from Presbytery to Episcopacy, the faith of the Church changed only in the direction of a narrower and stricter orthodoxy.

In requiring the adoption of the Five Articles James had imposed a most unwelcome task upon the Scottish bishops. They knew that the articles would arouse bitter controversy and strong opposition. The king was peremptory. He maintained that, as they concerned rites and ceremonies alone, and in no wise affected doctrine, he could of his own authority enforce them upon the Church, and that it was of his own good pleasure that he asked the concurrence of bishops or ministers. When the General Assembly met at Perth in August, 1618, a letter from the king was read in which he demanded obedience to his will. "We will content ourselves with nothing but with a simple and direct acceptation of these articles." Obedience to the royal wish was carried by a majority, and the Assembly sanctioned the articles proposed, viz.—

1. That the communion should be received kneeling.
2. That in case of necessity the communion might be administered in private houses.
3. That in case of necessity baptism might be administered in private houses.
4. That children on reaching eight years of age should be confirmed by the bishop.
5. That Christmas, Good Friday, Easter Monday, Ascension Day, and Whitsunday should be observed as holy days.

The sanctioning of these articles immediately gave rise to three parties in Scotland. Some regarded them as superstitious, idolatrous, and antichristian; others with equal zeal maintained that obedience to the will of the king and the resolution of the Assembly should be enforced upon all; and a third party, while not objecting to the articles themselves, disapproved of the manner in which they had been enacted, and viewed with grief the means employed to compel obedience. Dr. George Garden, himself a keen Episcopalian, looking back on that time through a vista of eighty years, notices the fact that the five articles of Perth were causing as general and bitter a controversy in Scotland as the five articles of Arminius were at the same time producing in Holland, and attributes the simultaneous commotion raised in each country to a cunning device of Satan, whereby he sought to overthrow religion itself by involving men in violent disputes regarding matters of very slight importance.[1] The opinion of the worthy episcopalian divine was not that of the men who resisted the ceremonies imposed on the Church in obedience to the will of the king. They believed that in their resistance they were maintaining the cause of truth against error, and it is this belief which brings the controversy within the range of doctrine.

The rite of confirmation was not insisted upon, and as it was not practised it did not form a prominent subject of disputation. When opposed, the opposition was based mainly on the ground that confirmation by the bishop implied that the bishop was superior to the presbyter, and could, in his official capacity, be the means of conferring a grace which the inferior presbyter was unable to bestow. This assumption, they maintained, was opposed to the teaching of the New Testament, in which bishop and presbyter were not two different persons, but two different appellations for one and the same person. Private communion and private baptism were optional, and so did not bulk largely in the controversy. The administration of the sacrament of the Lord's supper to the sick and infirm and to prisoners—for that practically was all that was aimed at—was acknowledged to be a means of grace, but was opposed on the ground that such a practice would encourage belief in the dogma that participation in the sacrament was necessary for salvation. For a like reason private baptism was opposed. It was regarded as fostering a belief in the absolute necessity

---

[1] Forbesii Opera, tom. i. p. 12, "Vita Forbesii."

of the ordinance, and in the cruel judgment of the Romish Church against infants who had died unbaptized. The arguments against these practices were confessedly weak. They were directed, not against the practices themselves, but against the abuses to which it was thought they might lead. In taking this position the opponents of these two articles stood alone. The authority of Calvin and other eminent Reformers, whose antagonism to the specified errors of Rome and to aught that was calculated to foster them was indisputable, was in vain adduced against them. The position, though weakly, was obstinately defended.

In resisting the observance of Christmas and the other festivals they stood on firmer ground. Whatever opinion might be entertained regarding the observance of them in itself, there could be no doubt that it was opposed to the belief and uniform practice of the Scottish Church. The question was decided when the Helvetic Confession had been, in 1566, presented to the Scottish Reformers for approval. That Confession was approved of in all respects, save in the matter of holy-days. These were rejected as having no warrant in the word of God, and from the position then assumed the Church had not up to this time ever withdrawn. If the premiss be granted, the conclusion necessarily flows; if no festivals are to be observed by the Church other than those prescribed in Scripture, then the observance of Christmas, Easter, and the others is inadmissible.

The contest, however, regarding these points was a mere affair of outposts; the fortress around which the main battle surged was kneeling at the Communion. This was regarded as an act of worship, and assuming this view its opponents were able to deliver a strong attack against it. When the Roman Catholic kneels in receiving the host, he kneels before his Saviour, who, he verily believes, is really present in the sacrament. The Scottish Protestants, who were now for the first time commanded to kneel, rejected the doctrine of the real presence. The elements, according to them, were, after the words of institution had been pronounced by the officiating minister, as really bread and wine as they had been before. Kneeling before mere bread and wine was therefore an act of worship rendered to a creature, and thus was idolatry. It was in vain urged on the other side that no one could duly partake of the Lord's Supper who did not while partaking adore the Lord Jesus, and that no posture was better suited for adoration than the posture of kneeling.[1] The essence of the controversy is pithily given in Calderwood's account of the disputation between Thomas Hogg, minister at Dysart, and Dr. Lyndsay, minister at Dundee, and shortly afterwards Bishop of Brechin, in the presence of the Archbishop of St. Andrews and several prelates and clergymen. Lyndsay adduced the case of two men who had communicated, the one sitting and the other kneeling. He who had communicated kneeling asked the other if he had kept his bonnet on at the Lord's table, and on being answered in the negative, argued that kneeling was no more an act of worship than uncovering the head. Hogg allowed that all reverence was due to the celebration of the sacrament, and therefore uncovering the head, which was only an act of reverence, was proper and becoming; but kneeling was a gesture of Divine worship, and should be rendered to God alone, and if used at the Lord's table was "a parting of God's honour betwixt God himself and the sacramental elements."[2] The issue put before the people was, broadly stated, obedience to King Jesus or obedience to King James: our earthly king has commanded the observance of these ceremonies; our heavenly King, the only head of the Church, has forbidden it—which of the two is to be obeyed? When a question is thus represented, and is submitted in this form to the decision of the Scottish people, there can never be any doubt as to the answer.

Unfortunately the conduct of James himself made it easy to submit the question to the nation in that form. The prelates did not wish the articles; it was the king who proposed them and insisted upon their adoption. In his letter to the Perth Assembly, and in the manner in which the question was there put to the vote, the will of the king was supreme. Lyndsay and Calderwood differ as to the exact terms in which

---

[1] "Forbesii Eirenicon," p. 380.
[2] Calderwood, anno 1619. Lyndsay's illustration of uncovering the head must have been popular with his party, as we find it referred to by Dr. John Forbes in his "Eirenicon," published in 1627.

the question was finally put, but there can be no doubt that it was not, "Are those articles right in themselves and expedient at the present time?" but actually, if not verbally, "Whether will ye consent to these articles or disobey the king?" The means were thus provided for raising higher questions than James had contemplated, and of reminding the people that there was One who was sole King in Zion, whose mandates they must obey, even should they in doing so disobey the behests of an earthly monarch.

CATECHISMS IN COMMON USE FROM THE REFORMATION TO THE INTRODUCTION OF THE WESTMINSTER LARGER AND SHORTER CATECHISMS IN 1648.

From the time that the Reformation obtained a permanent footing in Scotland the church had paid careful attention to the catechetical instruction of the people, and especially of the young, in the doctrines of the Christian faith; and it now remains to take a glance at the manuals commonly used. The most important of those which received the sanction of the Church was Calvin's "Catechism of the Christian Religion." It had been published at Geneva in 1556, the year in which Knox returned to that city, and must have been well known to him while he ministered there to the English congregation. An English translation was soon published. The First Book of Discipline enacted that every Sunday afternoon the children were to be publicly examined by the minister in this catechism in the audience of the people. It was to be gone through consecutively, and a portion was appointed for each Sunday. The minister was enjoined to explain to the people the questions proposed as well as the answers given, and to use all diligence to make them understand the doctrine which was taught. It begins with an exposition of the Christian faith on the lines laid down in the apostles' creed, of man's duty as summarized in the ten commandments, of the nature, manner, ground, and substance of prayer, of the Lord's prayer, and of the means of grace, which are the Word and the sacraments of baptism and the Lord's supper. The catechism, explained as the ministers were enjoined to do, was an invaluable means of making the people well acquainted with the doctrines contained in the Confession, and the Scriptural grounds on which these doctrines rested.

The Palatine or Heidelberg Catechism was also used in Scotland. It owed its origin to the same movement that had produced the Helvetic Confession. The Palatinate had, in the year in which Scotland adopted the Reformed faith, gone over from the Lutheran to the Calvinistic Church. The Elector Frederick III., under whom the change took place, caused a catechism to be prepared for the use of the schools in the Palatinate. It was received with great favour by all the Reformed churches, and passed soon into general use. An English version was printed in 1591 for the use of Scotland. In the Scottish Church it took much the same position with regard to Calvin's Catechism that the Helvetic Confession occupied with regard to the Scottish Confession. Its use was never formally authorized by an Assembly, but was favourably regarded. It was, like Calvin's Catechism, taught from beginning to end in the course of a year, a portion being assigned for each Sunday. The order followed is the same, the instruction being based on the apostles' creed, the ten commandments, and the Lord's prayer. Two subjects, the righteousness of faith and the assurance of faith, are explicitly and clearly taught in the sense which was condemned as heterodox in subsequent controversies.

In order that the reader might gain his modest annual stipend of forty merks he was expected, besides reading the Scriptures and common prayers in church, to teach the children of the parish in school. As his guide in their religious instruction a very brief manual was composed. It contains sixteen questions and answers, and must, when used, have been supplemented by the oral teaching of the minister, who was also required to take part in the instruction of the young. It was known as "the Little Catechism," and continued in use till 1592, when it was superseded by Craig's Catechism. Craig had, while minister at Aberdeen, drawn up a pretty full summary of Calvin's Catechism, which was eventually published at Edinburgh in 1581. Ten years after its publication the Assembly desired him to condense it into shorter compass. This was done, and in the following year the abridgment was laid before the Assembly, was approved, and appointed to be used in place of the Little Catechism. It continued to be the authorized manual of religious instruction for the young until it was superseded by the Shorter Catechism. It was specially designed to serve as "ane forme of examination before the Communion," and no better manual for instructing young communicants has been published since. The Shorter Catechism was substituted for it, not from any dissatisfaction with its teaching, but in order to have one and the same form for the three kingdoms. The most ardent admirer of the Shorter Catechism may truthfully acknowledge that, for the instruction of the young, Craig's was in some respects superior, and assent to the words of Edward Irving: "The Shorter Catechism is systematic, Craig's Catechism is scriptural and simple; the Shorter Catechism is intellectual, Craig's Catechism is vital."[1]

THEOLOGICAL WRITERS.

The theology of the times under consideration having been seen as exhibited in authorized Confessions and Catechisms, it now remains to glance at it as exhibited in the writings of the theologians of the period. In the early years of the Reformation the most prominent men are Knox, Craig, and Melville. Knox was a man whose theological opinions found expression not so much in books as in actions. His great theological work is the Scottish Reformation itself. His views on Christian doctrine, and on the manner in which he thought these views should be taught to a nation, are recorded in the Scottish Confession and the First Book of Discipline. The results of his teachings were the moulding of modern Scotland, and the impressing of its distinctive characteristics on Scottish Presbyterianism;

---

[1] Preface to "Confessions of Faith," p. cxxvii. In addition to the catechisms in English, there were also Latin versions of the Little and of the Heidelberg Catechisms, and others, for the use of grammar schools. The catechisms of the Scottish Reformation have been collected and edited by Dr. Horatius Bonar. The catechisms enumerated must have formed but a small proportion of those actually in use. Then, as now, every minister seemed to think himself at liberty to draw up a manual for young communicants for his own congregation. In his sermon preached before Charles I. on his visit to Scotland in 1633, Dr. Forbes complains that almost every minister uses one of his own, composed according to his own whims and beliefs, and laments that Scotland in his day presented a scene like that in Judah in the days of Jeremiah, when the prophet said, "According to the number of thy cities are thy gods, O Judah;" for in the Scotland of his days, he says, there were almost as many catechisms as parishes.

and though not now gratefully acknowledged, they are still to be descried in a Communion which, though exclusively episcopal, cannot obliterate all traces of having proceeded from "the Reformed Church of Scotland." Knox's great theological work stands conspicuous, and can still be known and read by all men. Besides performing that work, he wrote a purely theological treatise which is not by any means so well known. It is on predestination, a subject which has always bulked largely in Scottish theology. Dr. M'Crie, than whom there could be no more competent judge, speaks of it as being in his day rare and seen by few. Having been republished, it is no longer rare, but they are few in number who have not been content to believe M'Crie's word, that "it is written with perspicuity, and discovers his controversial acuteness with becoming caution in handling that delicate question."[1]

John Craig had a romantic history. Left an orphan by the death of his father on Flodden field, he joined the Dominicans, and for many years lived as a monk of that order in Italian monasteries. He became a convert to the Reformed faith, and after many perilous adventures, some of which have evidently lost nothing in the frequent telling, he reached Scotland and joined the Reformers. At first he preached in Latin, having so far forgotten his native tongue through his long residence abroad that he was unable to use it readily. He soon, however, became an eloquent preacher in the Scottish language, and after a brief ministry in Aberdeen became colleague to John Knox in Edinburgh. His doctrinal views are lucidly set forth in the Negative Confession and his two catechisms. The former supplies ample evidence of his detestation of the Romish doctrines in which he had been trained, and of the sincerity of his belief in the faith to which he had become a convert; while the latter bears as ample testimony to his soundness and orthodoxy. One thing learned among the Dominicans he had not forgotten. That order afforded, and still affords, the best educationists. Craig, while a monk at Bologna, had been the teacher of the novitiates. The fruits of his training and experience as a teacher in the monastery are seen in the manuals which he composed for the use of the Scottish Reformed

[1] M'Crie's Works, i. 299.

Church. The questions and answers are uniformly clear, short, and pointed.

The important work accomplished by Andrew Melville does not fall to be considered here. With the exception of a short Commentary on the Epistle to the Romans, he wrote no treatise of a purely theological character. The result of his labours is the form which he impressed on the church government of Scotland. In getting the Church to acknowledge that presbyterian parity was explicitly taught in the Word, he may be regarded as having added a new article to its creed, but otherwise he did little directly to influence theological opinion.

The doctrines which had now taken root in Scotland began to show their vitality by growth and development. Up till the time when the Perth Articles were passed, the most marked movement was in the direction of a much more pronounced Calvinism than was contained in the authorized standards of the Church. There were two men especially who contributed much to produce this result — Robert Rollock, principal of Edinburgh University from 1583 to 1599; and Robert Boyd, principal of Glasgow University from 1614 to 1622. Besides these two, William Cowper, minister at Perth, and afterwards bishop of Galloway, deserves to be mentioned. He was one of the ablest preachers of the time, and by his sermons and writings did much to further the movement. He was long a zealous champion of the Presbyterian cause. He got, as he himself declared, new light, and soon after obtained preferment to the see of Galloway. The Presbyterians never forgave his desertion of their cause, and the Episcopalians never forgot his former zeal on behalf of the party which he had abandoned. Calderwood speaks of him with virulence, and Spotswood with qualified praise. His published works merited another fate than the oblivion into which they have fallen.

Subjects which had been left undetermined, and others which had not been mentioned in Confession or Catechisms, were taken up, considered (often at great length and with much learning), and dogmatically settled in accordance with the narrowest form of Calvinism. Such questions as the absolute decrees of God —original sin, and how it was propagated—how it was that God invited to repentance those who by an eternal and irrevocable decree had been doomed to destruction—the extent of the atonement: was it for all or exclusively for the elect? with many others, were discussed and determined in this manner. This movement was so successful and so general that one of its results was apparent in a fact which has already come under our notice—namely, that the proposed Aberdeen Confession of 1616 was much narrower than the authorized Confession of 1560. The movement had resulted in a stricter and sterner Calvinism.

The reaction then came, and continued to show its vitality and power till it was crushed in 1638. One of the most influential pioneers of the movement was John Cameron, who in 1622 succeeded Boyd as principal of Glasgow University. Cameron was a native of Glasgow, studied there at the university, and was a first-year's student when Boyd was in his fourth year. After a brilliant career at college, he left in 1600 for France, received a travelling scholarship from the church at Bordeaux, studied at various universities, was pastor of the church at Heidelberg, professor of theology at Saumur, and on returning to his native country was appointed to be Boyd's successor. His stature was of middle height, his countenance open and pleasant, his eyes bright and expressive, his temper, as was natural to a Celt, fiery—readily roused and speedily appeased. He was a thorough hater of all sham and deceit. Such is the portrait drawn of him by a contemporary.[1] His reputation on the Continent was exceedingly high; in England bishops all pronounced him to be "the most learned man Scotland had ever produced." His published works do not give an adequate idea of what he really was. He hated writing and loved talking. Much that is published was never written by him, but compiled from notes taken of his *extempore* lectures by students and others. He did not stay in Glasgow above a year, but the presence of such a man, even for that brief period, gave an impetus to fresh theological investigation. A proof of the importance attached to his opinions is seen in the fact that, nearly a century afterwards, Wodrow in his "Life of Cameron" deemed it necessary to devote a space to their refutation.

The reaction against strict Calvinism was especially con-

---

[1] Johannis Cameronis Icon. præf. Operum, 3.

cerned with two subjects. The first was regarding the decree of God in electing from all eternity some to everlasting life. The question arose, Was this decree absolute or conditional? If God in electing from all eternity some men to everlasting life regarded them as being, like others, utterly corrupt and dead in trespasses and sins, their election to eternal life was absolute, proceeding from God's sovereign pleasure alone. If, on the other hand, God in electing from all eternity some to everlasting life regarded them as believing in Christ, then election to eternal life was conditional. That election was absolute was the current view of the extreme Calvinists; that election was conditional was the view of Cameron. He maintained that God decreed first to make men believers, and then to save those who believed. These two decrees were special, having respect to individual persons, but were made in a certain order; for God regarded man as believing before He regarded him as destined to be saved. Therefore in the decree faith went before salvation—or in other words, God first regarded man as a believer, and then predestined him to everlasting life.[1] In this manner the attack was made on one of the positions held by the Calvinists.

The second subject regarded the extent of the atonement. Did Christ die for the elect only, or did he die for all mankind? The former was the Calvinistic doctrine, the latter the doctrine taught by Cameron. He granted, indeed, that in one sense Christ might be said to have died for believers only, inasmuch as they alone become members of His body through faith; but on the other hand he said that Christ had died for all, had redeemed all, and that redemption was offered to all on the condition of faith in Him. It was in consequence of the want of faith that men were not sharers in the atonement which had been made for them. He has a favourite illustration which he repeatedly uses. The sun gives light for all, affords for all pleasure in beholding the light, but a man must not shut his eyes. If he does so he has no cause to complain that the pleasure of beholding the light is denied to him; for the fault is not in the light, which is shining around him, but in himself. Christ is the sun; the atonement made by Christ

[1] Cameronis Opera, 529.

is the light of the sun; the fruit of the atonement is the pleasure derived from seeing the light; and faith is the sense of sight.[1] These opinions startled and even shocked the orthodox in Scotland. Cameron returned to France, where he soon afterwards died, but the impetus which he had given to free thought continued to exert its power. His views, as expounded by his pupil Amyrauld, were adopted by Richard Baxter, and were in the following century widely known and strongly condemned in Scotland under the name of Baxterianism.

While these opinions were disseminated in Glasgow, similar views were making their appearance in Aberdeen, and found there a much more congenial soil than in Clydesdale and the west. Aberdeen was not to be startled by doctrines because they were opposed to received beliefs. In 1618 Dr. Wm. Forbes, the same minister who afterwards preached before Charles I., and inveighed against the number of Catechisms in use, held a formal disputation with the Principal of Marischall College, in which he maintained the lawfulness of prayers for the dead. There was nothing surprising in Forbes maintaining that opinion, but it is significant that when the Principal opposed that opinion he was regarded with suspicion and his opposition to such a view received with disfavour.[2] Forbes threw himself heartily into many controversies of that time, but the bulk of his labours we must pass over. There is one "modest consideration" which he urged upon those disputants who were engaged in propounding subtle definitions and making endless distinctions, to render their definitions more exact, which is applicable not merely to his own time—Why seek to define the indefinable, and draw limits around the illimitable, and compel men on pain of damnation to accept your definition and confine themselves within the limits which you have prescribed? This Forbes was minister of St. Nicholas' Church, afterwards the first bishop of Edinburgh, and must not be confounded with a much greater Forbes of Aberdeen, with whom we shall soon make acquaintance.

The theological chairs of the University of Aberdeen were filled by men eminent for their abilities, learning, and piety. For the most part their influence was exercised in promoting

[1] Cameronis Opera, 389, 533 ff. [2] Grub's "Ecclesiastical History," ii. 531.

the reaction against extreme Calvinism. Prominent among them was Robert Baron, a Fifeshire man, professor of theology in Marischall College. His teaching was similar to that of Cameron. The will of man was free. There was no necessity for acting in this manner or in that, imposed on man's will by God, either by an eternal decree or by subjecting it to the influence of an irresistible motive. The will being free, the actions were also free. God did indeed predestinate some to everlasting life, and others He left to perish; but this predestination was not absolute and arbitrary, but proceeded from His foreknowledge of the faith and repentance of some, and of the voluntary unbelief and impenitence of others. The atonement also was universal. Christ had died for all men, and therefore all men might become reconciled to God in Christ, provided only they believed the Gospel and repented. Such were the views held and taught by Baron. He was on one occasion challenged to defend the universality of the atonement by a formidable opponent. In 1636 Samuel Rutherford was forced by the High Court of Commission to leave his parish of Anwoth and to reside in Aberdeen. There he held a disputation, among others, with Baron, and maintained the opinion that Christ died, not for all men, but only for the elect. The doctrine on the extent of the atonement, which Cameron and Baron taught and Rutherford condemned, is now very generally acknowledged and preached by men who think themselves strictly orthodox. Rutherford was, and is still, held in high esteem in many respects; but it is somewhat strange that men should extol him for entering the lists in Aberdeen to oppose unfaithful and corrupt ministers, and for valiantly defending truth and smiting error, while they themselves preach the error which he smote, and ignore the truth which he defended.

In that theological school of Aberdeen by far the greatest man was the professor of divinity in King's College, John Forbes of Corse. By family ties he was connected with both the Episcopalian and the Presbyterian party. His father was Bishop of Aberdeen—his father's brother had been banished, along with John Welsh of Ayr, for faithful adherence to the Presbyterian cause. After a protracted residence on the

Continent, where he studied at several universities, he returned to Scotland in 1619, and in the following year, in the twenty-seventh year of his age, was appointed to the chair of theology. The form which his lectures on systematic divinity took was determined by a desire to supply a pressing want of the time. Able and skilful Roman Catholic emissaries were at work in Scotland, affirming, and in the opinion of some proving, that all Catholic antiquity was on their side, while the Protestant Confession was a mere upstart novelty. Their representations were gaining converts. The common method of combating these views was by direct appeal to Scripture; but however valuable this method might be in itself, it involved the disadvantage of abandoning all historical continuity. The church of the Reformation was linked on to the church of the apostles, but the space which intervened between the apostles and reformers was passed over. The church was thus not an historical development, but a new creation quickened into life by the Divine word. It was to promote more correct views, and to train men who could meet and conquer the advocates of Rome on their own ground, that the study of historical theology was recommended by the bishop and clergy of Aberdeen, and in John Forbes they found the man who was specially competent to discharge the duty. His method in discharging it was to establish and define Christian doctrines from Scripture, and then to trace their history from century to century. He availed himself of no second-hand citations, but thoroughly knew the fathers whom he quoted. It was by this method of procedure that he proved the Protestant doctrines to be no novelty, but on the contrary to be the truly ancient tenets of the Church, and that, if the charge of novelty were made, it could be justly made only against the tenets held by the Church of Rome, and against these tenets especially as defined and fixed by the Council of Trent.[1] His lectures on religion in its practical bearing were founded on the ten commandments, in the exposition of which he dealt to some extent with casuistry (taking that term in its original and best sense) or cases of conscience—a department in which Scottish theology is somewhat deficient.[2]

[1] "Vita Forbesii," 8 f.; "Instructiones Historico-Theologicæ." [2] "Theologia Moralis."

He was pre-eminently a man of peace, and took but little direct part in the controversies of his day. He was from conviction an Episcopalian, and in favour of the observances enjoined by the Perth Assembly. He wrote a treatise in their favour which drew forth the warm commendation of Archbishop Ussher, and which he humbly thought might tend to still the storm which was raging. An epigram of the time truthfully says that while his Eirenicon was intended for peace it only tended to rouse strife.[1] Appeals to moderation, charity, and the fathers were made in vain to men who were told that the choice before them was either to bow the knee to Baal, or to form a portion of the 7000 who still remained faithful to Jehovah. Tried by the severe test applied by the Purging Committee, he was found free from all Papistry and Arminianism, and quite sound in the faith. He was deprived of his chair, but his character was esteemed and reverenced even by the men who removed him. If a profound and wide knowledge of the works of the fathers, of the mediæval writers, and of the theological literature of his time; if a reverent regard for truth, and skill and courage in defending it; if fairness and charity in the treatment of opponents; if true piety and childlike humility—can give a man a claim to be regarded as a theologian, Scotland has not since produced a theologian like Dr. John Forbes of Corse.

The reaction against extreme Calvinism culminated in the Aberdeen school. The objects which the combatants on both sides had immediately in view was to settle in one way or another the doctrines of absolute predestination and particular redemption. So far as that end was concerned, no advantage was gained; the dispute left matters much in the same state that it found them. Indirectly some advantage was reaped. The controversy served to keep Scottish theology from becoming a mere system of formal tenets; it served to stimulate free inquiry, and free inquiry had borne some good fruit when the leaders in this reaction were willing to grant to others the same freedom of thought that they claimed for themselves. Free inquiry and freedom of thought were, however, not to settle in Scotland for a long period. They had appeared and produced some fruit, but the flood was now rising which was

---

[1] Εἰρήνην voluit cadere, cudit ἔριν.

destined to sweep away the small beginning of free inquiry and toleration, along with the Arminianism which they had produced.

The General Assembly which met in 1638 in the Cathedral Church of Glasgow effected, as we know, a complete revolution in the government and ritual of the Church. Episcopacy was abolished, the Five Articles of Perth were declared to be null and void, and the Church was restored to the condition in which she had been before King James attempted to introduce bishops and novel ceremonies. That return to Presbytery and to the former ritual of the Church was so important that it has diverted attention from another task which the Glasgow Assembly undertook and accomplished—the task of arresting the movement of free thought and inquiry in doctrine, and marking out the path of strict orthodoxy from which no deviation should be allowed. The proceedings on this subject began in the eleventh session by the Moderator calling on David Dickson, minister at Irvine, to speak in the Assembly against Arminianism. Dickson in his speech referred, in an unmistakable manner, to the prevalence in the Church of those opinions on election and the extent of the atonement which had been taught by Cameron and some of the Aberdeen school of theology. He spoke plainly of the origin of that doctrine, and of its propagation in the Scottish Church; both were the work of Satan, the Pope, the Scottish bishops, and worldly men. In opposition to the errors which had been taught he set forth the true doctrines which must henceforth alone be maintained. Instead of conditional election "we give this for our doctrine out of the Word of God: that there is a number severed out, in God's special purpose, from the race of mankind, and advanced above the state of nature to the estate of grace and glory, by a special designation; and that for no foreseen good works in the man, but for God's free grace and good purpose." He next stated, in the clearest manner, the orthodox opinion on the extent of the atonement: "That our Lord made no blind bargain, but knew well what He bought as the Father knew what He sold; and had His sheep before His eyes, and was content to lay down His life for them." For acquiring a sound view of these doctrines, Dickson urged upon the Assembly a deeper study of the Covenant theology which had been imported from Holland, and was destined to occupy a prominent place in the orthodox school in Scotland. In the brief summary of that theology which he gave in his speech, he sought to establish further the doctrines which he had announced. In the covenant of redemption, made between God and the Mediator Christ, the number and names of the elect, the gifts of grace and glory to be bestowed on them, and the time and means to bestow it were "all condescended and agreed upon, with the price to be paid." After another member had spoken to the like effect, the Moderator, Alexander Henderson, thanked God that the error had been nipped in the bud before it had spread very far.[1] It would be a mistake to imagine that this matter was brought on a sudden before the Assembly. The business to be taken in hand, the men who were to speak upon it, and the conclusion to be recommended were all carefully arranged beforehand. Government and ritual had been reformed, and the Assembly was proceeding, according to a settled plan, to the reformation of doctrine.

The Assembly having defined what opinions were heterodox and what were orthodox, proceeded at once to enforce its definitions by the summary deposition of men who were accused of holding Arminian views. These men might have pleaded for time for study and repentance, but no time was granted. The Church must be purged of heresy. A Commission was appointed to try suspected ministers, and numerous depositions took place. The inquisition extended not merely to a man's public teaching, but to his private opinions. Robert Rollock was accused, among other things, "of maintaining the universality of Christ's merits, and the falling away of the saints." He appeared personally before the Assembly of 1639, and declared "that he did not in preaching, but in private, affirm the foresaid points." He was condemned. Short work was made with the Aberdeen school. Dr. John Forbes was, indeed, declared to be free of Arminianism, but was deprived of his chair for declining to sign the National Covenant. Baron, who had disputed with Rutherford, was dead, but those of his colleagues who had favoured his views were deprived and deposed.

[1] Peterkin's "Records of the Kirk," 156-159.

No divergence from the straitest Calvinism was to be allowed in the Church of Scotland.

Orthodoxy in faith and church government was now established in Scotland, and a prospect opened of establishing the same in England. The Root-and-Branch Bill had been passed by the English Parliament, and Episcopacy had consequently been abolished. Proposals were made from England to three successive General Assemblies to have one Confession of Faith, one form of church government, and one Directory for Public Worship for the three kingdoms. The proposals were eagerly listened to. For thirty years attempts had been made by royal authority to bring the Church of Scotland into conformity with that of England, and now a way was opened up whereby the Church of England was to be conformed to the pure Presbyterian Church of Scotland. At the General Assembly of 1643, commissioners from the English Parliament appeared. Their real object was to obtain the aid of the Scottish nation in the war which the English were now carrying on against the king. The Assembly let it be clearly understood that there must be a religious covenant between the two parties before there could be a civil league. The terms were accepted. There were to be one Confession, one form of government, and one ritual for England, Scotland, and Ireland; and the document in which these terms were engrossed was THE SOLEMN LEAGUE AND COVENANT. It was partly conservative and constructive, and partly destructive. It pledged the signatories to endeavour, really, sincerely, and constantly, "the preservation of the Reformed religion of the Church of Scotland, in doctrine, worship, discipline, and government, against our common enemies; and the reformation of religion in the kingdoms of England and Ireland in doctrine, worship, and discipline, according to the Word of God, and the example of the best Reformed churches." It also pledged them in like manner, without respect of persons, to endeavour the extirpation of Popery, Prelacy, and whatsoever should be found contrary to sound doctrine and the power of godliness. In the Solemn League and Covenant Scotland was regarded as having attained purity, and therefore her religion is to be preserved. England and Ireland have not reached that point, and therefore religion in these kingdoms is to be reformed "*according to the Word of God and* the example of the best Reformed churches." The words in italics were not part of the original draft, but were inserted on the suggestion of Sir Henry Vane, one of the English commissioners.[1] The words seemed good in themselves; to the Scots they had only one meaning. Reformation according to the Word of God could result only in Presbyterianism. They did not think that to many of the English Puritans the clause would convey a very different meaning. Reformation according to the Word of God meant to some Puritans Independency, which the Scots detested; to others, tenets which were if possible still more detestable in their estimation. The same words could be used, and were used, in widely divergent meanings by different parties. The latter clause, "the example of the best Reformed churches," did not explain the ambiguous meaning of the former; for of course the Word of God was the supreme rule, and that was the best Reformed church which was most in accordance with that Word. The Solemn League was not a bond of uniformity either in its language or in its working. It had a fatal flaw from the beginning. The Scots were outwitted; and each member of the Assembly or of the Committee of the Convention of Estates who ratified the document in the hope of promoting uniformity of religion, had great cause to join in the prayer which Cromwell offered ten years afterwards with regard to the same astute politician, "Oh, Sir Harry Vane, thou with thy subtle casuistries and abstruse hair-splittings, thou art other than a good one, I think; the Lord deliver me from thee, Sir Harry Vane."[2]

The Solemn League and Covenant, containing the ambiguous clause, was accepted by the English Parliament, and sworn to by the House of Commons and the Westminster Assembly of Divines, and afterwards by the House of Lords. It was adopted with reservations. The Westminster Assembly declared that those who engaged to preserve and defend the Church of Scotland were bound only so far as they believed that Church to be according to the Word of God. In the sermon which he preached at St. Margaret's before the House of Commons and

---

[1] Gardiner's "Great Civil War," i. 269.
[2] Carlyle's "Cromwell," 20th April, 1653.

the Assembly when they swore to the Covenant, Philip Rye showed that they were not binding themselves to reform the English Church after the model of the Scottish. "If England," he said, "have attained to any greater perfection in so handling the word of righteousness and truths that are according to godliness, so as to make men more godly and more righteous; and if in the churches of Scotland there be any more light and beauty in matters of order and discipline, by which their assemblies are more orderly; or if to any other church or person it hath been given better to have learned Christ in any of His ways than any of us—we shall humbly bow and kiss their lips that can speak right words unto us in this matter, and help us unto the nearest uniformity with the word and mind of Christ in this great work of reformation."[1] These words show clearly the essentially different views of the object of the Covenant entertained by the two parties. The Scottish Presbyterians adopted it as a means of preserving a church which they regarded as a model of purity in doctrine and discipline, and of reforming England and Ireland according to that model; the English Puritans accepted it as pledging them to defend the Church of Scotland so far as they thought it agreeable to the Word of God, and in the work of reformation in the churches of England and Ireland, to strive after "the nearest uniformity with the word and mind of Christ."

The leaders of the dominant party in Scotland thought their object was now assured. The Solemn League and Covenant had been already approved by the Assembly and Convention of Estates, and a week after it had been sworn to in London by the House of Lords, the Committee of Estates and Commission of Assembly issued an edict commanding the Solemn League and Covenant to be sworn by every man and woman in Scotland, on pain of ecclesiastical censure and confiscation of goods. The edict was rigorously enforced; many subscribed gladly, others sorrowfully and reluctantly; the severe punishments denounced were, if possible, inflicted upon recusants; and thus Scotland became covenanted to defend the Church as it then was, to extend her doctrine and discipline to England and Ireland, and to extirpate Popery, Prelacy, and all other

[1] Gardiner's "Great Civil War," L 276, and reference.

errors. It was held, further, that the obligation thus assumed or imposed rested not only on those who of free will or compulsion signed the Covenant, but on their posterity throughout all generations.

THE WESTMINSTER CONFESSION.

The next step for securing uniformity was to prepare a Confession of Faith for the three kingdoms. That task was completed in 1647 by the Westminster Assembly. That Assembly was indeed composed of "learned and godly divines," but was undeniably Erastian in its origin and one-sided in its composition. It was called into existence by the Long Parliament; it derived its authority solely from Parliament; it was required to give its opinion only on the subjects which Parliament submitted to it for judgment; and its decisions were of no force until they were approved and ratified by the civil court to which it owed its being. It was entirely one-sided. A few Episcopalians had been designated as members of the Assembly, but of these few some declined to attend, and others were expelled. No testimonials, however ample and satisfactory, regarding the abilities, learning, and piety of the members, alter in any degree the Erastian origin and partisan character of the Assembly itself. The Confession drawn up by those men embodied, indeed, the beliefs of themselves and a large party in the country; but it was published as a Confession of Faith for the three kingdoms, which all should, under heavy penalties, be compelled to adopt as expressing the religious beliefs which they themselves held.

The Erastian origin of the Westminster Confession was partly atoned for in Scotland by the fact that it was approved by the General Assembly before it was ratified by the Scottish Estates. It was first sanctioned by the Church and then by the State. In August, 1647, the Assembly had the completed Confession before it, and after careful and deliberate consideration found it "to be most agreeable to the Word of God, and in nothing contrary to the received doctrine, worship, discipline, and government of this Kirk." The Assembly therefore approved "the said Confession as to the truth of the matter, judging it to be most orthodox and grounded upon the

THE DOCTRINE OF THE CHURCH. 221

Word of God, and also as to the point of uniformity, agreeing for our part that it be a common Confession of Faith for the three kingdoms."[1] It was not, as is sometimes alleged, accepted only in so far as it agreed with the Confession adopted at the Reformation; it was accepted absolutely. The Assembly first stated, as a matter of fact, that it was in no wise contrary to the received doctrine of the Church, and then approved and adopted it. The approval of the second section of the thirty-first chapter, regarding the power of the magistrate in calling assemblies of the Church, was qualified by an explanation. That section acknowledged the magistrate's power to call an assembly of the Church by his own authority. This acknowledgment was offensive to the Scots; it was therefore explained that this power of the magistrate could be exercised only in the case of churches not yet fully organized. There was a like reservation also with regard to the statement made in the same section concerning the power of ministers to meet in assembly of themselves, in virtue of their office and without delegation from their churches. The exercise of this power was also declared to be permissible only in churches not yet organized and settled. In all other respects the Confession was unreservedly adopted.

The Westminster Confession consists of thirty-three chapters, and contains 171 distinct and separate doctrinal propositions, almost every one of which shows the orthodox finding on fiercely contended and protracted controversies. It was truthfully described as not being contrary to the received doctrine of the Church, but it might with equal truth have been described as containing many doctrines on which the former Confession was altogether silent. It also defined what had been left indefinite, and amplified what had been briefly indicated. Adherence to the old Confession was consistent with the existence of a broad, liberal, and comprehensive church; adherence to the new made the existence of such a church impossible. The definitions of the true faith are so numerous, precise, and minute, the path of orthodoxy is so plainly marked out, the by-ways which lead into heresy are so carefully indicated and rigidly prohibited, that the straying wanderer must be

[1] Act of Assembly, 1647, approving the Confession.

culpably ignorant, or grossly negligent, or boldly defiant. A comparison of the two Confessions would shed a wonderful light on the history and character of the development of doctrine in the Scottish Church, but such a comparison would require a separate work for itself. In illustration of what has now been asserted, we give one instance of the amplification of doctrines which had been before received, and another of the addition of new doctrines.

THE CONFESSION OF FAITH OF THE CHURCH OF SCOTLAND, 1560.

Article I.   Of God.

We confess and acknowledge one only God, to whom only we must cleave, whom only we must serve, whom only we must worship, and in whom only we must put our trust; who is eternal, infinite, unmeasurable, incomprehensible, omnipotent, invisible; one in substance, and yet in three persons, the Father, the Son, and the Holy Ghost; by whom we confess and believe all things in heaven and earth, as well visible and invisible, to have been created, to be retained in their being, and to be ruled and guided by his inscrutable providence to such ends as his eternal wisdom, goodness, and justice hath appointed them, to the manifestation of his own glory.

WESTMINSTER CONFESSION OF FAITH, 1647.

Chapter III.   Of God and of the Holy Trinity.

1. There is but one only living and true God, who is infinite in being and perfection, a most pure spirit, invisible, without body, parts, or passions, immutable, immense, eternal, incomprehensible, almighty, most wise, most free, most absolute, working all things according to the counsel of his own immutable and most righteous will, for his own glory; most loving, gracious, merciful, long-suffering, abundant in goodness and truth, forgiving iniquity, transgression, and sin, the rewarder of them that diligently seek him; and, withal most just and terrible in his judgments; hating all sin, and who will by no means clear the guilty.

2. God hath all life, glory, goodness, blessedness, in and of himself; and is alone in and unto himself all-sufficient; not standing in need of any creatures which he hath made, not deriving any glory from them, but only manifesting his own glory in, by, unto, and upon them: he is the alone fountain of all being, of whom, through whom, and to whom are all things; and hath most sovereign dominion over them, to do by them, for them, or upon them whatsoever himself pleaseth. In his sight all things are open and manifest; his knowledge is infinite, infallible, and independent upon the creature, so as nothing is to him contingent or uncertain. He is most holy in all his counsels, in all his works, and in all his commands. To him is due from angels, and men,

and every other creature, whatsoever worship, service, or obedience he is pleased to require of them.

3. In the unity of the Godhead there be three persons, of one substance, power, and eternity: God the Father, God the Son, and God the Holy Ghost. The Father is of none, neither begotten nor proceeding; the Son is eternally begotten of the Father—the Holy Ghost eternally proceeding from the Father and the Son.

The one article presents a simple confession of the faith which we profess, the other gives a synopsis of a recondite dissertation on the being, attributes, and nature of God.

As a specimen of the way in which new doctrines are introduced, we take the chapter on election. The Scottish Confession is very brief on this subject. It merely affirms, in Article VIII., that God the Father, "of mere grace, elected us in Christ Jesus His Son before the foundation of the world was laid." The Westminster Confession, in Chapter III., treats of the subject of God's eternal decree, which includes election. "1. God from all eternity did, by the most wise and holy counsel of His own will, freely and unchangeably ordain whatsoever comes to pass; yet so as thereby neither is God the author of sin, nor is violence offered to the will of the creature, nor is the liberty or contingency of second causes taken away, but rather established. 2. Although God knows whatsoever may or can come to pass upon all supposed conditions, yet hath He not decreed anything because He foresaw it as future, or as that which would come to pass upon certain conditions. 3. By the decree of God, for the manifestation of His glory, some men and angels are predestinated unto everlasting life, and others foreordained to everlasting death. 4. These angels and men, thus predestinated and foreordained, are particularly and unchangeably designed; and their number is so certain and definite, that it cannot be either increased or diminished. 5. Those of mankind that are predestinated unto life, God, before the foundation of the world was laid, according to His eternal and immutable purpose, and the secret counsel and good pleasure of His will, hath chosen in Christ unto everlasting glory, out of His mere free grace and love, without any foresight of faith or good works, or perseverance in either of them, or any other thing in the creature as conditions or causes moving

Him thereunto; and all to the praise of His glorious grace. 6. As God hath appointed the elect unto glory, so hath He, by the eternal and most free purpose of His will, foreordained all the means thereunto. Wherefore they who are elected, being fallen in Adam, are redeemed by Christ; are effectually called unto faith in Christ by His Spirit working in due season; are justified, adopted, sanctified, and kept by His power through faith unto salvation. Neither are any other redeemed by Christ, effectually called, justified, adopted, sanctified, and saved, but the elect only. 7. The rest of mankind, God was pleased, according to the unsearchable counsel of His own will, whereby He extendeth or withholdeth mercy as He pleaseth, for the glory of His sovereign power over His creatures, to pass by, and to ordain them to dishonour and wrath for their sin, to the praise of His glorious justice. 8. The doctrine of this high mystery of predestination is to be handled with special prudence and care, that men, attending the will of God revealed in His word, and yielding obedience thereunto, may, from the certainty of their effectual vocation, be assured of their eternal election. So shall this doctrine afford matter of praise, reverence, and admiration of God, and of humility, diligence, and abundant consolation to all that sincerely obey the Gospel."

The chapter quoted gives an able and most carefully worded statement of the doctrines maintained by Calvinists on the general subject of predestination, and on the particular part of that subject which concerns the predestinating of some angels and men to everlasting life, and the predestinating or foreordaining of others to everlasting death.[1] The whole range of the controversy with the Arminians on this point is traversed, the Calvinistic conclusions are stated, and the grounds of the conclusions are indicated. Here the Westminster Confession goes far beyond the former received creed of the Scottish Church. The subject is much wider. It is God's universal plan, formed from all eternity by His own wise and holy counsel,

---

[1] In the Westminster Confession "predestinated" is employed with regard to the decree unto life, "foreordained" with regard to the decree unto death. There is no difference in the absolute nature of the decrees themselves implied; but there is, according to some Calvinists, a difference in the manner in which the decrees operate, which is indicated by the verbal variations.

unconditional, unchangeable, which is first taken up in the new Confession; in the old, election, which is only one part of that vast and all-comprehending plan, was little more than mentioned. In the new, the absolute, unconditional predestination of some to life and of others to death is clearly and fully stated; in the old, election to life is alone noticed. It may be truly alleged that the doctrines on this point which were explicitly expressed in the new Confession were at least implied in statements made in the old; that, for instance, the election of some to everlasting life necessarily implied the passing over of others and leaving them to everlasting death, and as both Confessions acknowledged that all events were ruled by God, therefore the saved must have been predestinated to life and the lost foreordained to death. All that may be granted. We are not concerned here with the truth of a doctrine, or the cogency of the reasoning by which one doctrine may be deduced from another; all that is affirmed is that the insertion of all those dogmas in a Confession, to be received as Divine truths, was going far beyond all that was contained in the old creed. If a man, under the former Confession, believed, for instance, that God did not foreordain men to death, he might perhaps quite fairly be regarded as deficient in the reasoning faculty, and so unable to draw just inferences from a dogma which he had accepted; under the new he would be condemned as denying a truth revealed in the Word, and expressly stated in the creed. Formerly he might be looked upon as illogical, now he would be regarded as heretical. As creeds expand, liberty of thought is narrowed.

The Westminster Confession is not so much a confession of faith for the people, as it is a most excellent and carefully arranged manual of Calvinistic doctrines for the use of theologians. Extensive reading in theological literature, and especially an intimate acquaintance with controversial divinity, are required in order to understand the nature and bearing of many of its statements. The results of controversies in the early days of the Church regarding the Trinity, the nature and person of the Saviour, the Holy Spirit, of the controversies between Rome and Protestantism, between the Lutheran and the Reformed Church, between Calvinists and Arminians, ranging from the Council of Nice to the Synod of Dort, and even later, are all embodied in the dogmas proposed for belief. To accept every one and all of the hundred and seventy-one propositions as the truths of God may be evidence of implicit faith in the learning, judgment, and godliness of the Westminster divines, but can hardly be the result of independent research and honest conviction founded thereon.

The approval of the Confession was followed by the approval of the Larger and Shorter Catechisms and the Directory for Public Worship; and now the object which the General Assembly had from the first contemplated seemed on the point of being realized. There was uniformity of doctrine and worship between the three kingdoms so far as uniformity could be secured by solemn league and covenant, confession, and acts of Assembly and Parliament.

It is from their principles and conduct during this period of success and supremacy that the Scottish Covenanters should be judged. At a subsequent period they were divested of place and power, they were oppressed and persecuted; and the popular descriptions of them belong to that time of oppression and persecution. It is right to exhibit their courage and endurance in a time of suffering; but if their conduct during that period be alone regarded, the judgment concerning them must be partial. They were the acknowledged rulers of the Church and the virtual rulers of the State from 1643, when the Solemn League and Covenant was approved and enforced, and the Scottish army marched into England to gain the religious uniformity which that bond contemplated, till 1651, when Cromwell at Worcester ended the career of Charles II. as Scotland's covenanted king. After 1651 their power was effectually crushed under the stern sway of Cromwell. There was thus a period of eight years during which the Covenanters exercised supreme power, and showed their principles in conduct. They believed with all their heart in God's absolute sovereignty, to which princes and potentates owed obedience equally with the lowliest, and hence when commands which they thought to be opposed to the will of God were issued by the civil magistrate they met them with resolute opposition. Election with all its consequent blessings was of free grace alone, and hence they bowed before God in deepest humility and fervent gratitude. Christ was the sole king of His Church, and therefore His voice must alone be listened to. They believed that they were justified by faith alone, but it was a faith which worked by love and showed itself in obedience, and hence was that stern discipline from which no rank was exempted. They had the deepest sense of sin. No one who reads the records of those times can fail to be struck with the accounts of men acknowledging their offences in public and private with bitter weeping. It is a shallow explanation to attribute such tears to hypocrisy. They very probably were in some cases hypocritical, but in many cases they were the genuine accompaniments of sincere self-abhorrence and penitence. They did not proceed from mental weakness or infirm will. The men whose faces were wet with tears at the remembrance of their own unworthiness and of God's holiness and love were the sagest counsellors in difficulty, and the sternest and boldest in peril. They made no distinction between essentials and non-essentials in the truths which God revealed. What was man that he should presume to say of the Divine injunctions that some were essential and must be obeyed, while others might safely be disregarded? It was not only the sacrifices that had been divinely prescribed, but the curtains, and the boards, and the very pins of the tabernacle. Presbytery, in their eyes, had been prescribed by God, and was the only effectual means of preserving unity and truth in the Church,[1] and hence they strove to maintain and promote it as they would maintain and promote any other truths of God. Their convictions on the one hand produced zeal for truth, on the other intolerance against error. The Covenanters have been represented as the champions of civil and religious liberty; they themselves would have repudiated such a charge. They claimed for the Church supreme control over the civil power in all matters affecting conscience. In the declaration of war, in legislation on duties between king and subjects, husbands and wives, parents and children, masters and servants, it belonged to particular ministers, and much more to the Assemblies of the Church, to declare

---

[1] "The Assembly's Answer to the English Ministers' Letter" (Peterkin's "Records of the Kirk," p 295 f.)

to the State the mind of God from the Scripture; and in difficult cases legislation on these duties formed a subject of cognizance and judgment for the Assemblies of the Church. In short, they claimed for the Church what the Pope now claims for himself, the right to be supreme judge in all matters of faith and morals, and further, the right of determining what was to be included in that category.[1] For some years the Assembly ruled the state.

Liberty of conscience they maintained, but it was liberty to follow truth and crush error; and of truth and error they themselves were the judges. Liberty of conscience, meaning thereby liberty for men to propagate what the Covenanters considered to be error and heresy, and to oppose what they regarded as truth, was a liberty which they repudiated and abhorred.[2] If doctrines were the truths of God, toleration was too little—they should have supreme and sole sway; if doctrines were the falsehoods of Satan, toleration was too much—they ought to be extirpated. Their conception of religious liberty is clearly expressed in the Solemn League and Covenant, and is fully explained by the means adopted to carry that covenant into effect. To secure uniformity in religion the Scottish army fought along with the forces of the English Parliament against the Royalists. The Scottish Commissioners to the Westminster Assembly relied not merely on the force of their arguments, but also on the prowess of their soldiers, to win converts to Presbyterianism. With Independency, writes Baillie, "we purpose not to meddle in haste, till it please God to advance our army, which we expect will much assist our arguments."[3] The Solemn League and Covenant pledged its subscribers to extirpate popery, prelacy, and other errors. Men who now laud the Covenant and advocate religious liberty in the sense detested by the Covenanters, affirm that the clause pledged its adherents to nothing more than persuasion and argument in their dealings with those who were so unfortunate as to cling to the errors indicated. Doubtless the delivery of anti-

---

[1] "The General Assembly's Answer to the Committee of Estates," Peterkin, p. 505 f.; Acts of Scottish Parliament, 10th June, 1648.
[2] "A Declaration and Brotherly Exhortation of the General Assembly to their Brethren of England," Peterkin, p. 469.
[3] Baillie's Letters, December, 1643.

popery and anti-prelacy tracts and lectures is one way of trying to extirpate popery and prelacy, but it was not on such means that the Covenanters, when in power, relied in order to attain the object which they had sworn to accomplish.

In order to extirpate popery, papists were excommunicated and their goods confiscated; they were commanded to remove from them all popish friends and servants, to abstain from mass and the company of all priests; their children were taken from them and educated in the Protestant faith under the superintendence of the presbytery of the bounds. In order to extirpate prelacy all the bishops had been deprived, and most of them excommunicated. The ministers were obliged to abjure episcopacy and sign the National Covenant and then the Solemn League and Covenant. Laymen who refused to sign the latter forfeited their estates. In religious matters the Covenanters demanded supremacy for their own views, and allowed no toleration to views which they condemned.

The year 1647, which witnessed the adoption of the Westminster Confession as a confession of faith for the three kingdoms, saw also the beginning of that controversy which was destined soon to rend the Covenanted Church of Scotland in twain, and range those who had hitherto been of one mind into two bitterly opposed parties, known as the Resolutioners and the Protesters. Nothing is easier than to ridicule and stigmatize the Protesters. The men who before the battle of Dunbar insisted on dismissing from the Scottish army thousands of its bravest soldiers, who excluded in a time of peril and perplexity the ablest statesmen from council and parliament, may well seem at first sight to have been fools and fanatics. In forming a judgment everything depends on the point of view from which we regard them. If they be considered simply as Scotsmen fighting in defence of their king and country against a powerful enemy, their conduct in rejecting the aid of fellow-countrymen as loyal, as patriotic, and at least as brave as themselves, cannot be too severely reprobated; but if they be considered as Covenanters, whose object was to have a covenanted king ruling over a people that acknowledged only Presbytery and the Westminster Confession, then the course which they followed was the only one consistent with principles which were professed by both

Resolutioners and Protesters. Both parties owned the Solemn League and Covenant. Both believed that the object which it proposed was the Lord's cause. Both believed that God by His direct agency guided and controlled all events. If the Lord hid His countenance from them they knew that horsemen and footmen were powerless to avert disaster; but if the Lord caused His face to shine upon them victory was assured to them, whether many or few were on their side. The Lord would be with them or against them according as they were faithful or unfaithful to His cause. It was on these principles that the Protesters caused the Scottish army to be purged before the battle of Dunbar, and attributed the subsequent defeat to the Lord's anger against them on account of the unfaithful that had been left; and it was for the same reason that they refused to pray for the success of the Scottish army when it went to fight and perish at Worcester. They had no warrant, they said, to pray for its success; they could only pray that the Lord would purge it of all malignants.

Nowhere in the whole ecclesiastical history of Scotland is a better instance afforded of men carrying out to its logical results a principle which they believed to be true. The Protesters had the courage of their opinions, and did not shrink from the consequences which their application involved. They were indeed unpractical, but they were consistent. If their conduct be condemned, the condemnation must begin with the Solemn League and Covenant, of which their conduct was the legitimate result.

The Scottish theologians of the period now considered were chiefly occupied with the fierce controversies then raging about church government and ritual. John Forbes had the option given him of signing the Solemn League and Covenant, or of leaving the country. He chose the latter alternative, and retired to Holland in 1644. After a residence of two years in that country, he was allowed to return, and to live in retirement at Corse, where he died. Alexander Henderson, who was moderator of the Glasgow Assembly of 1638, and who for eight years guided the policy of the Church, and in no small degree that of the State, was more a statesman than a theologian. The same may be said of Robert Douglas, whose position was only second to that of Henderson, and who continued to be a prominent leader of the Church till the Restoration. The story of his life has never been written. He opposed the Protesters; after the Restoration he declined the offer of a bishopric, but accepted the indulgence, and died in 1674 the presbyterian minister at Pencaitland. His name therefore was never inserted in the catalogue of Scottish worthies by writers who could discern worth only in the supporters of the party to which they themselves belonged. His writings, which were in existence in the time of Wodrow, have most likely perished, but if they could be recovered new light would be cast on many of the transactions in which he was so long a chief actor. The theological writings of David Calderwood and George Gillespie are storehouses of arguments in favour of presbytery and simplicity of ritual, but are only remotely connected with doctrine. David Dickson, who opened the campaign in the Glasgow Assembly against Arminianism and all tenets opposed to a rigid Calvinistic creed, was promoted to the chair of Divinity, first in the University of Glasgow, and subsequently in that of Edinburgh. It was under his superintendence that a commentary on the several books of Scripture, a work which had been sanctioned by the Assembly, was carried on. The work was never completed, but it was as part of this projected commentary that Dickson wrote on the Psalms, the Gospel of Matthew, and Hebrews; Durham of Glasgow on Canticles and Revelation; and Hutcheson of Edinburgh on Job, the minor prophets, and the Gospel of St. John.

The greatest, however, of the Covenanting theologians was Samuel Rutherford. No problem scares him by its difficulty. He was born too late to take part in the controversy which once divided the schoolmen, as to whether an angel could pass from star to star without traversing the intermediate space, but he delights in raising and discussing questions no less abstruse. The outcome of the reasoning may be lightly esteemed, but no one can fail to admire the ingenuity of the process. Like a true Scotsman, he is troubled with no doubts regarding the truth of the opinions which he entertains, and strikes down his opponents with a warrior's joy. His acute and daring intellect sometimes leads him to maintain positions which might almost be regarded as heretical by orthodox divines, who uphold the doctrine of the necessity of the atonement. The doom of sin, he indignantly asserts, proceeds solely from God's sovereign decree. God might, if He had so chosen, have left sin altogether unpunished—a doctrine which is not regarded as quite sound. But this is almost the solitary instance in which he deviates from the path of strict orthodoxy. In his voluminous writings he smites the Antinomian, the Arminian, the prelatist, and all heretics. He wrote the best book yet produced against religious toleration; and if any one think it allowable to take sexual love as the symbol of spiritual emotions, and expatiate at length on that seductive theme, he can find no collection of religious erotic prose-poetry at all to be compared with Rutherford's letters.

We shall, however, have only a partial conception of the theology of the period when Scotland was under the Solemn League and Covenant, if we limit our view to the school represented by Rutherford and his fellow-thinkers, and leave unheeded that school of which Robert Leighton was the representative.

Leighton the bishop was, for learning, moderation, and saintliness of character, by far the best of the Scottish prelates of the Restoration period, and his theological reputation is generally associated with the position which he then occupied. It should, however, be borne in mind that the writings of Leighton, on which his fame rests, belong not to the times of restored Episcopacy, but to the Covenanting times which preceded that restoration. It was not when he was Bishop of Dunblane or Archbishop of Glasgow that Leighton wrote his "Commentary on First Peter" and his theological lectures, but before he became a prelate, and while he was minister at Newbattle or Principal of Edinburgh University, in the Covenanted and Presbyterian Church. It is the theology of the times of the Covenant which they serve to illustrate. Leighton had sworn to keep the Covenant, and had administered the oath to others. Extant records show that he took an active part in the business of the Church. There may or may not be truth in the story that when questioned by his presbytery if he preached to the times, he replied that one poor brother might be permitted to preach Jesus Christ and eternity;

but there is no doubt that Jesus Christ and eternity form the themes of his published discourses. The din of passionate wranglings is there hushed, and a heavenly calm prevails instead. His writings serve to show that even in those dark and bitter times there were elements of light and sweetness, contributed by teachers in whose eyes church government and ceremonies were as nothing when weighed in the balance against the eternal verities of religion.

The period now considered began with prohibiting all freedom of thought regarding doctrine, with establishing extreme Calvinism as the only standard of orthodoxy, and again recognizing Presbytery as the only form of church government divinely appointed. Then followed an attempt to enforce this faith and government on England and Ireland. To accomplish this end, the Solemn League and Covenant was drawn up, and the old Confession of the Scottish Church was abandoned in favour of that of Westminster, which was to serve as a common Confession for the three kingdoms. The bond of Covenant and Confession produced even in Scotland only a nominal union. At last the strain became too intense, and the nominal union was severed. For ten years before the Restoration the Covenanted Church of Scotland was rent in twain. Each of the two parties pronounced the heaviest ecclesiastical censures on the other; and if ecclesiastical censures involved no civil consequences, that was owing simply to the strong government of Cromwell. Baillie, himself a Resolutioner, who was grieved at the division and foresaw its result, says that "the two parties looked on each other rather as of different religions than of different persuasions about things which were not fundamental." Such was the state of matters when the Restoration took place, and the supremacy of the Covenanters came to an end.

THE CHURCH WITHOUT A CONFESSION, CATECHISM, OR LITURGY, 1661–1689.

At the restoration of Charles II. it seemed at first that though Episcopacy was to be re-established in England and Ireland, yet Presbytery would continue to be maintained in Scotland. The king had avowed to the anxious Presbyterians his firm resolution to protect and preserve the government of the Church of Scotland as it was settled by law. The firm resolution, if ever entertained, was soon abandoned. When the Scottish Parliament met in the beginning of 1661, it might easily have been seen that Presbytery was doomed. The king was declared to be the only supreme governor over all persons and in all causes. The Solemn League and Covenant was declared to infer an obligation on Scottish subjects to interfere with the churches of England and Ireland, and was forbidden to be renewed unless by royal warrant. The famous Rescissory Act was passed, by which all parliaments since 1633 were declared to be null and void, and their Acts of no effect. The king at his restoration had promised to maintain the Church as settled by law, but now the laws by which she had been settled were all rescinded. The Presbyterian Church was thus overthrown. Episcopacy was then restored, and the government of the Church was to be determined by the king, with the advice of the archbishops and bishops and such of the clergy as should be nominated by the king.

The period between the Restoration and the Revolution teems with events of the highest interest, but with most of these we have here little or no concern. The ejection of hundreds of ministers for refusing to take presentations from patrons and collation from bishops, of others for refusing to attend diocesan synods and to yield obedience to their ordinaries, the violent means used to enforce Episcopacy upon an unwilling people, and the resistance which the people offered, can be alluded to only in so far as they serve to illustrate doctrinal truths.

The Rescissory Act accomplished more than its authors had contemplated. It rescinded the statutes by which the Presbyterian Church had been again established, but it rescinded also all those statutes by which the Westminster Confession, Catechisms, and Directory had been approved and adopted. These documents were all abolished along with the Church to which they belonged, and nothing was substituted in their room. It thus came to pass that the Scottish Episcopal Church, from the day on which it was established, in 1662, till the day on which it was overthrown, in 1689, stood alone among the national churches of Christendom as being the only one which had neither creed, nor catechism, nor liturgy. The Apostles'

Creed was recommended by the bishops to be repeated at the administration of baptism, but that recommendation was made by them to diocesan synods, and had no legal sanction. Burnet, indeed, alleges that "the Westminster Confession was the only one that was read in Scotland, and the bishops left it in possession, though the authority that enacted it was annulled." That is merely saying that the bishops did not interfere. Individuals among the clergy and laity might, if they pleased, believe its doctrines, but the fact of their doing so did not make it the Confession of the Church. The adoption of it by the Church could have been made only in a national synod, and such a synod was never convoked. More could be said in support of the allegation that the old Scottish Confession was restored by the rescinding of the Acts which had approved of that of Westminster. But the Rescissory Act alone no more involved the restoration of the former creed of the Church than it involved the restoration of Episcopacy. To accomplish the latter object a special Act was needed. John Knox's Confession had now fallen into almost total oblivion. Its name was introduced into the Test Act of 1681, which, when first drawn up, ordained that all persons holding a civil or ecclesiastical office should swear that they professed the true Protestant religion. It seemed advisable to give some definition of the true Protestant religion thus professed, and so the clause was added, "as contained in the Confession of Faith ratified by the Parliament of 1567." Burnet says that "the book was so worn out of use that scarce any one in the whole Parliament had ever read it; none of the bishops had, as afterwards appeared."

The insertion of such a clause was a proof of the ignorance which prevailed regarding the contents of the Confession. The clause made the test oath self-contradictory. The Confession enjoined obedience to kings and all in authority "not repuguing the command of God:" the test oath enjoined absolute obedience. The Confession condemned resistance to kings "while they pass not over the bounds of their office:" the test oath declared it to be unlawful to take up arms against the king on any pretence whatever. There is great probability in the suggestion of Burnet, that Sir James Dalrymple, who knew the Confession and was opposed to the oath, proposed the clause thinking that it would secure the rejection of the measure. When attention was thus called to the Confession, and some refused to receive it as a standard of their belief, the Privy Council issued an explanation of the oath, to the effect that those who took it swore only to the true Protestant religion contained in that Confession, as opposed to Popery and fanaticism. The Scottish Confession was not revived as a standard of the faith of the Church.

The Episcopal Church encountered from the first strong opposition, and a clear idea of the grounds on which that opposition was based is necessary in order to understand the history of the period. The king had been declared supreme ruler of the Church in matters of government, and Episcopacy was re-established by Parliament in obedience to his behest. His authority over the Church was extended. In 1669 Parliament enacted that the king had supreme authority in all ecclesiastical causes, that the ordering of the external government of the Church was an inherent right of the Crown, and that all ecclesiastical meetings, and all the matters to be determined by them, were subject to such orders and constitutions as His Majesty should think fit. By this Act the Church was entirely subjected to the Crown. Its government, policy, and even its doctrines, were liable to be modified, or altogether changed, according to royal orders.

The Presbyterians objected to Episcopacy itself, and also to the claim of the king's supremacy over the Church. In their eyes Presbytery was the system of church government appointed in the Word of God, while Episcopacy was a mere human invention. They repudiated the claim of the king to settle the government of the Church. According to them Christ was the sole head of the Church, and it was one of His prerogatives to settle the government of His house. The supremacy over the Church was an inherent right, not of the crown of Charles II., but of the mediatorial crown of the Redeemer. Hence to them the establishment of Episcopacy, in room of Presbytery, was setting up a human invention in the place from which a divine institution had been removed; and the acknowledgment of the king's supremacy over the Church was transferring a prerogative from the crown of Christ to the crown of Charles II. Adherence to the Covenants, and specially to the Solemn League and Covenant, was regarded as obligatory both on account of the righteous objects contemplated and the oath which had been administered. The principles advocated by the Covenanters were correctly summarized in the motto inscribed on their banners—"For Christ, His Crown, and Covenants."[1]

The maintenance of these principles involved severe penalties. The Scottish Parliament had set apart the 29th day of May to be observed as a "holy day unto the Lord" for all time coming by "prayers, praises, and thanksgivings unto God," with preachings in all churches for the transcendent mercy shown in restoring Charles II. This was the only holy day enjoined by law; the observance of Christmas, Easter, and the other festivals of the Church, which had been enjoined by the Perth Assembly, was never attempted to be revived. Presbyterians would not observe the 29th of May as a holy day unto the Lord. Ringing bells, drinking the king's health at the market cross and thereafter breaking the glasses, lighting bonfires, and similar observances, were all within the sphere of civil authority, but it was not within that sphere to command religious services. The old arguments against festival days were revived with much greater force. If there was no warrant in the Word for the Church to set apart holy days to commemorate the birth or the resurrection of the Lord, there certainly was no warrant for the Parliament to set apart the 29th of May as a holy day unto God to commemorate the restoration of Charles II. The restored Episcopal Church agreed with the Presbyterian in not observing Christmas, Good Friday, Easter, and the other festivals, but differed from it by observing as a holy day the anniversary of Charles' restoration.

The Scottish Parliament enjoined that the oath of allegiance, which declared the king to be supreme in all causes, must be

---

[1] Scotland, as "a covenanted country," was regarded as being bound for all time coming, according to Acts of Assembly and Parliament, to two Covenants: (1) the National Covenant, i.e. the Negative Confession of 1581, with the additions made in 1638; and (2) the Solemn League and Covenant of 1643. The latter became the more prominent, as it virtually specified the divine right of Presbytery and its claim to sole supremacy—articles which only by an arbitrary interpretation could be considered as implied in the National Covenant.

taken by all that should be required to do so by the Privy Council, or by any acting under their authority. The Presbyterians were quite willing to acknowledge the king's supremacy in civil affairs, but refused to acknowledge him as supreme governor over the Church. Parliament commanded all men to attend their parish churches. The Presbyterians would not attend the parish churches, as they regarded the Episcopal clergy officiating in them either as apostates, who had by their perjury forfeited their ministry, or mere hirelings, who had no mission to minister in the Church of Christ except from prelates, who had no mission to give according to Christ's appointment.[1] Thence resulted fines, imprisonment, exile, and other penalties.

Until 1669 the nonconforming Presbyterians were united; after that year they were divided into two bitterly opposed parties. The king, as supreme governor, had, by a letter to the Council, directed that some of the Presbyterian ministers who had been ejected in 1661 might, on certain conditions, be allowed to resume duty. Another indulgence was granted in 1672, and in 1687 all penal laws against nonconformists were, by royal authority, conditionally suspended. The question as to whether these indulgences should or should not be accepted, rent the Presbyterians asunder. The indulgences were gladly accepted by some; they were sternly rejected by others. The rejection was based on doctrine. The king and Parliament had at first forbidden ministers to preach the Gospel and administer the sacraments of the Church; and many had regarded, but some had disregarded, the prohibition. The king had in course of time been graciously pleased to grant an indulgence to some Presbyterian ministers—on certain conditions—to preach the Gospel and administer the sacraments; and some had accepted, and others had refused to accept, that indulgence. Those who disregarded the prohibition did so on the ground that ministers of Christ's Church had not received their authority to preach His Gospel and administer His sacraments from king and Parliament, nor could they be deprived by the civil power of that authority. They would not receive, as an indulgence granted out of the king's

[1] "Hind Let Loose," 131 f.

THE DOCTRINE OF THE CHURCH.

gracious pleasure, a limited liberty given to discharge their ministerial duties, while they claimed full liberty as a matter of right.[1] They subsequently refused to pay arbitrary cesses and taxations, contending that these taxes were used for employing bands of soldiers to suppress the Gospel, to destroy religion and liberty, and to entail slavery on Scotsmen to all succeeding generations.[2] Finally, they renounced all allegiance to Charles Stuart,[3] and excommunicated him and his brother, the Duke of York.[4]

The grounds on which these proceedings were based were doctrinal. Allegiance to Charles II. was renounced in consequence of his unconstitutional government; and in so far as that unconstitutional government was regarded in its civil aspect, the Scottish nonconforming Presbyterians at this stage of their proceedings may be looked upon as occupying the same ground that was taken at the Revolution of 1688. The principal reasons, however, of their renunciation of allegiance were—the perjury of the king in breaking and burning that Solemn League and Covenant which he had twice sworn to observe; the rescinding of the Acts which he had vowed to uphold; his persecution of the cause which he had professed to be the cause of the Lord; and his disloyalty to God, as shown in his own flagrantly immoral conduct.[5] They would have none but a covenanted king who showed the sincerity of his profession by living up to the covenants which he had sworn to observe. The civil liberties of citizens—simply as citizens—did not form the grounds of their actions. It was not the Presbyterians who accepted the indulgence and conformed to the conditions prescribed, but those Presbyterians who, on the doctrinal grounds just indicated, refused to accept it and braved the consequences, who were imprisoned, sold into slavery, hanged, shot, and drowned. This fact should be remembered in justice to all parties. Scottish Episcopacy has been condemned for merciless deeds, with which Episcopacy

---

[1] "History of the Indulgence, together with a Demonstration of the Unlawfulness thereof;" "Faithful Contendings;" "Cloud of Witnesses," &c.
[2] "Hind Let Loose," 150 ff.
[3] Sanquhar Declaration, June, 1680.
[4] Torwood Excommunication, September, 1680.
[5] "Apologetical Relation," 1684; "Testimony of the Reformed Presbyterian Church," historical part, 147 f

in itself had no connection. Presbyterians who do not know the difference between the National Covenant and the Solemn League and Covenant, and are profoundly ignorant of the obligations imposed by either, have claimed and do claim credit for the bold daring and patient endurance of the men who fought and died for the Covenants. The Covenanters themselves, when paraded as champions of civil and religious liberty, are represented as upholders of a cause against which, in its modern signification, they bore testimony even to bonds and death. Their conduct in action and suffering was guided by principles which, they were persuaded, were Divine truths. They tried conscientiously to act according to these principles; but their actions, and the grounds on which they were consistently founded, must be viewed as a whole. It is a partial, and therefore an unfair, judgment which is formed when their cruel sufferings as a persecuted people are alone regarded, and their despotic deeds, when virtual masters of Church and State, are overlooked.

Though Donald Cargill had excommunicated the king, the Duke of York, and others at Torwood, and "spared neither left-hand declensions nor right-hand extremes"[1] in the arduous task of keeping the Covenanters in the narrow path of rigid orthodoxy, yet there arose a party among them that disowned Cargill, and would hold no communion with his followers. Their leader was John Gib, a sailor in Borrowstounness. They were known as the Sweet Singers. Under Gib's guidance they soon reached a state in which they enjoyed heavenly raptures, and had no need of means of grace which were necessary to support the faith of others. They burned the Covenants, the Westminster Confession, the metrical psalms, and even, it is alleged, the Bible itself. The Covenanters strongly condemned the follies of the Sweet Singers, and the party, which never amounted to more than thirty, speedily disappeared.

Quakerism appeared and flourished in the north. George Fox had himself visited Scotland in 1657, but as he found the Lowlanders "dark and carnal," and the Highlanders so "devilish" that they attacked him with pitchforks,[2] he met with little success. About twenty years later Quakerism made more pro-

[1] "Hind Let Loose," 171. [2] Fox's "Journal," 264-269.

gress under the teaching of Robert Barclay of Ury. The doctrines inculcated were opposed on all sides. That inspiration was not limited to the sacred writers, but was common to all; and that the Scriptures were not the only, nor even the primary, rule of faith and manners; that all who had received Divine light in their souls might minister in holy things; that the sacraments were inward and spiritual; and that Christ's redemption was universal—were opinions obnoxious alike to Episcopalian and Presbyterian.

The persecuted and the persecutors united to invoke the execution of the penal statutes against Quakers.

At the eve of the Revolution, Episcopalians and Presbyterians formed the bulk of the nation. The Presbyterians were again divided into two classes—those who had accepted the indulgence, and those who would have none of it, but maintained the position which had been formerly taken by the Protesters. It would, however, be a mistake to imagine that in those sad and stormy years there was nothing but strife and warfare in the Scottish Church. The Christian life cannot be sustained on the dry husks of contentious wrangling. In the Episcopal Church there were many who regarded with indifference the points in dispute, and there had been many similarly minded in the Presbyterian Covenanted Church. The fact that nearly 600 ordained Presbyterian ministers at once conformed to Episcopacy, conclusively shows that the yoke imposed by the rulers of the Covenanting Church in the time of their supremacy had been uneasily borne. Some, doubtless, conformed from selfish motives, but there were many who looked upon the matters so bitterly contested as having little or no connection with the cause of truth and righteousness. There were in the Scottish Episcopal Church of the Restoration period, men who walked in the footsteps of the saintly Leighton. Lawrence Charteris, who for some years occupied the Edinburgh divinity chair, was a worthy successor of Leighton. He studied the Fathers, not to cull from their works arguments for speculative opinions, but to learn from them their high views of the duties of the Christian ministry, and of the preparation needed for the faithful discharge of those duties, and to see in them examples of self-denial, heavenly-mindedness, and Christian conduct. Practical and not speculative religion was what he sought to teach his students and exemplify in himself. He was singularly free from the besetting sin of Scottish theologians—absolute certainty of the truth of their own opinions, and of the error of the opinions held by those who differed from them. He was, on the contrary, positively certain on few points, and was opposed to large confessions of faith when used as tests of orthodoxy.[1] His address from his pulpit at Dirleton on the reasons for national humiliation,[2] and his work on "The Difference between True and False Christianity," show the estimate in which he held forms of Church government, as compared with holiness and righteousness.

Henry Scougal, son of the Bishop of Aberdeen, was a man of like character. He was for four years professor of divinity in Aberdeen, and died in 1678, when he was only twenty-eight years of age. The testimony of his contemporaries and the writings which he has left bear witness to his piety, meekness, and charity. His work, "The Life of God in the Soul of Man," lifts us up to a spiritual region which the din and roar of controversy never reach. The book belongs to the literature of the universal Church, and has served for many generations to quicken the piety of Christians totally irrespective of the denominations to which they may belong.[3] We get a false idea of the Episcopal Church of the period, if we look at it only in the light in which it was presented by its suffering and conscientious opponents. It was a calamity to the Church which had such men as Leighton, Charteris, Scougal, and many others like-minded, that it never had an opportunity of meeting in national synod and officially declaring its doctrine and regulating its worship, but having been established and controlled by external authority, bore the odium of the arbitrary and tyrannical measures adopted for its maintenance.

The indulged Presbyterian clergy found sufficient employment for their theological activities in defending the consistency of the position which they occupied with the principles

---

[1] Burnet's "History of his own Time," anno 1666.
[2] Grub's "Ecclesiastical History of Scotland," iii. 325 ff.
[3] Ibid. 270, and authorities there quoted.

which they professed. The non-indulged Presbyterians in Scotland were engaged in maintaining the covenanted cause, both against the Episcopalians, whom they regarded as open and professed enemies, and against those Presbyterians who, having accepted the indulgence, were scorned and condemned as cowards and traitors. The theological literature of the Scottish Covenanters of the period was written by expatriated ministers who had found a refuge in Holland. Their works are mostly controversial, and are designed to uphold those views of church government for the maintenance of which the writers had been banished. John Brown, who had been minister at Wamphray, and who had been obliged to retire to Holland in 1662, besides contributing largely to the literature connected with government and ritual, wrote a great and orthodox work on justification; and in his valuable and ponderous book against the anti-Sabbatarians has maintained the Divine origin and sanctity of the Sabbath with an ability, research, and copiousness that no subsequent writer on that subject has ever approached.

THE WESTMINSTER CONFESSION THE ONLY CREED OF THE CHURCH, 1690 TO THE PRESENT TIME.

In 1689 the Scottish Parliament declared that James had forfeited the Crown, that the throne was vacant, offered the sovereignty of Scotland to William and Mary, and abolished Episcopacy. In the following year it ratified and established the Westminster Confession as the public and avowed Confession of the true Church of Christ in Scotland, and vested the government of the Church in those ministers who had been ejected for nonconformity in and after 1661, and those who had been or should be admitted by them. The re-establishment of the Presbyterian Church and of the Westminster Confession as its creed was thus a purely Erastian Act. In 1560 the Church produced its creed to the State, and the State adopted it; in 1690 the State established the creed, and the Church received it. An apology for this mode of procedure in 1690 might be found in the fact that in no other way could the Westminster Confession and Presbyterian Church government be restored; and it might be argued that the Act came under the exceptional case provided for in the Second Book of Discipline, that when the Church is corrupted, and all things out of order, kings and princes may, by their own authority, restore the true service of the Lord. Such reasoning did not satisfy the Covenanters. The Covenanted Church of Scotland, they rightly maintained, still existed. It had indeed only one minister and two probationers, who afterwards conformed, but the truth of God is not affected by the paucity of its adherents or the lapse of time. If the objects contemplated by the Solemn League and Covenant were Divine truths when they were popular in 1643, they had not become false though they were unpopular in 1690. Therefore they maintained that the Church acknowledging the Covenants and their perpetual obligation should now be re-established; that those ministers in whom the government of the Church was vested by the civil power should be admitted only on the condition of acknowledging their sin and giving public evidence of their penitence and reformation; and they strenuously denied the right of the State to prescribe to the Church of Christ its faith and government, even should that prescribed faith and government be in accordance with the Word of God. The real Covenanters never joined the Church of the Revolution settlement. Their distinctive principles are still maintained in theory, though not in practice, by the Reformed Presbyterian Church, and by the Synod of the United Original Seceders, and by them only.

The Presbyterian Church had now been re-established. In 1690 the General Assembly met, and at once took measures for the maintenance of purity of doctrine as defined in the Westminster Confession of Faith. All ministers and elders to be received into the Church were required to subscribe their approbation of that document. Commissioners were appointed to visit the whole of Scotland, for the purpose of purging the Church of those ministers who should be found to be negligent in the performance of duty, immoral in their lives, or erroneous in their doctrine.[1] A general agreement with the doctrines of the Confession was not sufficient to secure immunity from a charge of heresy. The Assembly of 1696

[1] Acts vii. and xv., Assembly 1690.

forbade "all ministers and members of the Church to publish, by speaking, writing, printing, teaching, or preaching, any doctrine, tenet, or opinion contrary to or inconsistent with the Confession of Faith, or any article, part, or proposition therein."[1] When the number of propositions and the wide field which they cover are considered, it will be seen that no heresy had a chance of entering the Church, or lurking within it undetected and unpunished. Orthodoxy of belief was secured so far as Acts of Assembly could secure it.

The history of doctrine in the re-established Presbyterian Church, and in those churches which separated from her, may be summarized as proceeding on one or other of three lines:— (1) All doctrinal opinions shall rigidly conform to the Westminster Confession; or (2) divergent opinions shall be explained in such a way as to give them an appearance of conforming; or (3) the attempt to secure real or seeming conformity shall be abandoned, and large freedom of opinion shall be allowed. The action of any or all of the said churches, on the alleged discovery of heretical views, has been on one of these three lines.

Conformity was required under severe penalties. No one acquainted, in even a moderate degree, with the literature of the Restoration can be ignorant of the fact that the reaction from Puritanic rigidity in faith and morals had led, in many cases, to profanity and debauchery. The Assembly in 1690 mentioned denial of the existence of God, of the life to come, of the immortality of the soul, among the prevalent sins which necessitated a national humiliation. In 1696 the Assembly specified denial of the Trinity, of the incarnation, of the resurrection of the dead, and other doctrines, as being not uncommon, and enjoined all ministers to instruct and admonish seducers; and if after instruction and admonition the seducers remained impenitent, they should be proceeded against in the ordinary course.

A case soon occurred which called for the enforcement of the Act against publishing any doctrine inconsistent with the Westminster Confession. Dr. George Garden, one of the ministers of St. Nicholas' Church, Aberdeen, had in 1692 been deprived of his charge, and had continued to minister

[1] Act xxi., Assembly 1696.

to those of his former congregation who remained Episcopalians. In 1699 he published a defence of the opinions of Antoinette Bourignon. The Commission appointed to take cognizance of Aberdeenshire reported to the Assembly of 1701 that Garden had refused to disown the authorship of the book, and had expressed a general approval of its contents, and had been cited by them to appear at the Assembly bar. He did not appear. The Commission reported further that he had given positive proof of being infected with infamous and blasphemous error, by declaring that the defence which he had published represented the great end of Christianity, which was to bring us back to the love of God and charity, and that no sentiments in it were opposed to any article of the Christian faith. The Assembly found that "the writings of Antonia Bourignon were fraught with impious, pernicious, and damnable doctrines, as they are represented in the very apology that exhibits an epitome of them to the world in the fairest dress:—(1) The denying of the permission of sin, and the infliction of damnation and vengeance for it; (2) the ascribing to Christ a twofold human nature, one of which was produced of Adam before the woman was formed, and the other born of the Virgin Mary; (3) the denying of the decrees of election and reprobation, and the loading of those acts of grace and sovereignty with a multitude of odious and blasphemous aspersions, particularly wickedness, cruelty, and respect of persons; (4) that there is a good spirit and an evil spirit in the souls of all men before they are born; (5) that the will of man is unlimited, and that there must be in man some infinite quality whereby he may unite himself to God; (6) the denying of the doctrine of Divine prescience; (7) the assertion of the sinful corruption of Christ's human nature, and a rebellion in Christ's natural will to the will of God; and (8) the asserting a state of perfection in this life, and a state of purification in the life to come; that generation takes place in heaven; that there are no true Christians in the world, and several other errors contained in the said book."

The Assembly thereupon, "being moved with love to the truth of God and zeal for His glory, as also an earnest desire to purge this kirk of error and heresy, and everything that is contrary to sound doctrine," deposed Dr. Garden from the office of the ministry.[1]

This deliverance is remarkable in several respects. It shows the extensive jurisdiction assumed by the Assembly. Dr. Garden had received Episcopal ordination; he had never been a minister or member of the Presbyterian Church, and yet the Assembly tried and deposed him. It shows, further, that neither the Commission nor the Assembly had read the writings which they condemned. It is plain on the face of the Act that the list of heresies is compiled from Dr. Garden's book; if the writings themselves had been consulted, it would have been found that the account is rather a caricature than a description of Bourignianism. It is, of course, that caricature which for the last 180 years every minister of the Church of Scotland has solemnly renounced on receiving license and ordination.

Antoinette Bourignon had been twenty-one years in her grave when the Assembly passed this unfavourable verdict on her writings. She was born at Lisle in 1616, and was educated in the Roman Catholic faith. When sixteen years of age she parted from all her relatives in order to live a solitary life for the perfecting of her soul, and after having been expelled from various countries, died at Franeker in 1680. She read little, and wrote much. Her collected writings, which are composed in French, fill twenty-six volumes; and there is no doubt that, tried by the Westminster or any other orthodox Confession, they will be found to contain much erroneous doctrine. She did not attempt to solve the problem of the Divine permission of sin, but she saw in mankind little except sin, and strenuously taught that a sinful life was a life in a temporal hell, which would terminate in an eternal one. She speaks frequently of the elect, though she does not believe in the doctrine of election and its counterpart, reprobation, according to the Calvinistic system. She recognizes a good and an evil spirit ever present with us—the one inciting us to holiness, and the other tempting us to evil. She believes in God's foreknowledge, though not in the consequences which have sometimes been drawn from that truth.

[1] Act xi., Assembly 1701.

It is scarcely correct to say that she asserted the sinful corruption of Christ's human nature. No one asserts more strongly the perfect sinlessness of Christ, but while asserting this in the strongest terms, she taught that Christ took upon him our common nature, so that He, feeling our diseases and infirmities, might, in our nature, contend with and overcome the principle and root, as well as the effects and fruit of sin. The Assembly had, in effect, the same doctrine before it which 130 years after was taught and defended by Edward Irving.

As a contrast to the Bourignianism described by the Assembly and renounced by all ministers of the Church, we give the following account in the words of Antoinette Bourignon herself:—"Anthoinette Bourignon's Confession of Faith, publicly presented by her to the Court of Holstein, to oppose the malicious reports which some had industriously raised to make the purity of her doctrine and sentiments suspected: (1) I am a Christian, and believe all that a true Christian ought to believe; (2) I am baptized in the Catholic Church, in the name of the Father, of the Son, and of the Holy Ghost; (3) I believe the twelve articles of the Creed, or the Apostles' Symbol, and do not doubt any one article of it; (4) I believe that Jesus Christ is true God, and that He is also true man; and likewise that He is the Saviour and redeemer of the world; (5) I believe in the Gospels, in the holy prophets, and in all the holy Scriptures both of the Old and New Testaments. And I will live and die in all the points of this faith, which I protest, before God and man, to all whom it may concern. In testimony whereof I have subscribed this my confession with my hand, and sealed it with my seal. Anthoinette Bourignon. At Sleswick, the 11th of March, 1675." It is surely not Bourignianism as set forth in that authentic creed which for nearly 200 years every minister of the Church has been required to renounce.

We may safely say that Antonia Bourignon was both misunderstood and misrepresented; and that there was much truth and beauty, if also some error, in her teaching. The retirement from the world, which she urged, the quiet calm, the piety of life, and aspiration after perfect holiness, had great attractions for Garden, wearied with controversy and harassed by Commission and Privy Council with suspension and deprivation, and led him at last to feel with her in whose writings he had found solace, "it were better to give over all study and speculation, and with humility of heart to pray, as the Church has so long done—Come, O Holy Spirit, fill our hearts and renew the earth."[1]

After the condemnation of Bourignianism and the punishment of its Scottish advocate, the Church remained for some years free from all taint or suspicion of heresy. Theological thought was rigidly confined within the limits prescribed in the Confession, and the Commission appointed to watch over the purity of doctrine had no occasion to report any cases of erroneous teaching. This period of purity and peace soon came to an end. Rumours spread abroad that James Simson, professor of divinity in Glasgow, was teaching unsound doctrine to his students, and thus poisoning the fountain of which the future teachers of the Church were drinking. An investigation was immediately instituted, and when it had been completed and its results laid before the Assembly of 1717, that court found that in his public lectures, and in some private letters, he had used expressions which had been used by some in an unsound sense, though he disowned using them in that way; and that for answering the cavils and objections of adversaries, he had adopted some hypotheses different from those commonly used among orthodox divines, which hypotheses had no foundation in Scripture, and tended to attribute too much to natural reason and the power of corrupt nature. Mr. Simson was forbidden to use such expressions or propose such hypotheses, and all professors of divinity, ministers, and preachers were enjoined to adhere strictly to the Confession in their teaching.

The objections urged against Simson show the extreme orthodoxy of the Church, and the sensitiveness which prevailed regarding any departure from it. Simson had ventured to say that the heathen, by considering the light of nature, the works of creation and providence, and the traditions of pure religion

---

[1] Four, at least, of Antoinette Bourignon's treatises have been translated into English, viz. "The Light of the World," "Solid Virtue," "The Light risen in Darkness," and "The Renovation of the Gospel Spirit."

which still lingered among them, might arrive at some dim knowledge of the truth that God and man could be reconciled. No attempt was made to show that such a truth was unknown in any heathen religion, or if known, that it was borrowed from Christianity; no appeal was made to matters of fact, but the erroneous and dangerous character of such a statement was deduced as a necessary consequence from an assumed premiss. It was assumed as an incontrovertible truth that Scripture was the only source from which it could be known that reconciliation was possible, and therefore, it was argued, Simson's statement disparaged the Word of God, involved the Arminian heresy of the sufficiency of natural reason to enlighten man, and, worst of all, implied that Christ had satisfied Divine justice for at least some of the heathen. All these dreadful results were, it was maintained, the necessary consequences of admitting that any religion not founded on the Old and New Testament contained a dim intimation of God's mercy to man, and therefore such an admission must be unsound and dangerous. Again, Simson had in his lectures suggested that God from among the sinful mass of mankind elected a certain number to grace in Christ, and regarding them as possessing grace had elected them to glory. He might have been much more profitably employed than in trying to define with accurate precision the order in which election to grace and election to glory took place in eternity, but the order in which they occurred does not affect the absolute nature of the election. Simson did not, like Cameron, who occupied his chair a century before, teach that God first regarded men as believing in Christ, and then elected them to eternal life; but that out of the sinful mass of mankind, God, of his mere good pleasure, chose some as sinful and miserable as the rest, appointed them to grace in Christ, and then, regarding them as thus endowed with grace, appointed them to the possession of glory. Election, according to Simson, is free and absolute. Some would not regard his hypothesis in this light, and so the cry was raised that he taught his students the pernicious doctrine that God elected men to eternal life on the foresight of their faith and repentance, and so made election conditional on man's good works.

Simson cannot be so easily defended against another charge

of unsoundness made against him. He was alleged to have asserted that all children dying in infancy were in the number of the saved. The statement in the Confession, that "elect infants, dying in infancy, are regenerated and saved by Christ," may be taken in a wide and comprehensive sense, though it may also be doubted if the Confession means the word "elect" to be synonymous with "all." Be that as it may, there were many who resolutely maintained that the words were not synonymous, that an elect number of children could not possibly comprise all children within it, and that therefore the professor was in direct opposition to the standard of faith in saying that all infants dying in infancy were regenerated and saved.

The decision of the Assembly in this case has been, and is still, represented as the first declension of the Revolution Church from purity of doctrine, and forms one of the stock accusations against her. It is usually represented as a formal sanctioning of Pelagian and Arminian doctrines. A vague charge of Pelagianism and Arminianism may mean anything or nothing; it is the specific facts which determine how much or how little truth it contains. The men who in that day wrote and argued against Simson believed sincerely that the doctrines specified were heretical and dangerous. It would be interesting to know how many of those who continue to repeat the statement, that the Assembly of 1717 was unfaithful to Christian truth in the decision which it gave, really believe that no religion except the Jewish and the Christian contains even a dim intimation of Divine mercy, and that of babes who die in infancy a number pass into eternal torment.[1]

Another instance of extreme zeal for orthodoxy came before the same Assembly from the presbytery of Auchterarder. That court, besides requiring the applicants for license who appeared before them to answer the questions and sign the formula prescribed by the Assembly of 1711, tried the soundness of their belief by tests of their own devising. They had asked a student to declare as an article of faith, "I believe that it is not sound and orthodox to teach that we must forsake sin in order to our coming to Christ and instating us in covenant

---

[1] The work chiefly consulted on the nature of the first Simson case has been "The New System of Doctrine," by John M'Laren of the Tolbooth Church, 1717.

with God," and on his declining to assent to that proposition had refused to give him an extract of license. The meaning of the presbytery was orthodox, though that meaning might have been more happily expressed. All that they intended to imply was that the forsaking of sin was a result of our coming to Christ, and not a preliminary condition which we must fulfil in order that we may come. The meaning, though not the language, of the Auchterarder presbytery is contained in the authorized hymnal of the Church in such lines as—

> "Just as I am, and waiting not
> To rid my soul of one dark blot,
> To Thee whose blood can cleanse each spot,
> O Lamb of God. I come."

At that time, however, there was a tendency in some ministers, if not actually to disparage the duty of personal holiness, at least to keep that duty in the background, in order that the grace of God in man's salvation might be alone exalted, and it was that tendency which the Assembly wished to repress. The language of the Presbytery might easily have been regarded by ordinary people as conveying the impression that holiness of life was not required of a Christian. In that sense the Assembly condemned the statement, but they did not condemn the doctrine which it was intended to express. The proposition was declared to be "unsound and detestable *as it stands and was offered by the said Presbytery to be subscribed.*"[1]

The decision forms another of the stock illustrations of the Church's departure from Gospel truth. It is adduced in the Secession testimonies to prove the corruption of the Church; in these testimonies the words printed in italics are invariably omitted, and the Assembly is represented as condemning the proposition absolutely and unconditionally.[2] The ministers of the Auchterarder presbytery appeared before the Commission, and offered an explanation of the sense in which they had used the words. In the following year the Assembly expressed themselves satisfied with the explanation, but declared that however sound and orthodox the meaning of the Presbytery

---

[1] Act x., Assembly 1717.
[2] "Testimony of Associate Synod of Original Seceders, 1827," part i. p. 43; "Testimony of the United Associate Synod, 1828," part i. p. 31.

had been, it had been expressed in very unwarrantable and exceptionable words.[1]

The matter seemed now to be at rest. The Presbytery had explained, and the explanation had been accepted; but the controversy did not cease. It burst forth anew, agitated the country for some years, and virtually rent the Church asunder. In the discussion of the Auchterarder case by the Assembly, Mr. Boston, minister of Ettrick, observed to Mr. Drummond, minister of Crieff, that he had become acquainted with a book entitled the "Marrow of Modern Divinity," and recommended it as a masterly production on the subject which was then debated. Mr. Drummond read the book, and was as highly pleased with it as Boston had been. Eventually it was resolved to republish it, with a recommendatory preface by Mr. Hog of Carnock. It appeared under its old title, though Boston, after it had been condemned by the Assembly, sadly remarked that "The Marrow of Ancient Divinity," now discarded, would have been a more appropriate title. It at once commanded a wide sale, and gave rise to the most important discussion on doctrine that ever agitated the Church of Scotland.

The Assembly had strictly forbidden all ministers to preach any doctrines inconsistent with the Confession, and especially such as, on the one hand, attributed too much to corrupt human nature, or on the other tended to relax the obligations to personal holiness. Presbyteries were enjoined to see that this Act was observed by ministers, and the Commission was ordered to see that presbyteries obeyed the injunction. The courts of the Church were on the alert to detect any divergence from rigid orthodoxy, and when men were thus keenly and suspiciously watching each other, cases which seemed to call for the exercise of discipline speedily appeared.

A sermon condemning the suspected book, preached by Principal Haddow of St. Andrews at the opening of the Synod of Fife, had been published, and Mr. Hog of Carnock had replied to it; and the controversy between the supporters and opponents of the "Marrow" was raging fiercely when the Assembly of 1720 met. The question was raised as to whether the "Marrow of Modern Divinity" was sound or

[1] Act viii., Assembly 1718.

unsound. The subject was first debated for a whole day before a committee of the house, and two days afterwards was briefly discussed before the Assembly. All the ministers, except four,[1] and all the elders voted for a resolution which condemned the "Marrow" as unsound, inasmuch as it taught five heresies:— (1) That assurance was of the essence of faith; (2) that the atonement was universal; (3) that holiness was not necessary to salvation; (4) that fear of punishment and hope of reward were not motives of a believer's obedience; and (5) that the believer is not under the law as a rule of life. The book was also declared to contain dangerous paradoxes and objectionable propositions, and all ministers were enjoined to warn their people against it, and earnestly exhort them not to read it—which warning and exhortation resulted in the book being more extensively circulated and diligently read.

The "Marrow" was now condemned as containing erroneous and dangerous doctrine, but those who had recommended the book were not inclined to acquiesce in a condemnation which they considered unjust and unwarranted. The controversy, instead of being quenched, burned with greater vehemence. It was asserted that in condemning the propositions cited from the "Marrow" they had condemned some essential truths which were universally acknowledged by the Reformed Churches. To ward off this objection, which had a basis in fact, it was answered that the Assembly had not condemned the statements in the abstract, but only in the sense in which it had regarded them. This reply laid them open to the charge, which was immediately made, that though the meaning which the Assembly attributed to the "Marrow" was heretical, it was not the meaning of the propositions themselves, but that which the Assembly had mistakenly read into them. In short, the Assembly was charged with first making a heresy, and then imputing the heresy which they themselves had made to the "Marrow of Modern Divinity."

The growing feeling of dissatisfaction against the Act of Assembly condemning the "Marrow" found expression in a representation and petition presented to the Assembly of 1721.

---

[1] The four were—Gabriel Wilson, Maxton; John Grant, Auchinleck; Andrew Brugh, Madderty; and Robert Willock, Echt.

THE DOCTRINE OF THE CHURCH.

This document had been drawn up by Thomas Boston, and after revision by Ebenezer Erskine and others, was signed by twelve ministers, thence known as the Remonstrants or the Marrow men. It begins by acknowledging two tendencies in human nature, both of which have to be carefully guarded against—the tendency to pervert the grace of God into an encouragement to sin, which shows itself in teaching that holiness is not necessary to salvation; and the tendency, on the other hand, to seek salvation, not by faith in Christ, but by the good works which a man himself performs. It then specifies the points in which it was considered that the Act erred through inadvertence. It imported that a believer could not be under the law as a rule of life unless he were under it as a covenant of works. In the "Marrow" there were unmarked quotations from great divines, and the Act in representing the book as repudiating personal holiness had condemned a number of propositions which were not written by the author, but quoted by him from Luther on justification by faith. As regarded faith itself, the Assembly had confounded two different things—the sure faith, by which a man receives and rests upon Christ for salvation; and the assurance of faith, which a man can have only by possessing the graces which are its invariable fruits. Finally, it was asserted that in condemning the universal offer of salvation, the Assembly had condemned the Divine commission to preach to all men salvation through the Lord Jesus. The Assembly was in effect accused of misunderstanding the "Marrow," and of condemning, in their mistaken zeal for truth, the teaching of Luther on justification, and the teaching of the Confessions of the Reformed Churches, including that of the Church of Scotland. The Remonstrants kindly added that they did not for a moment imagine the Assembly to have been intentionally heterodox, but to have been led into error only through an oversight. While this representation afforded ample evidence of the learning and ability of its compilers as theologians, it also afforded as ample evidence of their unskilfulness as ecclesiastical tacticians. To charge the Assembly with condemning sound doctrine and favouring heresy, and to suggest as a palliation of the offence that it was done in ignorance, was more than ecclesiastical flesh and blood could stand. There had been a pretty general dissatisfaction with the Act, a feeling that it had been passed without due investigation into the accuracy of its statements, and a disposition, if not to recall, at least to modify it; but now when it was alleged that the Assembly had erred in matters of fact and of doctrine, not intentionally indeed, but by carelessness and ignorance, it was felt that no concession could be made, and that the battle must be fought till the bitter end.

The Assembly of 1721, before which the representation had been laid, was brought to a premature close by the illness of the commissioner; and the Commission of the Assembly was instructed to consider the document, and prepare a final report, to be submitted to the supreme court in the following year. The Remonstrants were repeatedly called before the Commission. A report was agreed upon which vindicated the Act complained of, and adduced additional proofs of the Antinomian character of the "Marrow." Up to this point the Remonstrants had been the assailants, and the Commission had been engaged in repelling their attacks; but at the meeting in November the Commission became the assailants, and, to use Boston's words, "turned the cannon directly against us." Twelve queries were drawn up, which the Marrow men were enjoined to answer. The questions bore upon the several points of the Remonstrance, and were designed to elicit answers which might afford ground for counter-charges against the soundness of the assailants. The Remonstrants, while protesting against being subjected to an examination in order to furnish materials for a charge against them, as being a form of process "unconstitutional, inquisitorial, and ensnaring," agreed to have their answers to the queries ready to be laid before the Commission in March.

The answers were draughted by Ebenezer Erskine, extended and amended by Gabriel Wilson, and finally revised and subscribed by all the twelve Remonstrants. The questions were ingeniously and skilfully prepared; they were as ingeniously and skilfully answered. There were pitfalls on every side, but the pitfalls were seen and avoided. The distinction between the direct and reflex acts of faith, between the moral law as a covenant of works and as a rule of life, were made once more. Sometimes the answers implied a rebuke to the examiners for asking the questions which were put. The second query asked if the believer was now bound, by the authority of the Creator, to personal obedience to the moral law, though not in order to justification. It was replied that the passage in the "Marrow" on which the question was founded, was almost in the words of the Confession, and therefore of indubitable orthodoxy, but since the Commission had seen it meet to put the question, they had no hesitation in saying that the believer is certainly bound to personal obedience, as in becoming a new creature he does not cease to be a creature. When asked if the moral law, before it was a covenant of works, had a threatening of hell annexed to it, they replied that sin deserved hell, whether there was a covenant of works or not, but that they declined to enter into the question as to the manner in which God ought to nave disposed of man if man had sinned before a covenant had been made. The Marrow men had objected to an expression used by the Assembly of 1720, enjoining ministers to preach the necessity of a holy life in order to the obtaining of everlasting happiness; and they were now asked if preaching the necessity of a holy life, in order to the obtaining of eternal happiness, was of dangerous consequence to the doctrine of free grace? In reply they gave fourteen reasons on account of which a holy life was necessary, but dared not approve of the Assembly's language. Holiness of life was not to be regarded as so much work done, in return for which eternal life would be bestowed; for eternal life was the gift of God through Jesus Christ our Lord. They said that the natural interpretation of the Assembly's words gave heretical doctrine. They were far from imputing this doctrine to the Assembly, but though the words might be explained into an orthodox meaning, they had at least an appearance of evil, and their use had been industriously shunned by Protestant Churches and divines. In short, the meaning of the Assembly and Commission was good, but it was badly expressed—the very censure which the Assembly had passed on the presbytery of Auchterarder, and had thereby originated the Marrow controversy.

The task of reconciling the offer of the benefits of Christ's death to all mankind, on the ground that Christ was dead for all, with the received dogma that Christ had died for the elect, and for them alone, was not so successfully performed. Those who maintain that the Saviour died for all, and that consequently salvation, through His death, is offered to all, are consistent, though, according to the Confession, utterly heterodox. But the Remonstrants and the Commission were at one in holding that Christ had purchased salvation for the elect alone, and that the rest of mankind had been left to perish. How, then, it was asked, was every man without exception warranted to believe, as the "Marrow" said he was, that Christ was dead for him? The Remonstrants attempted to solve the difficulty by drawing a distinction between a giving of Christ in possession, and such a gift of Christ as warranted man to receive Him; the latter was offered to all, the former was limited to the elect. Boston quotes with approval the distinction which had been made between the phrases, "Christ died" and "Christ is dead." That Christ died for all is heretical doctrine, that Christ is dead for all is orthodox.[1] It is only some experts in theology, not all, who can detect the vital difference between these two phrases. The Marrow men were really, though unconsciously, on the verge of the doctrine regarding the extent of redemption, on account of which John Macleod Campbell was a century afterwards expelled from the Church.

The Commission received the answers, and prepared a long report to be submitted to the ensuing Assembly. The report was keenly debated at the Assembly by a sub-committee, then by the committee on overtures, and finally by the house itself. It was then adopted; 134 members voted for its approval, 5 for its rejection, and about 17 declined to vote. The Assembly therefore vindicated its Act of 1720, condemning the doctrines of the "Marrow" specified as erroneous, and forbade all ministers to teach either publicly or privately the opinions mentioned or any of like tendency, refused to repeal the Act of 1720, and because of the injurious reflections contained in the representation, ordered the twelve Marrow men

---

[1] "Marrow," Boston's works, vii. 264.

to be rebuked and admonished.[1] They were then called in, rebuked and admonished, and thereupon they laid a protest upon the table, and, as Wodrow informs us, "gave gold with it" for the Assembly clerk, both of which were refused.

The protest was remarkable for its plainness and boldness. The men who had just been rebuked declared in it that they still regarded the fifth Act of Assembly 1720 as contrary to the Word of God, the Confession, and the Covenants; and protested that they would continue to preach the truths which the Assembly had now once more condemned. They expected the Assembly to take further means against them in consequence of this bold step, in which case the Secession would have taken place ten years sooner than it did, and on other grounds; but the Assembly thought they had vindicated their authority by their Act and rebuke, and the Remonstrants thought they had freed their conscience by their protest, and the Secession was for the time averted.[2]

The condemnation of the "Marrow," and the censure passed upon its supporters, have been attributed by partisan writers to the Church's indifference, or hostility, to sound doctrine. Such a view is a mistake. The resolution to condemn the book and censure its advocates was practically unanimous, and was supported by many whose orthodoxy was unquestionable. The "Marrow" contained many startling statements, which, though capable of a sound explanation, were very liable to be perverted. Great pains were needed to show that their apparent meaning was not their real meaning. That a holy life was not necessary in order to the obtaining of everlasting happiness, was a statement which could be explained in such a way as not to affect the necessity of holy living; but there was a danger that the explanation might be overlooked, and a belief entertained that everlasting happiness might be secured without holiness of life. Sinners might be told that their sins were pardoned before their lives were reformed; but such teaching, unless carefully guarded, was apt to lead to the persuasion that reformation of life was a

---

[1] Act vii., Assembly 1722.
[2] "Marrow of Modern Divinity," with notes, by Rev. Thomas Boston; Queries agreed upon by the Commission of the General Assembly, with the Answers; Dr. M'Crie's account of the Marrow Controversy, in *Christian Observer*, 1831.

superfluity. The assertions that in one sense assurance was of the essence of faith, while in another it was not; that pardon of sin is offered to all because Christ is dead for all, while the pardon offered is limited to the chosen number for whom Christ died—might be shown to be consistent with the teaching of the Confession; but the fine-drawn distinctions by which the consistency was defended were to many inappreciable, and there was a danger that the teaching of the Confession, for which all were zealous, should be corrupted. It was not indifference or hostility to the doctrines of the Confession which animated those who condemned the "Marrow," but a sincere, though it may have been a mistaken, belief that the interests of sound doctrine and pure morality were imperilled by its teaching.

The character of that theology, the purity of which was then so zealously guarded, and subsequent departures from which have sometimes been so deeply lamented, is shown at its best in such treatises as "Human Nature in its Fourfold State" by Thomas Boston. The author was a typical Scottish minister. His profound and varied scholarship, his faithfulness in the discharge of all ministerial duties, his soundness in the faith, and his fervent piety, show him to have been one of the many saintly worthies which Scotland has produced in her various schools of religious thought. His panegyrists do not err so much in the praises which they bestow upon him, as in the disparagements which they cast upon his equally good and faithful, though perhaps less gifted, contemporaries. In Boston's theology man is entirely and utterly corrupt and depraved. Adam fell as the representative and progenitor of all mankind, and in eating the forbidden fruit broke all the ten commandments. Since all mankind were represented by him, they are born guilty of the breach of the ten commandments; and as they are descended from him, they are born with a nature entirely corrupted. To man in this condition belongs Divine wrath and wrath alone. The wrath of God endures for ever. The unregenerate must sin eternally. Sin is an infinite evil, and therefore the infinity of God makes infinite wrath the doom of sin. The Divine anger against the unregenerate is described in this manner in order to serve as a basis for an earnest exhortation to flee to the refuge provided; for a refuge has been provided for a definite number, known to God, but unknown to man. Christ has suffered in the room of this definite number. Faith unites man to Christ, and faith is the special gift of God to the elect. Unregenerate man can use the means of grace, and it is his duty to use them. If he be in the number of the elect, God will in the use of the means give him faith, and grace, and glory. If he be not in that number, he will be all the better of using them, as he will through them be kept from the commission of some graver sins, though at last he must suffer that wrath of God from which he has not been redeemed by Christ, and he must suffer for ever. Immortality is bestowed on the lost soul in order that it may be eternally tormented. It is repeatedly affirmed in the work that God will through eternity hold up the lost soul with the one hand, and pour the full vials of wrath into it with the other. Boston was a man of a mild, gentle, and loving nature. He preached these doctrines because he believed them to be essential elements of the Gospel, and yearned in proclaiming them to lead men to seek salvation. His preaching was a full and faithful exhibition of what was then regarded as alone constituting pure Christian doctrine, and served for many years to shape and nourish a religion which was stern and joyless, and which in later days has seemed to proceed from an imperfect and partial conception of the glad tidings of salvation. The deity depicted has been justly regarded as possessing features more akin to the Moloch whom human sacrifices were thought to delight, than to the God of love revealed in Jesus Christ.

The Marrow controversy, besides showing the zeal of the Church for the purity of Calvinistic orthodoxy, indicated also a line of cleavage in Scottish theology which afterwards became much more distinct. On the one side of this line were those who gave greater prominence to doctrinal teaching, on the other those who gave the greater prominence to ethical instruction. After the decision of the Assembly the controversy itself was continued in presbyteries and synods, but gradually died away. The doctrinal calm which succeeded lasted but for a brief period. Rumours arose that Simson, who had formerly given the Church trouble with regard to his alleged Arminian teaching, was now instilling into the minds of his students unsound doctrine regarding the Trinity; and in 1726 the Assembly was overtured by several presbyteries to inquire into the grounds of these rumours. An investigation had already been instituted by the presbytery of Glasgow, under whose jurisdiction Professor Simson was, and the Assembly immediately took steps to make the investigation thorough and effectual. It appointed a committee of ministers and elders, which included men whose theological learning, doctrinal orthodoxy, and legal acumen were universally acknowledged, and instructed them to make an independent inquiry into the truth of the allegations, and also to aid the presbytery in their efforts. The task was difficult. There were no publications by the professor to bear witness to his soundness or heresy. The evidence adduced consisted mainly of students' reminiscences of theological lectures, which had been delivered in Latin; and of hearsay statements which were alleged to have been made in private conversation. On the evidence adduced and sifted, Simson was ultimately accused of denying the necessary existence of the Son, or at least of saying that the necessary existence and independence of the Son were philosophical niceties of which we had no real knowledge, and also of asserting that the Trinity was not numerically one. Such were the heresies which, after long and careful investigation, were alleged against him. On the other hand, he affirmed that he adhered strictly to the Westminster Confession, and that he believed and had taught the necessary existence of the Son. With regard to the charge of denying that the Trinity was numerically one, he protested that his teaching had been misunderstood and misrepresented, that he had in his theological lectures taught "that the three persons of the Trinity were of one substance in number, not in the sense in which that phrase is applied to creatures, which would restrict it to one person, but in a sense importing the strictest unity of the Godhead, in opposition to a plurality of Gods, yet consistently with there being three persons in opposition to one person." Such was his own statement of the nature of his teaching on the subject of the Trinity, as opposed to the opinion imputed to him from hearsay reports. His teaching on this point, as stated by himself, is the orthodox faith, and is directed, as he maintained it was, against the heresy of Sabellianism, which, asserting the unity of God in effect, denies the Trinity of the Godhead. It was not, however, to this subject, but to that of the necessary existence of the Son, that the inquiry was chiefly directed. The work of Dr. Samuel Clarke on "The Scripture Doctrine of the Trinity" was at the time exciting much controversy in England. In that work Dr. Clarke maintained that the Son derived His being from the Father, not by necessity of nature, but by an act of the Father's will. The result of this view was necessarily semi-Arianism. Simson was accused of having taught Dr. Clarke's view, though he asserted that he repudiated the conclusion which certainly must flow from that premiss. The investigation gradually narrowed itself into the question as to whether Simson in his teaching had or had not denied the necessary existence of the Son, which again depended on the further question as to whether he had taught that the generation of the Son was a free and voluntary act of the Father, or had taught that the generation of the Son was by necessity of nature. For if the generation of the Son was a free and voluntary act of the Father, then it might or might not have been—that is, the Son might or might not have existed; and also the Father might have communicated to Him as many or as few of the Divine attributes as He pleased. If that premiss be granted, it necessarily follows that the divinity of the Son, or the semblance of divinity in the Son, or the existence of the Son at all, is a mere matter of privilege, and Arianism is unquestionably the result. If, on the other hand, the generation of the Son was by necessity of nature, necessary existence belonged to the Son by nature, and not by privilege, and the Catholic doctrine of the divinity of the Son as defined by the Council of Nice was the result.

The investigation occupied two years. The ultimate decision on the merits of the case was arrived at by the Assembly of 1728, which found that Professor Simson did assert the necessity of the existence and generation of the person of our Lord Jesus Christ; also that the titles of the Most High God and the only true God were equally applicable to the Father and the Son, and not in any lower sense to the Son than to the

Father; likewise that he affirmed that the three persons in the Godhead are one substance or essence in number, but that he had taught and uttered such things, and expressed himself in such terms, as were subversive of the doctrines which he now professed—doctrines taught in the Scriptures and laid down in the Confession. He was thus found to be orthodox in his belief in 1728, but to have been erroneous, consciously or unconsciously, in his teaching. The question as to the punishment which should be inflicted was remitted to the presbyteries to consider, and to the next Assembly to determine. Meanwhile he was suspended from preaching and teaching. The Assembly of 1729, after long discussion, passed an Act in which, after declaring their thankfulness that in all this protracted process there had been nothing but unanimity regarding the doctrine of the glorious Trinity and the proper supreme deity of the Lord and Saviour, they found that though Mr. Simson owned the orthodox doctrine, renounced all the errors with which he had been charged, and expressed his regret for the ambiguous expressions which he had used; yet, considering the offence which he had given, they could not, while tempering judgment with mercy, allow him to act longer as professor or preacher. His suspension was made perpetual.[1]

Professor Simson seems to have viewed favourably, if he did not adopt, Dr. Clarke's method of fathoming the unfathomable and explaining the inexplicable. Like many who have subsequently appeared, he dabbled in heresy so long as such dabbling gained a repute for liberal thought, but shrank back when the consequences of the assumed heresy became apparent. Judging from the accounts given in the trial, he was not an original thinker even in heterodoxy. His opinions on the Trinity and the Sonship are evidently borrowed from Dr. Clarke; but while adopting the statements, he asserted that he repudiated the conclusions which that theologian had quite consistently deduced from them, and thus he saved his credit for orthodoxy at the expense of his credit for courage and ratiocination.

[1] Assembly 1729, Act vi. For an excellent account of the Simson case, Dr. Cunningham's "Church History" (ii. 264-275) should be consulted.

The Assembly's decision in this case forms another of the stock charges made against the Church for unfaithfulness in maintaining sound doctrine. The charge is unfounded. The case was thoroughly investigated. The Church was unanimous in asserting the orthodox faith and in condemning even the appearance of error. The only question on which there was a difference of opinion was regarding the punishment which should be inflicted on Simson, after he had made a full profession of orthodoxy and declared that he had never taught nor intended to teach error. Was he, in his old age, to be deposed and beggared, or was he to be simply prohibited from the discharge of his professional and ministerial duties? The Assembly adopted the latter and more merciful judgment. The only member of the Assembly who protested against this decision was the worthy Thomas Boston, who, however, withdrew his protest. The long, anxious, and thorough investigation of the case, the able speeches delivered during its progress, the unanimity of the Assembly in maintaining the Nicene Creed—all show its unfeigned and hearty zeal for the purity of the faith. The case shows also the falsity of the opinion which was long adopted in Scottish ecclesiastical history, but is now in process of being abandoned, that the alleged looseness of doctrine was introduced and fostered by the conforming Episcopalian ministers. Simson was trained in the strictest school of orthodoxy. His father had been ordained minister at Renfrew in 1655, had been expelled at the Restoration, restored at the Revolution, and died in 1715, the last, according to Wodrow, "of the Antediluvians," by which term the ministers ordained before the Restoration had come to be designated. He was lineally descended from that Andrew Simson, schoolmaster at Perth, who, according to John Knox, became a convert to the Protestant faith by reading David Lyndsay. The sentence of suspension, instead of deposition, was carried by the votes of the members from the Synods of Glasgow and Ayr, and of Galloway, the very districts in which the Episcopal clergy had been rabbled. The conforming Episcopal ministers were comparatively few in number; they did not figure as leaders in the Church courts; their sympathies might have led them to support an improvement in the services, but not an alteration in the doctrines of the Church. If Simson had gone beyond the confessional limits, which he denied, his doing so was simply an instance of the truth which history uniformly discloses, that it is impossible to confine living thought within the narrow bounds of rigid creeds.

This perplexing and protracted case having been finally disposed of, it seemed not unreasonable to hope that the Church would now enjoy a period of repose undisturbed by doctrinal controversies. The hope was fallacious. A controversy arose, which for years engrossed the attention of the Church and the nation, and finally effected a permanent secession. The causes which led to it had long existed; the occasion of its appearance was comparatively insignificant. The Secession controversy was but remotely and indirectly connected with doctrine at the beginning, and was only at a subsequent stage brought, by an after-thought, into direct contact with it. We are concerned with the controversy only as it affects doctrine.

In 1730 the Assembly enacted that reasons of dissent from the judgment of church courts should not be entered in the records of the court, but be retained in the custody of the clerk; and in 1732 it enacted that in all cases in which a patron had delayed or neglected to present a minister to a vacant parish, the regulations for the election of a minister should be observed which had been in force from the Revolution settlement till the restoration of patronage in 1712. These two enactments, so harmless in appearance, occasioned the Secession. The controversy began with the latter Act. Ebenezer Erskine spoke strongly against it at the Assembly, preached against it from his own pulpit, and published his sermon. He had in the summer of 1731 been inducted as third minister at Stirling, and when the Synod met there in the following April he was chosen moderator. In this capacity it fell to him to preach the opening sermon at the October meeting in Perth. There was no anticipation of anything unusual happening, and that meeting of Synod was in point of numbers undistinguished from any others. Mr. Erskine accompanied by an elder came from Stirling, the minister of Dunblane joined them, and the rest of the Synod comprised thirty-eight ministers and thirty-four elders from the presbyteries of Dunkeld,

Perth, and Auchterarder. The subject of the opening sermon was chiefly the iniquitous character of the Act of 1732. Doctrinally considered, that Act, it was maintained, was opposed to the principles which God had laid down in Scripture. There is a twofold call to the ministry, "the call of God and the call of the Church. God's call consists in qualifying a man for His work. . . . The call of the Church lies in the free choice and election of the Christian people." The divine right of the people to elect their ministers was the doctrine very vigorously maintained by Erskine. The doctrine was undoubtedly new in the practice of the Church. In the Assembly's Act which he condemned, the election was vested in the elders and heritors of the parish. In the only two brief periods in the history of the Church during which patronage had been abolished, the divine right of the people to elect a minister to a vacant parish had never been recognized. The Act of Assembly merely revived the law which was passed on the re-establishment of the Presbyterian Church. In the period between 1649 and the Restoration, which has been regarded by some as the golden age of the Church, the election of the minister was vested in the kirk-session. In both periods the people had only the right to object, and the Church courts were the sole judges of the worth of the objections. Erskine had no historical grounds for asserting that the right, and much less the divine right, of the Christian people to elect the parish minister had been the law and practice of the Scottish Church. He had said in his sermon that the ministers who had not been elected by the people should be looked upon as thieves and robbers; and in the discussion which arose on this point it was urged in the Synod that he thereby excluded the whole ministers of the Church of Scotland, and himself among the rest, from having the call of God, as the body of the people had never been allowed to vote in their election. Erskine replied that he did not exclude the whole ministers of the Church or himself, since he was not aware of any settlement having taken place from the Revolution till the Act of Patronage came into force, in which the people had not concurred, and till of late they were, in practice, allowed to vote. The people were, indeed, in many instances allowed to vote, but this liberty was always granted to them as a favour, and not given as theirs by divine right. The doctrine, new to the Church, which he proclaimed was in effect that the election of parish ministers by male heads of families was a divine institution.

There was another subject which was merely glanced at in the sermon, which took a prominent place in the early proceedings of the Secession Church—the necessity of going back beyond the Revolution, to the attainments which the Church had reached in the covenanting period, and from which it subsequently declined. "During the times of persecution and tyranny which preceded the Revolution, encroachments," Erskine said, "had been made on the crown rights of Christ, which no subsequent Assembly had testified against by an express Act." Dissatisfaction with the Church of the Revolution, even in its purest state, and a desire to restore it to the position which it occupied in the times when the covenants were supreme, sentiments which were more fully and clearly expressed in the Testimony afterwards published, were here, at the very beginning of the controversy, distinctly enunciated. Erskine's sermon gave offence to some, not because of his disapproval of the Act of the last Assembly regarding the election of ministers, but because of the strong, and, as it seemed to them, vituperative language in which that disapproval had been expressed. A committee was appointed to confer with him, "to see if he would acknowledge that he was in the wrong in emitting such expressions, and would promise before the Synod that he would not express himself on public occasions in time coming after that manner." He told them "it was in vain, for he was fixed." After a discussion which lasted three days, the Synod, by a majority of six, "found Mr. Erskine censurable on the account of the expressions he emitted in his sermon before the Synod." From this decision Mr. Moncrieff of Abernethy and twelve other members dissented, and Mr. Erskine along with Mr. Fisher of Kinclaven dissented and appealed to the Assembly.[1]

The Assembly of 1733 found the expressions in Mr. Erskine's sermon quoted in the Synod's minutes "to be offensive, and to tend to disturb the peace and good order of the Church; and

[1] The quotations are taken from the Synod record, on which also the statements relative to the Synod's proceedings are based.

appointed him to be rebuked and admonished by the Moderator at their own bar, in order to terminate the process, which was done accordingly."[1] Erskine protested against the censure, as implying that he had in his doctrine departed from the Word of God and the standards of the Church; and protested further that he would preach the same truths, and testify against the same or like defections. The gauntlet was here thrown down. The Assembly was defied—on mistaken grounds, as it might seem to an impartial onlooker. Neither Synod nor Assembly had censured anything but the alleged violent and offensive language which Mr. Erskine had used. It would have been far wiser to have taken no notice of the language, but prudence and calmness did not characterize the discussion on either side. A committee was appointed to confer with the protesters, but they refused to withdraw or to modify their protest. The case was remitted by the Assembly to its Commission, which summoned the protesters before them, and found them firm in refusing to yield an inch of the ground which they had taken. At length, at the meeting of the Commission in November, it was resolved, by the casting vote of the Moderator, to proceed to censure the protesters, and on the question being proposed whether they should be deposed from the ministry or declared to be no longer ministers of the Church, the latter alternative was adopted, whereby their ecclesiastical connection with the Church was severed, and their respective parishes made vacant.

The charge which the Synod and Assembly had first found proved was the use of intemperate language by Erskine; and on the refusal of Erskine and his friends to withdraw or modify their protest, the further charge of insubordination and contumacy was found proved by the Commission. On the other hand, it was maintained by Erskine, that if he was to be censured for speaking against the defections of the Church, and if he was to be precluded from having his reasons of dissent against the resolution of a church court entered in the record of that court, he was, within the Church, absolutely fettered in his ministerial freedom and faithfulness in testifying against error and in behalf of the truth. Therefore when the "four brethren" were expelled from the Church, they found themselves, sup-

[1] Act vii., Assembly 1733.

ported by numerous and enthusiastic sympathizers, in a position in which they could exercise all freedom and faithfulness unrestrained by the fetters with which Synod and Assembly had vainly tried to bind them. A fortnight after they had been expelled by the Commission, they formed themselves into a presbytery.

Erskine and his three brethren had been expelled from the Church by the Commission, but the Commission was not a court of the Church, and before its proceedings could have legal authority, they required to be ratified by the next Assembly. The Assembly of 1734 tried to undo the mischief which had already been wrought. Erskine had denounced, in intemperate language as was thought, the Act of 1730 about not recording mere reasons of dissent, and of 1732 about planting of vacant churches to which patrons had failed to present: both Acts were repealed. He had denounced patronage: the Assembly along with Synods, and specially Erskine's own Synod of Perth and Stirling, with presbyteries and kirk-sessions, had heartily and continuously denounced it since it had been restored; but it now sent an influential deputation to London to endeavour to get patronage abolished. The Church and the world were assured that the Act of last Assembly censuring Mr. Erskine for the expressions he had used in his sermon neither did restrain, nor was intended to restrain, ministerial freedom and faithfulness; and the Assembly even empowered the Synod of Perth and Stirling to restore the four ministers to the communion of the Church and to their respective ministerial charges. In accordance with the instructions of the Assembly, the Synod held a special meeting at Stirling on the 2nd of July. There were laid before it petitions from the town councils and kirk-sessions of Stirling and Perth, and the kirk-session of Kinclaven, praying that the four ministers should be restored to their charges. The Synod unanimously restored the four brethren to ministerial communion with the Church, and to their respective parishes; the representatives of the several town councils and kirk-sessions declared themselves well satisfied, and, so far as the Synod and public bodies interested were concerned, all ended happily.

One slight circumstance alone transpired which tended to

disturb for a moment the general satisfaction. It was reported by the presbytery of Dunkeld that a presentation in favour of Mr. Adam Fergusson, minister at Killin, to the vacant parish of Kinclaven, together with his letter of acceptance, was in the hands of their clerk. The Synod strictly forbade the presbytery of Dunkeld to receive the presentation, as the Church was not vacant, and enjoined them to inquire into Mr. Fergusson's conduct in accepting it.

This Act of the Synod, and its results as affecting the position of "the four brethren," must be borne in mind in order to form a fair judgment of the subsequent conduct of the Assembly. If it had not been passed, the parish of Kinclaven and the other three, which at the time were actually vacant, would have been supplied with other ministers; but in consequence of it "the four brethren" were restored, and so continued to preach in the parish churches, and to enjoy all their rights and emoluments as parish ministers. In so far they homologated the Act and reaped its benefits; but in all other respects they refused to be restored to the Church. Their names appeared once more on the roll of presbytery and Synod, and continued on the roll till 1740, but they neither sat in the courts nor acknowledged their jurisdiction. The Assembly had rescinded the Acts about the settlement of vacant parishes and not recording reasons of dissent, but had not confessed its sin in having passed them; it had enjoined all ministers to preach the pure doctrine of Christianity as set forth in the Confession, but it had given no guarantee that the injunction would be obeyed in all time coming. "The four brethren," who had already constituted themselves as a presbytery, now assumed jurisdiction as a court. Their adherents, who were still members of the Established Church, were to be subject to that court alone. Meantime they had been joined by four other parish ministers, who, without resigning their livings, repudiated all allegiance to the courts of the Church of which they were still ministers. They occupied, unquestionably, a most anomalous position. They drew a distinction between the Established Church of Scotland and the Church of Christ in Scotland. The former, they said, had driven the latter into the wilderness, and they saw it to be their duty to tarry in the wilderness with her. So far their position was intelligible, and in accordance with their convictions. But all the time that they were tarrying with the Church of Christ in the wilderness they were, as ministers of the unfaithful, corrupt, and persecuting establishment, preaching in the parish churches, living in the manses, and receiving the stipends. This latter fact has generally been either kept in the background or conveniently ignored. It is evident that such a state of matters could not continue, and so at length, in 1740, the General Assembly, which had taken action against the eight ministers for declaring that the judicatories of the National Church were unlawful courts of Christ, and for declining all authority over them which the courts of that Church might claim, deposed them for insubordination and contumacy; and their parishes were declared vacant.

This Act of the Assembly is, in sectarian narratives, sometimes represented as crowning the Church's unfaithfulness and corruption. These men's soundness in doctrine, purity of life, attachment to the true constitution of the Church, are held up for admiration, and the sentence is denounced as unjust and tyrannical. No representation could be more unfair; it may safely be asserted that no Church ever displayed greater forbearance. She had for six years seen her authority defied, her character traduced, and her members alienated by men who were all the while eating her bread. When the eight ministers at last appeared at the bar of the Assembly, they appeared as a presbytery, only to decline its jurisdiction, and to present a series of accusations which, they maintained, justified them in their declinature. They might, at the same time, have given the Church some credit for having, during the past six years, exhibited to them an uncommon instance of the exercise of meekness, patience, and long suffering. There was a difference of opinion in the Assembly as to whether the men should be deposed: there can scarcely be any difference of opinion as to whether the Assembly had not ample reasons for declaring them to be no longer ministers of the Established Church. When they repudiated the authority of the ecclesiastical courts, and constituted themselves into a separate court which disclaimed connection with the Church, they should also have voluntarily resigned the material advantages which they enjoyed only in virtue of being connected with it.

The aim of the founders of the Secession was to have a church which should be not only free from all taint or suspicion of unsound doctrine at the time, but which should never harbour heresy in all time coming. Their ideal of purity was borrowed from the covenanting period. The years from 1638 to 1650 seemed to them an age of gold and glory, though to the majority of those who lived in them they seemed rather a time of iron and blood. To connect themselves firmly and indissolubly with the Church as it then existed, they enacted that all who were admitted to the ministry should have renewed the covenants, while such of their members as opposed or slighted the duty of covenanting should not be admitted to sealing ordinances. Theological thought was to be put back a century and fixed for ever in the position which it had then occupied, and no divergence therefrom was to be tolerated.

An attempt has sometimes been made to represent the Secession movement as being a continuation of the Marrow controversy. It is true, indeed, that in the doctrinal testimony of the Secession Church, prominence was given to the expressions in the "Marrow" which the Assembly had condemned as being of dangerous tendency, and they, together with the Auchterarder test, were represented as containing vital truths which had been unrighteously condemned; but the Secession was not supported by those who had been the chief defendants in that controversy. Of the twelve Marrow men who had been rebuked at the bar of the Assembly in 1722, ten were alive when the Secession began. Ebenezer Erskine and his brother Ralph were the only ones who took part in it. The other eight stood aloof from the movement, and some published their reasons for disapproving the step which had been taken.

It was not in order to have liberty to preach evangelical doctrine that Erskine seceded. That liberty he and all others possessed, and were enjoined to exercise, while the preaching of any other doctrine was strictly forbidden. It was patronage extending in its range, and hardening in its exercise, which mainly originated the Secession, and contributed to its support and extension. There was, on the one side, the proclamation of the divine right of the Christian people to elect their ministers; on the other, patronage, resulting often in violent settlements. In the Established Church many ministers were still to be found who preached the purest Calvinistic doctrines, inculcated the duties of covenanting and the binding obligation of the covenants, and testified strenuously against all defections; but popular election was not found there, and it was gradually becoming evident that it was not to be found. That patronage propagated the Secession is evident from one undoubted fact. The settlement of an unpopular presentee was either followed by the erection of a Secession church in the parish, or by an accession of members to one that might have already existed in the neighbourhood.

The attempt of the Secession to restore the spirit and practice of the covenanting age resulted in absolute failure. It could not be otherwise. The fashions of a past century may be temporarily revived, but the modes of thought which then prevailed cannot be restored. The covenants were at that time steadfastly and consistently maintained by a small body of Presbyterians, who were the legitimate representatives of the men who had never accepted indulgences, and who had refused to join the Revolution Church as being Erastian and uncovenanted. If the seceders were to go back a century and restore the Church which then flourished, it was this small remnant that had ever been faithful to the cause which they should have joined. One of the eight seceding ministers, Mr. Nairn, saw eventually that this step was the logical result of this attempt, and accordingly joined the Society people. The others held on their own way, and so the duty of covenanting and the perpetual obligation of the covenants were in the Secession Church quietly allowed, in course of time, to drop into oblivion.

The subsequent history of the Secession Church, its divisions and reunions and alliances, lies beyond our province. That church is now large and influential, but it has reached that state only by abandoning principles for which the first seceders contended, and which they deemed essential. The real representatives of "the four brethren" and those who first joined them are not the United Presbyterians, but the Original Seceders.

After the Secession had taken place, the Church for a lengthened period enjoyed comparative rest from doctrinal controversies. The Assemblies were indeed agitated by keen and incessant disputes regarding patronage and forced settlements, and the baneful results which they involved, but it was only at rare intervals that a case of mild heresy cropped up to increase their many perplexities. New influences were now at work outside of the domain of theology, but destined to effect changes on its character by expanding and liberalizing the spirit of the age. From the time of the Reformation Scotchmen had been almost entirely engaged in theological controversy. Their writings were on theological subjects, and generally of a polemical character. They were incessantly engaged in attacking and refuting ecclesiastical opponents, and had neither time nor inclination to enter on the field of literature. In reading the works or memoirs of Scotchmen of those times, one is struck by the almost total absence of allusions to the literary productions of contemporary English authors. Bacon, Shakespeare, Milton, and others are never mentioned. They possessed no attractions to men whose energies were absorbed in the church controversies which raged fiercely around them. Bacon had invented some new system of philosophy to supplant that of Aristotle, Shakespeare was a strolling actor who had composed some stage plays, Milton had written scoffingly of Presbytery and its divine authority, and in "Paradise Lost" his theology was tinctured with Arianism. Why should these and similar productions be studied by men who had to defend Presbytery against Prelacy, Calvinism against Pelagian-Arminian errors, and the supremacy of the covenants against careless Gallios and lukewarm Laodiceans? Scottish poetry may be said to have died with Sir David Lyndsay, and to have revived after two centuries in Allan Ramsay. Histories were composed, but they related to Scottish ecclesiastical politics and opinions, and were written in a partisan spirit. Even works designed to nourish piety were largely controversial. The writers were few in number who, like Leighton, rose above sectarian disputations, and reached the serene heights of pure spiritual religion.

Scottish intellect could not be doomed to move continuously

in this beaten path. Poetry revived—not imitations of the Italian school, like the sonnets of Drummond of Hawthornden, or Latin verses embodying Calvinistic dogmas in sapphic metres, as in Boyd's "Hecatomb," but genuine poetry, racy of the Scottish soil and descriptive of the life of the Scottish peasantry. Philosophical investigation was prosecuted on new lines. Hutcheson struck out new paths in philosophic thought. Adam Smith's lectures on the "Theory of Moral Sentiments" could not fail to excite the students to independent thought. The freedom of the human will and cognate subjects began to be discussed, without reference to the results which the decisions arrived at might have on orthodox doctrine. Hume had assailed the very foundations, not only of Christianity, but of religion itself, and other weapons were needed to defend them than the fulminations of the Assembly's Commission against the authors of books tending to error. These would have been unheeded by the thinkers who acknowledged that in argument Hume had been worsted by Dr. George Campbell. Historical investigations, in which the ecclesiastical questions of the time were not concerned, were prosecuted, and their results published in such works as those of Dr. Robertson. Dramatic literature, which had for two centuries been unknown once more appeared. The novel, though sternly denounced, found its way into Scotland. The productions of Richardson, of Fielding, and of Smollett—himself a Scotsman—were read, and soon a Scottish novelist appeared in Henry Mackenzie, the first of a brilliant host. All these facts show that the Scottish mind had now burst through the ecclesiastical environments which for two centuries had mainly confined its energies.

The liberalizing influence of the wider and freer range of thought extended to the pulpit. In the previous century there had been, as Baillie tells us, complaints of such preachers as Leighton, Grey, and Binning, who, abandoning the good old way of expounding and dividing a text, "ran out in a discourse on some common head in a high, romancing, unscriptural style, tickling the ear for the present, and moving the affections in some, but leaving little or nothing to the memory and understanding." A hundred years after Leighton and his companions had, as young preachers, startled staid congregations by their new methods of preaching, complaints were again made that instead of discourses embracing doctrine and uses, mere moral harangues were often delivered from the pulpit by young aspirants to the ministry. The Assembly in 1736 not only enjoined the preaching of sound doctrine, but enunciated a scheme of Christian truths and duties which ministers were required to teach. The method was literally followed by many, and was known as "preaching on the system." There are still traditions telling of men who began every sermon, if not at the bliss of paradise, at any rate at the misery which immediately succeeded that bliss, and who, after treading the customary round, ended it by consigning saints and sinners to their respective destinations. Much of what was called evangelical preaching came to be of this character, but there was much also of a far different and higher kind. There were in the Church many able, earnest, and spiritual preachers, who faithfully taught the truths of Christianity and the influence which these truths should have on daily life and conduct; but while this description is true of many, it becomes untrue when it is applied to all the ministers of the evangelical school. The influences which were changing the spirit of the age produced naturally and inevitably a change in the pulpit. Hence arose what was termed the Moderate School in theology, which must be carefully distinguished from the Moderate School in church government. The men under the influence of the new tendencies put the duties of Christianity in the foreground. They did not deny the doctrines nor did they ignore them, but insisted mainly on the practical duties which they involved. Their best representative as preachers is Dr. Hugh Blair, who, like others of the leading Moderates, was descended from faithful Covenanters. He by no means ignores doctrine in his sermons, but regarding religion as "a calm, sober, and rational principle of conduct," his aim is to make that principle regulate common life. There was a danger in this mode of preaching of presenting religion exclusively on its practical side; and this danger not being guarded against, led, in some cases, to the production of pulpit discourses which were merely dry, cold, and uninteresting moral dissertations. But, again, it is unfair to represent that description as applicable to all Moderate preaching.

There was another line of cleavage in the Church, caused by a difference of opinion on the administration of the Act of Patronage—an Act which in itself had no connection with doctrine. One party in the Church, which contained men who approved and men who disapproved of the Patronage Act, were united in thinking that so long as it was the law it should be obeyed, and that the authority of the Church in enacting obedience should be vindicated. Another party, while reluctantly submitting to its operation, sought to give some effect to the wishes of the people in the settlement of a minister, and were inclined to excuse or overlook the conduct of those members of ecclesiastical courts who refused to obey the injunctions of the courts, when the wishes of the people were disregarded. The former class was also called the Moderate party, the latter was known as the Popular party. This cross division has led to confusion in considering the history of the period. Many of those who were Moderates—that is, on the side of strict law and order as regarded the carrying out of the Patronage Act—were Evangelicals as regarded their preaching. It was the contentions of these two parties on the Patronage Act and its administration, and not doctrinal differences, which mainly disturbed the peace of the Church. The description of that period given by a leader on the Moderate side, who yearned to find a means by which the Patronage Act, which could not be thrown off, could be reconciled with the popular claims, which the legislature would not grant, is strictly accurate in its main features. "In doctrine there are no divisions among us. Our people are in no danger of being distracted by jarring theories from the pulpit in their most momentous concerns; the word heresy is not once mentioned among us; and we do not meet in our church courts to discuss articles of faith or to divide on the orthodoxy of opinions."[1]

The liberalizing influence of the new tendencies of thought showed itself in greater mildness and toleration. Keenness to detect the faintest trace of heresy, and rigour in punishing it, were no longer encouraged. Several instances occurred which show the spirit of toleration that began to prevail. Tindall's book entitled "Christianity as Old as the Creation," which

[1] Dr. Hardy, "Principles of Moderation," 1782.

endeavoured to establish that men are fully able of themselves to discover all the articles of natural religion, and that articles of faith which lie beyond the reach of human discovery can never be admitted as a Divine revelation, had been published in England, and was regarded as an able argument in favour of deism and against revelation. The book called forth many replies, and one of the best was written by Dr. Archibald Campbell, professor of church history in St. Andrews. Dr. Campbell maintained the necessity of Divine revelation, and wrote to prove "that mankind, left to themselves, without supernatural instruction, are not able to discover the being and perfections of God, and the immortality of the soul, in the knowledge and belief of which all religion is founded." He had also in another publication, designed to prove that the apostles were not visionary enthusiasts, as deists affirmed, but men of calm and sober judgment, given it as his opinion that during the interval between the death of Christ and the descent of the Holy Spirit, the apostles had lost faith in Jesus as the Messiah. It frequently happens that a man, arguing in defence of what he regards as a vital truth against a real opponent, expresses himself more strongly than he would do if he were writing an abstract treatise on the same theme. He is apt, in the heat of the contest, to press his argument unduly. Dr. Campbell was thought by some to have in his ardour made some rash assertions, but no doubts were entertained by any regarding the purity of his motives or the sincerity of his purpose in defending revelation against deism. Some propositions which in themselves were suspected of having an unorthodox tendency were selected and submitted to the consideration of the Assembly in 1736. The Assembly acquitted, and righteously acquitted, Campbell of upholding or even of harbouring erroneous doctrine, but recommended to him and to all ministers and professors of divinity "to be cautious in their preaching and teaching and writing, not to use doubtful expressions or propositions, which may be constructed in an erroneous sense, or lead the hearers or readers into error, however sound such words or propositions may be in themselves, or however well intended, but to hold fast the form of sound words."

The case of Dr. Campbell shows not only the good sense and fairness of the Assembly in refusing to be actuated by a panic-dread of heterodoxy, but it shows also the spirit and practice of those who posed as the defenders of sound doctrine. To select some sentences from a writing, to draw from those sentences, separated from their context and considered apart from the motive of the book in which they appeared, the consequences to which they, taken by themselves, might lead, and then to attribute all these consequences to the author as being the opinions which he held and meant to inculcate, would be a proceeding manifestly and grossly unjust. It would be wrong-doing under the guise of zeal for truth. The decision of the Assembly in this case is adduced in the Secession Testimonies as another proof of the Church's unfaithfulness.

The growing spirit of toleration and fairness was shown three years afterwards in the case of Mr. Glas, founder of the denomination of Glassites or Sandemanians. Mr. Glas, who also was the descendant of a covenanting and protesting minister, had become convinced that the covenants were unwarranted by the Word of God, and that those who suffered for them were unenlightened; that there was no warrant in the New Testament for a National Church, and that the civil magistrate had no concern with upholding true or suppressing false religion; and finally, that a single congregation is subject to no jurisdiction under heaven. For holding and teaching these views he had been deposed in 1728. The Assembly of 1739 were of opinion that Mr. Glas had been too hardly dealt with, and that he should have been simply declared to be no longer a minister of the Church. The sentence of deposition was accordingly recalled.

The liberal spirit displayed by the Assembly in this case was in reality a greater defection from doctrinal purity than the decisions in the cases of Campbell and Simson. In these cases erroneous opinion was, at the most, only a matter of inference; in the Glas case the errors of Independency, of pure Voluntaryism, of denying not only the obligations but the righteousness of the covenants, were maintained and taught as Divine truths; and yet, in the full knowledge of his persistence in these errors, the Assembly restored him to his status as a minister, though not to his office as a minister of the Church.

THE DOCTRINE OF THE CHURCH. 281

The case of Dr. Leechman, professor of divinity in Glasgow, which, after passing through the inferior courts, came before the Assembly of 1744, shows the morbid sensitiveness which still existed with regard to heresy, and the frivolous grounds on which a suspicion of heresy was sometimes based. Dr. Leechman had published a sermon on prayer, for the special purpose of counteracting the effects of a pamphlet which had been circulated in the West of Scotland, and which represented prayer as a practice absurd in itself, and impious in its design of altering the eternal and fixed purpose of God. The pamphlet attacked prayer itself, the offering up of our desires unto God, and said nothing against offering them up in the name of Christ; for if prayer is not to be offered, there is no need to add that it is not to be offered in the name of Jesus. Leechman's sermon was designed to be a vindication of prayer, and not a full treatise on its nature. Objections were at once raised, not with regard to what was said, but with regard to what was omitted. He had not affirmed in that sermon that our desires to God should be offered in the name of Christ, through the merits and satisfaction of the Mediator, as the only grounds of our acceptance with God, and of our obtaining the pardon of sin; and therefore, it was argued, he must be unsound in these points. Leechman replied that he held these doctrines, and appealed to his other published sermons as proof that he had faithfully taught them; and affirmed that their omission in the sermon in question proceeded only from his persuasion "that it was necessary to convince men of the reasonableness of offering up their desires to God before they can be convinced that it is a reasonable thing to offer them up in the name of Christ; and that it might be of some use, through the Divine blessing, to endeavour to do the first of these at the time when, and in the place of the country where, he attempted it."[1] Leechman was unanimously and righteously acquitted. If heresy were to be inferred from silence, and a man held guilty of disbelieving or denying all the doctrines connected with a subject on which he publishes book or pamphlet that he has not therein expressly avowed or defended, no one could be regarded as pure in the faith.

It was not till the year 1790 that another case of heresy

[1] Assembly 1744. Act ix.

relieved the monotony of the incessant disputations regarding patronage and violent settlements, which had for long mainly occupied the attention of Assemblies. It originated from a work by Dr. Macgill, one of the ministers of Ayr, entitled "A Practical Essay on the Death of Christ." He was accused of teaching Socinianism in a disguised form, of representing the priestly office of Christ as being metaphorical, and of representing repentance to be the proper atonement for past transgressions, and faith and sincere obedience to be the foundation of the hope of future happiness. Macgill's case has attracted more notice than it really merits, on two accounts. The opinions which he was accused of teaching were thought to be pretty widely diffused; and they found a champion in a young Ayrshire poet named Robert Burns, who, in the "Kirk's Alarm" and other pieces, attacked the orthodox party, not with theological argument, but with sarcasm and ridicule. Macgill himself was not worthy of such an advocate. As a heretical teacher he lacked backbone. It is comparatively easy to deal with a heretic who stands firm and erect, but it is difficult to reach one who collapses as soon as a blow is aimed at him. Dr. Macgill succumbed. He declared that he was heartily sorry to find that there were in his publication ideas which might appear improper, and modes of expression, with respect to some things, which were ambiguous and unguarded. These ideas and expressions he disclaimed, and asserted his belief in the Confession of Faith as the authorized interpreter of Scripture and the confession of his own faith. The provincial Synod was satisfied; and when the case came before the Assembly it was dismissed, on the ground that it had been already adjudicated upon.

Though Macgill disclaimed holding the doctrines imputed to him, there can be no doubt that the theological views adopted by some of the clergy were very different in many things from those set forth in the Westminster Confession. A desire to be freed from the confessional trammels, and to be at liberty to teach the truth as they apprehended it in their own minds, and not as it was dictated to them from without, was felt and expressed by them. There had always been some dissatisfaction with a large, comprehensive, and minutely specific creed. It had found expression when the old Scottish Confession, which in simplicity contrasted favourably with the Westminster, was the symbol of the Church's faith. Wodrow speaks of men in his time who wished to be emancipated from the bonds of the Confession, not because they objected to its doctrines, but because they desired a freer range for investigation. The desire at length found expression in periodicals. It was said that the right of private judgment, which had been so strongly asserted at the Reformation against the authority of the Church of Rome, had come to be practically denied and condemned in the Church of Scotland, inasmuch as the dogmas of the Confession were placed before the investigator as the conclusions at which he must arrive. The movement never took practical shape. Its supporters had not the courage to avow their purpose openly in the courts of the Church, where it was certain to have met with a general opposition, and soon ceased to advocate it. The tradition of it long remained as an index of opinions once entertained by a few daring and heterodox thinkers, and served to mark the depth into which extreme Moderatism had sunk. Within recent years the same movement has been revived, not only in the Church of Scotland, but in other Presbyterian Churches whose profession of orthodoxy is unquestionable, and it gives fair promise of attaining a success which, a century ago, it did not even attempt to claim. The support given to it now, compared with the almost universal condemnation with which it was received at the close of the eighteenth century, is a significant token of the change in theological thought which has silently been effected.

The growing liberality of the Church was shown also in the position which the Church assumed with regard to such subjects as religious revivals, and the repeal of the penal laws against the Roman Catholics. When George Whitefield visited Scotland on a revival mission, the Secession, then in the enthusiasm of its early youth, would allow him to officiate in their churches only on the condition of his confining his ministrations to themselves; and on his refusing to come under such a stipulation they rejected his ministrations, and denounced him as an agent of Satan. Many of the pulpits of the Church were unconditionally thrown open to him. When the revival movement which began at Cambuslang, and spread over some parts of the country, was in progress, the Secession ministers could not regard it as the work of the Holy Spirit wrought by the agency of others than themselves, but humbled themselves in fasting before the Lord, who had in His anger suffered the land to be visited with such Satanic delusions. Ministers of the Church, and even some who had taken an active part against Mr. Erskine, and had been forced upon reclaiming parishes, were active and successful revival preachers.

When the penal laws against Roman Catholics had been repealed in England, and there was a prospect of a similar measure being passed for Scotland, the subject was discussed in the Assembly of 1778, and a resolution in favour of religious toleration was carried by an overwhelming majority, greatly in consequence of the efforts of Principal Robertson. The Secession joined with the minority in opposing the proposed repeal. There can be no doubt that in refusing to countenance Whitefield, "a priest of the Church of England who had sworn the oath of supremacy and abjured the Solemn League and Covenant," the Seceders and those of the National Church who sympathized with them, were acting in accordance with Covenanting principles, and there can be as little doubt that the evidences of liberality and toleration in the Church were evidences also of a falling away from past attainments.

On one point, the rigid enforcement of the Patronage Act, no toleration was at length allowed. Implicit obedience to the Assembly's orders, to intrude presentees upon parishes, contrary to the will of the people, was enjoined upon presbyteries. The carrying out of this resolution led to the formation of the Relief Church. That Church did not originate in a secession, but in an expulsion, in which doctrine was in no way concerned.

The credit for liberality in doctrinal matters which the Moderate party had so long enjoyed was forfeited by themselves, and transferred to their opponents by a tactical blunder. Mr. Leslie, an eminent scientist, had been elected to the mathematical chair in Edinburgh University in preference to Mr. Macknight, one of the city ministers. It might be thought that no doctrinal discussion could have arisen in the Church out of such an appointment. The Edinburgh ministers, who had zealously supported the candidature of Mr. Macknight, discovered that Leslie, in a note appended to a scientific work, had expressed his approval of Hume's theory of causation. According to that theory, the only connection between cause and effect that we can see is that of invariable sequence: when the one occurs the other invariably follows. They professed to be greatly alarmed at the dangerous results which might be anticipated from the academical teaching of a man who regarded such a theory with favour. In an evil moment the ministers gave a statement of what they considered the orthodox theory of causation, which was that the cause had power in itself to produce the effect. The tables were at once turned upon them. Hume's theory could be held, it was said, quite consistently with the belief that it was the Divine will which produced the effects, that it was God who caused the sun to shine, and the rain to fall, and the earth to yield her fruits; while the theory advanced as the orthodox one led necessarily to materialism, for if matter had an intrinsic power in itself to produce effects, then matter with its inherent forces accounted for all phenomena. The case came before the Assembly of 1805. The Moderates condemned the appointment in the interests of orthodoxy; their opponents supported it in the interests of liberal thought. The former position of parties was completely reversed. At the close of the discussion, which lasted for two days, and was characterized by exceptional ability, the Moderate party received the defeat which in this case they so richly deserved. The real subject of controversy was not the comparative merits of two different theories of causation, or the disastrous results to religion which either of them might occasion, but it was to determine the question as to whether university chairs should or should not be an appanage of the Church, to be held by the Moderate party.

During the first quarter of the present century the Evanglical party continued to grow in strength. An interest in missions to the heathen was awakened. It is incorrect to say, as has sometimes been done, that the cause of missions was promoted by the one side and opposed by the other. The apathy which had formerly prevailed had been shared by all, and the new missionary movement found some of its ablest supporters among men who, judged by the opinions which they held with regard to the Patronage Act and its administration, belonged to the Moderate party. Theology was keeping within its confessional limits. If there was some preaching which might truthfully be described as dry morality, there was as much that with equal truth might be described as dry doctrinal orthodoxy. Views now emerged which were taught by men who had little sympathy with Moderates or Evangelicals. They took a different and, in the opinion of many, a higher position. There were truths of God revealed in His word which the Westminster Confession did not contain, and other truths which it stated in a partial and imperfect manner. At no period of her history, and certainly not in the early part of the nineteenth century, did the Church of Christ reveal "all the light which was contained in her living Head." It was maintained, further, that the Church should ever seek to grow in the knowledge of Divine truth, and that it was a failure in duty in a Church, as it was in an individual Christian, to remain satisfied with the light possessed, and refuse to receive more. No Confession of Faith should be interposed between the Church and the truth revealed by our Lord.

These views were advanced by men who were thoroughly in earnest, and who would not keep silent regarding them. No prospect of censure from ecclesiastical courts could stay them from proclaiming what they believed to be the fuller message of God. The Church, in the interests of orthodoxy, took steps to arrest the movement. Proceedings were commenced against John M'Leod Campbell, minister at Row. Mr. Campbell was then thirty years of age, and had been for five years a minister of the Church. He regarded the confessional teaching as deficient in its exhibition of Divine truth, as based largely on God's sovereignty, and too little on God's character. It is a truth that God is almighty; it is also a truth that God is love. It was the character, and not the power, of God that Christ came to reveal, and of this character He was himself the fullest revelation. The feelings and actions and motives of Jesus reveal to us the feelings and actions and motives of God, so that in Christ we see God. Then looking at the life of Christ, he saw that Jesus, who showed the universal range of the command which enjoined every man to love his neighbour as himself, loved all men, and showed His love by His deeds, and finally and specially by His dying. If Christ, then, loved every human being, and showed His love by humbling himself and becoming obedient unto death, and if He be a revelation of the Father, then the love of Christ the Son shows in its nature and extent the love of God the Father to man. The love of God therefore embraces all. The work of Christ, which, as He is the revelation of the Father, is the work of God in Him, has for its object the return of man to his Father from whom he had so far strayed; and as the first step to this return, the remission of sin. The pardon of sin is as wide as the love of God to man. "In Christ God came forth testifying to every man that his sin is forgiven."

The person who believes this testimony "is enjoying an assurance of God's love *towards him*, and of *such a love* in God towards him as produces in him a trust, a confident and undoubting trust, in God for all that is good, as what God is willing to give to him, and what he may, with confidence, ask God for." This firm trust in God he held to be inseparable from the exercise of true faith.

The teaching, of which this is a brief outline, was charged with containing two dangerous heresies—the first, the heresy that Christ had made atonement for all men; the second, that assurance was of the essence of faith. For these Campbell was in 1830 libelled and tried. He wished that the question as to whether these tenets were or were not Divine truths, should be settled by comparing them first with the teaching of Scripture, and then with that teaching as interpreted by the old Scottish and Helvetic confessions, as well as that of Westminster. The proposal was rejected; one member of Presbytery declared that they must not go back to any confession before the Westminster, for to it they must bow; while another gave what seemed to him an irresistible reason for refusing to entertain Mr. Campbell's proposal—"We are far from appealing to the Word of God on this ground; it is by the Confession of Faith that we must stand; by it we hold our livings."[1] The

[1] Proceedings in case of Rev. John M'Leod Campbell, Greenock, 1831, pp. xxvii.-xxix.

case proceeded from Presbytery to Synod, and from Synod to Assembly, where, by a majority of 119 to 6, the two articles libelled were declared to be heresies, Mr. Campbell was found to be guilty of teaching them, and was accordingly deposed from the ministry of the Church.

The same two points—universal redemption and assurance of faith—had been brought before the Assembly, but not declared so distinctly and fully, in the Marrow case, and had then been condemned. After the lapse of more than a century, confessional orthodoxy on these points still maintained its supremacy. The decision which condemned these tenets alleged to be in the "Marrow," was nearly unanimous. The same thing occurred in Campbell's case. Moderates and Evangelicals laid aside their differences for the time, and cordially joined in thrusting out of the Church one of her most earnest and saintly ministers for teaching the dangerous and deadly errors that God loved all His children of mankind; that this love was revealed in Christ, who had procured remission of sin for all; and that man's faith in this revelation must be firm and sure.

The opposition to Campbell was remarkable for its intensity and unanimity. The Church had tolerated tenets much more inconsistent with the Confession, and when charges had been made against individuals of holding erroneous opinions, nothing like the spirit displayed in opposing what was called the "Row heresy" had been excited. But on the only two occasions in which universal pardon and assurance of faith ever came before the Church courts, all parties combined in condemning those two heresies with a burning zeal which all other heresies failed to rouse. The fact is singular; it surprised Campbell himself. He thought he had at last found the explanation. "The key to it all is, *this* is a personal demand upon every man for a personal religion, *i.e.* a personal faith, a personal hope, a personal love, a personal regeneration, a personal new life. Few have those personals to meet the demand, and they can only keep their false peace by casting doubt and contempt upon the authority that makes the demand."[1] There were doubtless other reasons; but whatever the explanation of the fact may be, the fact itself is undoubted, and is peculiar to Scotland.

[1] Memorials of John M'Leod Campbell, D.D., i. 68.

Two years after the Assembly had deposed John M'Leod Campbell, a like sentence was pronounced by the Presbytery of Annan on Edward Irving. He too had, like Campbell, firmly believed and earnestly taught the doctrines of universal pardon and assurance of faith. Towards the close of his brilliant career he became convinced that if faith were only strong enough in believers, the Holy Spirit would manifest His presence and power in them, by bestowing the gifts which Christians in the apostolic age had received. Then he believed, on what he regarded as sure evidence, that the Spirit was manifesting His presence in some by the gift of healing, the gift of tongues, and inspired utterances. It was not, however, for the teaching of these doctrines, or his belief in these manifestations of the Spirit, that he was arraigned and deposed. Irving had for years taught that Jesus in His human nature was sinless and undefiled, not because that nature was in itself incapable of sinning, but because it was kept sinless and undefiled by the indwelling of the Holy Spirit. To Irving the tenet seemed identical with the doctrine of Christ's real humanity; for if the human nature in which the Word tabernacled was created incapable of sinning, then, he argued, it must have been essentially different from the nature of man even in the state of innocency, for that was capable of falling, and it must in fact be not human but superhuman. He had preached this doctrine for years without ever suspecting that it was other than orthodox. In fact he held unwittingly the doctrine which had been held by Antoinette Bourignon and her Scottish apologist, George Garden. The Assembly of 1701 had condemned and deposed Garden, and the same fate now awaited Irving. In both cases the victims protested that the doctrine had been misapprehended. They were charged with maintaining "the sinfulness of Christ;" they indignantly repudiated such a charge. In the last speech which Irving, as a minister of the Church of Scotland, delivered in the parish church of Annan, on the day on which he was deposed, he denied the accusation in terms which could not be surpassed in strength. "As to my maintaining that Christ is other than most holy, I do protest that it is not true. It is not true!—before the living God, I do declare it is false. And though all men should say it is true, I say it is false, and that it proceeds from the father of lies. Ah! was He not holy? Did He not gain for us a victory? Holy in His mother's womb; holy in His childhood; holy in His advancing years; holy in His nativity; holy in His resurrection; and not more holy in one than in another; and He calls upon you to be holy—and this is what He says, 'Be ye holy, for I am holy.'"[1] The presbytery unanimously found Irving guilty of teaching "the doctrine of the fallen state and sinfulness of our Lord's human nature," and accordingly deposed him from the ministry.

The two men thus cast out of the National Church for heresy were in many respects of kindred minds. They had, independently of each other, arrived at the same views regarding the universality of the atonement and the assurance of faith. They were alike in the earnestness and courage with which they proclaimed the doctrines they believed to be Divine truths. Their influence still continues, though operating in widely different directions. When Irving stood before the presbytery of Annan, in 1833, his bodily and mental vigour had sadly decayed, and his earthly race was near its end. He died in the following year. His views developed into the doctrine, ritual, and government of the so-called Catholic and Apostolic Church. When Campbell was deposed, a long and active and honoured life still lay before him. It was in some respects good for him, and for the cause which he had at heart, that he had been expelled from the Church, for he was thereby left at liberty to pursue his investigations untrammelled by the necessity of arriving at certain definite conclusions laid down beforehand, or of incurring severe penalties if he arrived at others. His views, expanded, developed, and matured in the course of years, have been an important factor in modifying and liberalizing, not confessional theology, for that is fixed, but living theological thought in Scotland, both within and without that Church which drove him out as a heretic.

The doctrine of universal atonement, with the consequences which flowed therefrom, did not cease to make way, though the voices of Campbell and Irving were no longer heard in the pulpits of the National Church. A report arose that

[1] Oliphant's "Life of Irving," 392, 393.

it had been taught in the very citadel of orthodoxy, the divinity hall of the United Associate Synod—the training school of the ministers of the Secession. As the result of a careful inquiry it was found and announced that the tenet taught had been only that the atonement was *in itself sufficient* for the redemption of the whole human race, but actually was *efficient* only for the elect. As thus explained, the teaching turned out to be the mere reiteration of a distinction which had been made centuries before, and had become a well-worn truism. Some students who had listened to the teaching failed to follow out the distinction. It seemed to them, as it had seemed to some many centuries before, that an atonement which was in itself sufficient for the redemption of all mankind, but which, in reality, was applied only to a select number definitely and unconditionally fixed from eternity, did not differ in effect from an atonement made solely for that select number; more especially when the allied doctrines of man's total corruption and inability in himself to believe and repent were taken into account. They maintained that the pardon procured by Christ was not only in itself sufficient for all, but had actually been procured for all, and that no eternal decree hindered any man from accepting it. A young Secession minister, Mr. Morrison, in Kilmarnock, who taught this doctrine was deposed. He was joined by some fellow-thinkers, and the "Evangelical Union" was the outcome of the movement—a Union which is not fettered by the Westminster or any other rigid Confession of Faith. Dr. Morrison has lived to write some good works, mainly exegetical, which also have had some influence in promoting a liberal theology.

Meanwhile a revival of zeal and activity had taken place in the National Church. The revival showed itself partly in closer adherence to the Calvinistic doctrines of the Confession, and under its influence Mr. Wright, of Borthwick, was deposed for heresy in 1841, though he strenuously denied all the charges that were made against him. With this victim zeal for purity of doctrine was satisfied, and so far as heresy was concerned the Church had rest for forty years. The revival, however, showed itself chiefly in resuscitating the doctrines contained in the Scottish Confession and Second Book of Discipline, regarding the Church and the authority which she had derived from her Divine Head, and resulted in the controversy which ended in the Disruption. At first that controversy had little or no connection with doctrine. Whatever importance may be attached to the Veto Act or the Chapel Act, it can scarcely be maintained that they were Divine truths revealed in the Word, and imperatively binding on the conscience. But when these Acts, which had been passed by a majority in the Assembly, were challenged in civil courts by parties who alleged that they injuriously affected their civil rights, and the highest judicial tribunals decided that the Acts were illegal, and when the Assembly resolved, by a majority, to disregard the decision and enforce the Acts, the reasons assigned for adopting that course at once transferred the controversy from a matter of church expediency to the domain of Christian doctrine. The question submitted for the verdict of the people was so shaped that they were asked to decide—Shall the Church of Christ yield obedience to the commands of her divine Lord and Master, or shall she disobey her Lord and obey the civil magistrate? By Scotsmen who viewed the question in that aspect only one answer could be given. The effect of representing the controversy in that light was immediately apparent. Thousands who were quite contented with the law of patronage, who cared little about the Veto and Chapel Acts, and were utterly indifferent about the Auchterarder case in itself, zealously ranged themselves on the side of the Non-intrusionists when this question was put before them—Shall Christ or Cæsar be the ruler in Christ's Church? The opposite party maintained that the doctrine of the supremacy, or headship, of Christ over the Church, which they held as firmly as their opponents, was in no wise affected by the decision of the judicial tribunals, which declared that the Veto and Chapel Acts passed by the Assembly were inconsistent with the civil statutes under which the Church had been established. Those who saw in the judicial interpretation of those statutes an encroachment on the crown rights of Christ, went out of the National Church, charging those who remained with the crime of disowning the Lord Jesus in so far as regarded His authority as only

King and Head of His Church; while those who remained as strenuously repudiated the charge, and affirmed that the judicial interpretation of the civil statutes did not affect the spiritual independence of the Church.

Influences originating outside of the Presbyterian Churches, and even resisted by them, have within the last thirty years effected a revolution in Scottish theology.

Before sketching an outline of that revolution we shall glance at the development of doctrine which has taken place in the Roman Catholic Church since the Reformation in Scotland, and any changes of doctrine which may have been effected in the Scottish Episcopal Church since the Revolution. In the Roman Catholic Church the decrees of the Tridentine Council, of course, remain unaltered as articles of faith. Two dogmas which the Council of Trent left undetermined have lately received authoritative sanction. These are the immaculate conception of the Blessed Virgin, and the infallibility of the Pope when, as head of the Church, he decides on matters of faith and morals. The pre-Reformation Scottish Catholic Church adhered to the doctrine of the immaculate conception, and therefore the recent authoritative decision added no new article to the belief which it had explicitly professed. From the absence of any mention of the Pope's supremacy in Archbishop Hamilton's Catechism, the recognition of that dogma by Scottish Catholics immediately before the Reformation has recently been called in question.[1] The argument from silence is always unsafe. But whatever may be the opinion formed on that point, there can be no doubt, judging from the addresses lately presented to the Pope by Scottish Catholics, of their ample recognition now of the papal authority in faith and morals as it has recently been defined.

The Episcopal Church, while established, in the period between the Restoration and the Revolution, had, as we have seen, no liturgy, and with the exception of the Apostles' Creed, no authoritative symbol of doctrine. After its disestablishment the use of the English Book of Common Prayer was gradually introduced, and at length became universal. The communion office contained in the Scottish prayer-book, which had been

[1] By Mr. Gladstone in his preface to Law's edition of the Catechism.

prepared in the reign of Charles I. but had never been introduced into the church services, was with some modifications not unfrequently adopted. The chief doctrinal distinction between the English and the Scottish office was that, by the omission in the latter of the words "militant here on earth" from the rubric on the prayer for Christ's Church, prayers for the faithful departed could be allowed. Until 1804 the creeds contained in the English prayer-book had been the only ones recognized; but in that year the Thirty-nine Articles of the Church of England were formally adopted as the Church's authoritative confession of faith. In adopting these articles it was stated that the Calvinistic interpretation of some expressions in them was rejected, and that the belief in the Eucharist as a commemorative sacrifice was still retained. These explanations do not form a part of the resolution to adopt the Thirty-nine Articles as the doctrinal standard of the Church, but they clearly indicate the views of the Convocation. The opinions thus unequivocally expressed were essentially different from those which prevailed in the Episcopal Church while it was established. The confession drawn up by Scottish Episcopal theologians in 1616 was more Calvinistic than that of John Knox. Though the Westminster Confession had no authoritative position in the Episcopal Church of the Restoration period, yet practically it was for the most part the standard to which the doctrinal teaching of that Church conformed. Arminianism did not prevail in it till after the Revolution. Calvinism, as a doctrinal system, has nothing to do with the form of church government. It has been held firmly by an Episcopal, and has been as firmly rejected by a Presbyterian Church. The view which regarded the Eucharist as a commemorative sacrifice also revealed a change in doctrine. The belief formerly entertained on this point was that set forth in the Westminster Confession, and still professed by the Presbyterian Churches, that "in this sacrament Christ is not offered up to his Father, nor any real sacrifice made at all for remission of the sins of the quick and the dead; but only a commemoration of that one offering up of himself, by himself, upon the cross, once for all, and a spiritual oblation of all possible praise unto God for the same." Accordingly neither in the Presbyterian Church nor in the old Scottish Episcopal Church is there any place found for sacrifice, or altar, or priest.

In so far as official profession is concerned, the theological opinions of Scottish Presbyterians are all in harmony with the Westminster Confession. There has been no development and no change for two hundred and forty-two years. The standard which was adopted in 1647 still remains, in its wide sweep and minute details, the rule of faith to which all conform. One Presbyterian church may slightly differ in doctrine from another, but it differs only in bearing more faithful testimony to the truths of the Confession, and adhering to them with greater tenacity. Such in theory and profession is the present condition of doctrine in the Scottish Presbyterian churches. Facts reveal a different state of matters. The Confession is no longer the standard to which the faith of the churches is rigidly conformed. The only Presbyterian bodies in Scotland that maintain the confessional faith in its integrity are the Reformed Presbyterians and the Original Seceders, and the smallness of their numbers is a pretty clear indication of the popular favour with which rigid adherence to the Confession is regarded. The extent and character of the change cannot be closely defined. The evidence regarding it is somewhat vague and fluctuating. Speeches, sermons, articles, and books, the productions of individual ministers, have of course no official authority, and can only furnish evidence of the opinions held by the speaker or writer, and not of the doctrines held by the Church to which he belongs. But if distinctive and important doctrines of the official creed be habitually ignored, and other doctrines inconsistent with or contrary to tenets in that creed be openly avowed and proclaimed, and the churches in which this ignoring of Confessional truth and teaching of Confessional error occur take no steps to provide a remedy, it is evident that the bond between such churches and their professed creed has been considerably slackened. Freedom of thought and large toleration of divergent views may be good things in themselves; but they cannot be regarded by any as evidences of rigid adherence to a rigid creed, and they certainly prove the existence of innovation, and even a radical change, if not in doctrinal purity, at least in the method by which doctrinal purity was wont to be preserved. A hundred and fifty years ago a minister was accused of heresy on the ground that he had published a sermon which contained no heretical doctrine, but which did not contain all the sound doctrine that could have been taught on the subject. He escaped condemnation, but his escape was then regarded and long adduced as a proof of the degeneracy of the Established Church. If the same measure were now applied to the published sermons and other productions of Presbyterian ministers, and the lack of stringency in its application, once so sorely lamented, were now supplied by the enforcement of rigorous discipline, the number of ministers who would be relieved of their official duties could not indeed be even approximately guessed at, but it is certain that by such a procedure the proposal lately made to remedy Scotland's ecclesiastical ills by removing a thousand of her ministers would be effectually carried out. Calvinism is in many cases so toned down as to lose its special characteristics. Its distinctive doctrines do not, if we may judge from published sermons, figure prominently in the modern Scottish pulpit. The harrowing descriptions of the abode of the lost, with its exquisite and never-ending torments, which were formerly regarded as a potent means of frightening men to repentance, if given now as they were wont to be given by faithful preachers, would empty most of the churches. Calvinistic doctrines are sometimes mentioned only to be repudiated. In a recent sermon, for example, by an able Presbyterian minister, not of the Established Church, the doctrines of reprobation, of a limited atonement, of elect infants, and of verbal inspiration, are described as unauthorized additions to the truth of God. The fact that such a sermon was preached and published, and attracted no special notice, is a proof of the great change in doctrinal teaching, which has been silently effected since John M'Leod Campbell was deposed.

While this change has been going on the church courts have been singularly free from cases of heresy. The United Presbyterian Synod felt itself obliged to vindicate the doctrine of eternal punishment by declaring one of its number, who was unsound on the point, to be no longer a minister of the Church.

The Assembly and inferior courts of the Free Church were for years occupied in investigating a charge against one of its ablest and most scholarly professors, which virtually was a charge of unsoundness on the doctrine of inspiration, and at length disposed of the case by relieving him of his professorial duties, but continuing him as a minister of the Church.

In 1880 a book entitled "Scotch Sermons" was published. It contained discourses written by some ministers of the Church of Scotland, and was intended to show the direction in which thought was moving. It attracted no special notice till attention was drawn to it in the Assembly of the Free Church. Strong statements were made regarding the dangerous tendency of its teaching, and earnest warnings were uttered against its perusal. The immediate effect of the statements and warnings was to create a demand for the volume, and edition after edition was rapidly disposed of. One sermon, on "The things which cannot be shaken," had been selected for special animadversion. A charge of erroneous or at least defective teaching was made against the author in his presbytery, and the case came before the Assembly of 1881. Ultimately, in answer to a question agreed upon by the court, and put by the moderator, the writer declared "that the sermon to which exception had been taken was preached with a view to meet special objections that had been urged against certain doctrines in the Church's belief, and was not intended to contain more than an answer to those special objections." He also stated that his intention was not to identify himself with the objectors, but to meet their objections. He was then admonished to be careful to avoid in future what might give occasion of offence, and the case ended.[1] The volume of sermons need scarcely have been mentioned if it were not for the prominence still given to it in the supposed interests of orthodoxy. The finding of the Assembly, and the declarations of the writer of the sermon, are overlooked. The views of some sceptical modern theologians given in the sermon, and given, as the author declared, in order to be refuted, are still represented as his own, and the Assembly is charged with conniving at erroneous teaching. This is unfair. It may be questioned if those who, in

[1] Proceedings of Assembly of 1881, pp. 43, 45, 47.

their zeal for orthodoxy, called attention to the book and uttered solemn warnings against it, could not have found nearer home fit subjects for the exercise of that fervent zeal.

The movement to relax the stringent formula by which ministers bind themselves to accept the whole doctrine contained in the Westminster Confession as the truths of God and the confession of their faith, is also an unmistakable proof of a change in theological opinions. A century ago such a proposal was spoken of with bated breath in a few private circles, or timidly suggested in magazine articles, but was never mooted openly in the church courts. Now the proposal has been openly made and zealously advocated by leading men not only in the Established but also in the Free Church, with the result, in the case of the former, that a relaxation of the formula has been unanimously adopted by the General Assembly of 1889.

Behind the questions as to how far the Church is to be bound to the Confession, and how far the doctrines of the Confession are to be received as the truths of God, there lies the infinitely more important question, which sooner or later the Church must face, as to the sense in which the Bible is to be received as the inspired Word of God. Changed views on the nature of inspiration are also tolerated in all the churches. Scripture was formerly regarded as the Word of God dictated to man by the Holy Spirit, or at least so communicated to man by the Spirit that it exhibited in all its statements the truth free from all admixture of error. This same revelation it pleased the Lord to commit wholly unto writing, and these writings have, by His singular care and providence, been kept pure in all ages.[1] In accordance with this view all Scriptural statements are to be implicitly received and believed as Divine truths. Other views have recently been entertained, avowed, and tolerated. The Bible has been regarded as containing the best thoughts on religion and morality of the most highly-gifted and religious men that ever lived, but not as containing a direct revelation supernaturally imparted to the writers, and therefore to be received in all its statements as teaching absolute truth. That the Bible contains some mistakes in science, history, and morals, has been publicly and repeatedly asserted by Presby-

[1] Confession of Faith, chap. i.

terian ministers, and the assertions have entailed no censures from church courts. Not one Presbyterian church can reproach another with tolerating such opinions, for the opinions are freely expressed in all, with the exception of the two small denominations already indicated. In comparison with this question of inspiration, the controversy about the Confession and the formula which pledges ministers to it is insignificant. The Westminster divines would never have compiled the Confession if they had not believed that the Scriptures, on which they sought to found it, "are given by inspiration of God," and are to be believed and obeyed because the author of them is God, who is truth itself.[1] They would never have set about the task of preparing a systematized summary of the best thoughts of religious men, found in the remains of old Hebrew literature and the extant writings of the earliest Christians. Objections to statements in the Confession become sometimes objections to statements in the Bible. It needs but the stroke of a pen to delete from the Confession the statement that God created the world in the space of six days, but after deleting it from the creed we still read in the Book of Exodus that "in six days the Lord made heaven and earth, the sea, and all that in them is." If the statement be true in the Book of Exodus, it cannot become untrue by merely being transferred to the pages of the Confession. By the denial of that and many other assertions in the Westminster symbol, the question of the inspiration of Scripture is at once raised.

Of the many and various influences which have contributed to produce the undeniable change which has taken place in theological thought, we can here merely indicate a few. In the previous century the rise of a literature wholly unconnected with theology, the independent investigation of moral and metaphysical questions, and the revival of native poetry had produced results which affected to some extent the religious views of the age. In the present century all these influences have continued to operate, but far more powerfully, and, in the latter half of it especially, new ones have been introduced. In early times the General Assembly, and afterwards the Secession, endeavoured, as one means of keeping the faith of

[1] Confession, chap. i.

Scotsmen sound and orthodox, to prohibit them from reading or learning aught that was unsound or heterodox; and in this way they certainly succeeded to some extent in maintaining a sound, though it might be a stern and narrow, faith. This method is no longer available. The range of popular reading is wide and catholic; and the wide diffusion of secular literature has had a part in softening the stern and rugged features of old Scottish theology.

Natural science has made great advances in old fields, and has discovered many that are new. Some of its recent researches have brought to light results which, whether they be accepted as ascertained truths or only as probable theories, cannot fail to have a reflex influence on theology. The scientific method, which investigates and questions, and accepts nothing as true simply because some one has affirmed its truth, has also been to some extent imported into theology, and has had an influence in modifying previous conceptions.

Two new factors have been actively at work during the last half-century—Biblical criticism and the comparative history of religions. Fifty years ago, or even later, Biblical criticism was unknown in Scotland—unknown, we mean, as that science which not merely seeks from various readings to select the original one, but which seeks to examine and question the writing itself, to find what it really teaches, and to ascertain how far its teaching may have been influenced by the age in which it was produced, and how far it contains truth for all time. That work has been done almost entirely by Continental scholars. Free investigation has not been admitted into the Scottish Churches; but the results of that investigation cannot be excluded, and are unquestionably contributing to effect a change on traditional orthodox doctrine.

The comparative history of religion is also a new factor. It is only of late that such a history has been possible. The view long prevalent in Scotland, and still pretty common, was that all religions save Christianity—for the old Hebrew religion was but Christianity partially revealed—were merely gross superstitions invented by the father of lies, for the purpose of deluding and destroying their votaries. There is a change, and the extent of the change may be illustrated by a single incident. In the early part of last century a Glasgow professor of theology suggested in his class that man might, by the light of nature, dimly perceive that God was reconcilable. He barely escaped conviction for teaching heresy. This year a course of lectures was delivered in the same university, in which the lecturer mentioned as the sources from which he would seek a definition of religion, or at least of natural religion, the sacred books of the East—of which the Bible was one—mythology, laws, and language. He was heard by a numerous and applauding audience, which included divinity professors, theological students, and "ministers of all denominations." Imagination cannot picture the horror with which such a proposal would have been received 170 years ago, nor the storm of orthodox indignation which it would have raised.

Through the operation of these and other influences doctrines have been greatly modified. God and man and nature are regarded in another aspect than that in which they were once viewed. In modern Scottish theology there is much more of the love and much less of the wrath of God. The universal Fatherhood, with all the results which that doctrine infers, has been brought into clearer light. Formerly all men were represented as being born and (save the elect) as living and dying under God's wrath, and as enduring that wrath to all eternity. Higher views prevail. The love of God to all His children of mankind—His sinful, erring, and rebellious children—Christ as the revealer of that love, His work and death as procuring redemption for all, are brought into the foreground. There is a kindlier view of nature. Formerly the view was very prevalent that nature was accursed on account of man The world was regarded as illumined by the glare of the flames of Tophet rather than by God's blessed sunshine. The thoughts on nature embodied in the poetry of Wordsworth could not have been conceived by a consistent adherent of the old theology, or if conceived it would be in spite of that theology. The beauty of the earth and sky, the warmth and sunshine, the genial springs and the bounteous harvests, that fill men's hearts with food and gladness, are no longer regarded as given to God's non-elect children through the medium of the curse of a broken covenant.

There is one feature of the change which merits special attention. We are going back, in some respects, to the old Catholic doctrines held by the Church when it was still undivided. Scotland started from these doctrines, became more Calvinistic than Calvin himself, and is now, in some things, returning to the point from which she started. The love of God to all men, and the manifestation of that love in giving Christ to die for all, are old Catholic doctrines; the modification of the account given in the Confession of man's total corruption and depravity marks a return to the old Catholic belief. Campbell's view of the doctrine of the atonement—a view which largely influences much of modern Presbyterian preaching—does not differ greatly from that still held by the Catholic Church; and in the larger hope which is cherished by some, we have an approach to that still larger hope which Origen held—that the benefits of Christ's redemption would ultimately extend not only to all the fallen race of men, but to all the fallen spirits whom God had created. Since 1843 there has been a retreat all along the line from the Calvinism of the Westminster Confession, and in drawing back from the doctrines once so tenaciously held there is, in the opinions now so extensively entertained regarding the sinfulness of man and the goodness of God, an approach to the doctrines of the Church as they were when Ninian and Columba first preached the Gospel of Christ to pagan Scotland.

www.ingramcontent.com/pod-product-compliance
Lightning Source LLC
Chambersburg PA
CBHW030737230426
43667CB00007B/751